ST. AUGUSTINE'S CONFESSIONS

O'CONNELL, Robert J. **St. Augustine's Confessions, the Odyssey of Soul.** Harvard, 1969. 199p bibl 69-12731. 6.50

CHOICE   JUNE '70

Philosophy

In *St. Augustine's Early Theory of Man A.D. 386–391* (1968), O'Connell attracted the interest and the criticism of Augustine scholars. He now uses the ideas he presented there to clarify the meaning and unity of the *Confessions*, and he thereby seeks to buttress further his basic thesis that Augustine's psychology was much more Plotinian than has been heretofore admitted. This work will undoubtedly be much discussed by scholars but may present somewhat rough going for others, since it presupposes a familiarity with Augustinian philosophy and theology and the vast literature about them. Nevertheless, even the nonscholar will be able to enjoy it, for it outlines with exciting clarity the path of Augustine's development and is as intriguing as any detective story as it fits in bit by bit the pieces of evidence for the author's position. It will then, without replacing them, take a place along with such other works as Courcelle's *Recherches sur les Confessions de Saint Augustin*. Graduate philosophy and patristic collections will need it, but smaller libraries should first get some of the more general surveys, such as *Augustine's Quest of Wisdom* (1945, o.p.) by Bourke. Index.

ST. AUGUSTINE'S CONFESSIONS
THE ODYSSEY OF SOUL

ROBERT J. O'CONNELL

THE BELKNAP PRESS
OF
HARVARD UNIVERSITY PRESS
CAMBRIDGE, MASSACHUSETTS, 1969

For my students, over the years.

PREFACE

The reader should be warned at the outset of what he
would soon find out for himself: this book makes no claim to
being a comprehensive interpretation of the *Confessions*. It
does not pretend to say all that could, or even should, be said
about that rich and often baffling work. Rather, it aims to
extend an exploration of Augustine's thought on man that I
have already presented in a series of articles and then, more
fully, in my study of *St. Augustine's Early Theory of Man,
A.D. 386–391*.[1] That book represented the slightly reoriented
and much-expanded version of my previous efforts to demonstrate that the fundamental matrix of Augustine's early view,
especially of man as "fallen soul," is far more faithfully Neo-
Platonic and, more specifically, Plotinian than heretofore commonly acknowledged.

The present work is very much a sequel to its predecessor,

1. Cambridge Mass.: Harvard University Press, 1968. The articles in the order of their conception are: "*Ennead* VI, 4–5 in the Works of St. Augustine,"
Revue des Études Augustiniennes, 9:1–39 (1963); "The Plotinian Fall of the
Soul in St. Augustine," *Traditio*, 19:1–35 (1963); "The *Enneads* and St. Augustine's Image of Happiness," *Vigiliae Christianae*, 17:129–164 (1963); and "The
Riddle of Augustine's *Confessions*: A Plotinian Key," *International Philosophical Quarterly*, 4:327–372 (1964).

and as such, a "thesis book," with, I hope, some of the vir-
tues, but more likely all of the defects inherent in that genre.
It can be viewed from two angles: as confirming the hypothesis
embodied in my studies of Augustine's early anthropology, by
illustrating its substantial applicability to the *Confessions;* but
also, more justly, as explicating that same theory of man as
Augustine presents it, slightly modified at points, at a later
period in his development. What that theory of man implies
I have attempted to suggest in the Introduction and then systematically to summarize in the first chapter of this book. For
additional detail and for the proof that this summary does
represent Augustine's earlier view, I must refer the reader to
St. Augustine's Early Theory of Man.

Much of what I say here deals with matters scholars have
disputed about for decades and more. The admittedly provisional answer I present to some of those issues emerges from
the view to which my own research has led me, a view of how
the early Augustine used Plotinus in his effort to elaborate
an "understanding of the faith." The special character of this
optic, then, may explain at least in part why I have not chosen
to turn this exposition of the *Confessions* into a continued
altercation with rival views. What is all too often at stake in
my differences with other writers is the fundamental set of
interpretative suppositions I have tried to validate in *St. Augustine's Early Theory of Man* and to summarize in the Introduction and opening chapter of this book. In the notes to
those two chapters the reader will find references to the many
studies with differing interpretations from my own. These
notes may also stand as some small excuse for the relative
sparsity of notes to the subsequent chapters.

There is an obvious danger in the business of examining
a labyrinthine world such as that of the *Confessions* from the
kind of perspective I have assumed. Any optic one chooses
risks setting certain features into a prominence that may turn
out to have been exaggerated; it may at the same time mini-
mize the importance of features which, examined through a
wider lens, turn out to be far more prominent than the nar-
rower vision could allow. Every scholar fears the moment
when he may have become prisoner to a point of view he has
cultivated far too long than was good for his objectivity. And
yet, his only therapy is to present the findings that his point
of view enabled him to uncover, even at the risk of being premature. Others, then, may succeed in widening his vision be-

fore it is too late. In presenting his findings, he must (for sweet clarity's sake if for nothing else) suppress the ever-nagging temptation to resort to the subjunctive: "If my view of the matter be correct, then it would follow that Augustine means this." But the indicative mood, habitual in English exposition, tends to convey an air of greater confidence than the writer himself often enjoys: give me a scholar and he will know what I mean. My hopes are that whatever features of the *Confessions'* landscape I may have left in the shade were not deliberately ignored, or half-consciously excluded, because their message positively militated against the thesis propounded here, and that the Augustinian scholar will be sensitive to the number of hesitant subjunctives that still tremble behind my regular use of the indicative mood.

I am grateful to Doubleday and Company, New York, publishers of John K. Ryan's translation of *The Confessions of Saint Augustine,* for the kind permission to quote from that translation. I must thank the editors of *The International Philosophical Quarterly* both for the real assistance they gave at the time of publishing "The Riddle of Augustine's *Confessions:* A Plotinian Key" in their review, and for their kind permission to reproduce substantial portions of that article here.

The students, both graduate and undergraduate, who have aided me in sharpening the views presented here, will see how much I owe to their resilient minds; so will the patient members of Harvard University Press's editorial staff. Finally, I must thank the authorities of Fordham University for having accorded me the Faculty Fellowship year during which the substance of this work came to be.

Fordham University   R.J.O'C.
June 1968

FORMS OF CITATION

WORKS ON THE CONFESSIONS

The following frequently cited works are referred to throughout this book by the name of the author or translator only.

Critical editions

Gibb, John, and Montgomery, William. *The Confessions of Augustine*. Cambridge, Eng.: Cambridge University Press, 1908, 2d ed. 1927. Latin text, with still valuable expository notes.

Skutella, Martin. *Confessiones*. Leipzig: Bibliotheca Teubneriana, 1934. The best critical edition to date; reproduced with slight emendations in Solignac's edition, below.

Solignac, Aimé, S.J. *Les Confessions. Bibliothèque Augustinienne* series of *Oeuvres de Saint Augustin*, vols. 13 and 14. Paris, 1962. Hereafter cited as *BA* 13 and 14. Skutella's text with French translation; Solignac is responsible for textual emendations, Introduction, and Notes.

Translations

Rouse, W. H. D. *Confessions*. Loeb Classical Library. Cambridge, Mass., 1912. A revision of William Watts's translation dating from 1631.

Bourke, Vernon J. *Confessions. Fathers of the Church* series, vol. 21. New York, 1953.

Ryan, John K. *The Confessions of St. Augustine*. New York: Doubleday (Image Books), 1960.

Tréhorel, Eugène, and Bouissou, Guilhem, translators of the *Bibliothèque Augustinienne* edition listed above.

General studies

Courcelle, Pierre. *Recherches sur Les Confessions de Saint Augustin*. Paris: de Boccard, 1950.

Pellegrino, Michel. *Les Confessions de Saint Augustin*. Paris, 1960. Translation, with revisions and enlargement, of *Le Confessioni di Sant' Agostino*, Rome, 1956.

WORKS BY ST. AUGUSTINE

In citing from Augustine's works the chapter numbers are omitted and only the book and section are given. For example, *Conf* IV, I, 1 is shortened to *Conf* IV, 1. Works are cited by title abbreviations taken (in slightly adapted form) from those suggested by the editors of *Folia*, Supplement II, Worcester, Mass., November 1954. Latin titles (in chronological order), English translations, and corresponding abbreviations as used throughout the book are as follows:

Contra Academicos	Against the Academics	*Acad*
De Beata Vita	On the Happy Life	*Vita*
De Ordine	On Order	*Ord*
Soliloquia	Soliloquies	*Sol*
De Immortalitate Animae	On the Immortality of the Soul	*Immort*
De Quantitate Animae	On the Greatness of the Soul	*Quant*
De Genesi contra Manichaeos	On Genesis, against the Manichees	*Gen Man*
De Libero Arbitrio	On Freedom of Choice (or: of the Will)	*Lib*
De Magistro	On the Teacher	*Mag*
De Vera Religione	On True Religion	*Ver*
De Utilitate Credendi	On the Usefulness of Believing	*Util*
De Musica	On Music	*Mus*
Confessiones	Confessions	*Conf*
De Trinitate	On the Trinity	*Trin*
De Civitate Dei	The City of God	*Civ*

CONTENTS

ST. AUGUSTINE'S CONFESSIONS

INTRODUCTION

The translator of the *Confessions* does not have an easy task. When, for instance, Augustine writes *Et quis homo est quilibet homo cum sit homo* (IV, 1),[1] one can easily understand the translator's hesitation. The literal sense, "and what man is any kind of man while he be a man," does not, on the face of it, make very good sense. But it is, nevertheless, literally what Augustine wrote.

Nor is the example unique. *Tu assumsisti me ut viderem esse quod viderem et nondum me esse qui viderem,* he writes in his account of the Neo-Platonic vision of Milan (VII, 16). And translators differ, as one might expect. John K. Ryan's version represents a typical solution: "You took me up so that I might see that there was something to see, but that I was not yet one

---

1. For simplicity and convenience, citations from the *Confessions* will normally appear in parentheses in the text, as above. Gibb and Montgomery, p. 79, translate: "And what kind of a man is any man when he is merely a man," explaining the sense as implying that no one is "truly a man" when he is "only a man." Ryan translates: "What manner of man is any man since he is but a man." Tréhorel and Bouissou render the same phrase more freely: "Et qu'est-ce que l'homme, n'importe quel homme, dès lors qu'il est homme." Vernon Bourke changes the sense: "And *what* is man, any man, since he is but a man" (my italics). Excerpts from *The Confessions of St. Augustine,* translated by John K. Ryan, copyright © 1960 by Doubleday & Company, Inc., are used by permission of the publisher.

1

able to see it." [2] Yet had he meant that, Augustine could have put it into much better Latin; even more to the point, he could not have been more insistent throughout this entire account that he *did* "see." [3]

The "inability" underlined throughout is one that forbids him to "take a stand" on these contemplative heights, long endure the radiance of the vision, feast on the supernal "food for grown-ups" (*cibus grandium*) he has glimpsed and whose fragrance so attracts him. His weakness, from the weight of the corruptible body that drags him down, is equated with iniquity and with an unhealth from which he needs to be cured before he can "hold fast" and "enjoy," take up permanent "dwelling" in the "homeland of happiness" (*beatifica patria*) which he has merely espied from a distant hill. [4]

Augustine was, then, able to see, and (however cloudily and momentarily) *saw*. In that case, how is one to translate the troublesome phrase? Does he mean (as a literal rendition would suggest) that God took him up that "I might see that what I

---

2. Ryan, p. 171. Compare Tréhorel and Bouissou: "Tu m'as soulevé pour me faire voir qu'il y avait pour moi l'Etre à voir, et que je n'étais pas encore être à le voir," and Solignac's note (*BA* 13, pp. 616–617), where he suggests the possibility of a more literal rendition, in which case Augustine is playing on the opposition of God as *Esse* and himself as *nondum-esse*. This latter is faithful to the literal sense of the text, and I have tried to prove that, in a Plotinian interpretation of St. Augustine's work, literal translations of both these texts make excellent sense. See my article, "The *Enneads* and St. Augustine's Image of Happiness," *Vigiliae Christianae*, 17:129–164 (1963), esp. pp. 143–146; here-after cited as "Happiness." See also my book, *St. Augustine's Early Theory of Man, A.D. 386–391* (Cambridge, Mass., 1968), pp. 214–216; hereafter cited as *Augustine's Early Theory*.

3. Cf. VII, 16, *intravi et vidi;* 17, *inspexi . . . et vidi;* 18, *Et manifestatum est mihi;* 18, *vidi et manifestatum est mihi;* 20, *vidi te infinitum . . . visus iste non a carne;* 21, *respexi alia et vidi. . . . Et vidi;* 23 (*ratiocinans potentia*) *pervenit ad id quod est in ictu trepidantis aspectus. Tunc vero invisibilia tua . . . conspexi;* 26, again, but summarizing the entire experience, *invisibilia tua . . . conspexi.* In VIII, 1, Augustine alludes to the certainty won here, despite the fact that *in aenigmate et quasi per speculum videram.* It is clear, then, that Augustine claims to have "seen." For the sense of *videre* in this context, see my article, "*Ennead* VI, 4–5 in the Works of St. Augustine," *Revue des Études Augustiniennes,* 9:15–17 (1963); hereafter cited as "*Ennead* VI, 4–5." See also *Augustine's Early Theory,* pp. 43–48.

4. The *nondum me esse* here (VII, 16) is repeated in VII, 23, but now in connection with the term *cohaerere (deo).* Augustine there laments that *non stabam frui deo meo, sed . . . diripiebar abs te pondere meo.* The *pondus* in question is equated with *consuetudo carnalis* and is immediately linked with the "corruptible body" which (Wisd. of Sol. 9:15 quite literally taken) *adgravat animam.* This, the Saint goes on to say, is why *aciem figere non evalui et repercussa infirmitate redditus solitis,* he is left with but a "memory" of that *cibus grandium* which, he says, *comedere non possem.* Cf. (VII, 26) *per tenebras animae meae contemplari non sinerer; nimis . . . infirmus ad fruendum te;* note here the distinction *non tantum ad cernendam* [*scil. beatificam patriam*] *sed et habitandam* and its companion distinction, *non solum ut videat . . . sed*

saw *existed,* and that I, the seer, *did not yet,* exist?" In a Plotinian framework, such a literal translation makes excellent sense,
and Augustine's return to these themes, especially in Book XII,
strongly suggests that he is working inside that framework.[5]
    Whether or not one admits that a literal translation of such
thorny phrases makes sense, there is no doubt that they cause
difficulty. But they may, after all, be more than merely incidental; indeed, I mean here to propose that they root organ-
ically in the soil of an extremely difficult work. The recent and
invaluable edition of the *Confessions* published under the
auspices of the *Bibliothèque Augustinienne* [6] reminds the
scholarly world that there are many such tormented issues still
bothering the interpreter of Augustine's masterpiece, and the
importance of those questions is hardly to be gainsaid. Augustine's influence on occidental theology, both Catholic and
Protestant, has been literally incalculable. He enjoyed incomparable prestige in the thirteenth century when St. Thomas
attempted the synthesis on which the Church is still, to a large
extent, living; he continues to exercise a strong fascination on
Christian thinkers dissatisfied with the Thomistic synthesis and
searching for another to replace it. It is, therefore, more than
ever imperative that scholarship unearth solid findings respecting trouble-spots that go deep, at times very deep, into the
import of his teaching.

THE PROBLEM OF THE *CONFESSIONS*

Three Related Problem-Areas

    The three major problem-areas [7] in Augustine's *Confes-
sions* may be summarized as bearing on its sources, its historicity

---

etiam sanetur ut teneat. Hence there can be *videntes* (the Neo-Platonists,
doubtless) who do not "embrace" Christ the *via, non-videntes* (believers, one
may assume) who "walk" in His "way," but the implication is that *frui, tenere,
habitare* is conferred only on those "cured" and "strengthened" by acceptance of
the Incarnate Christ, *cibus miscens carni.* Note that the object and content of
the vision, to the enduring fullness of which the believer-become-seer eventually
attains, seems on the face of it substantially identical with that already momentarily attained to by the Neo-Platonist! And the stages in the soul's progress,
from the texts above, would seem to be (1) belief, (2) vision (following on
belief's having been complemented by "understanding") , and finally (3) permanent "enjoyment" of vision.
    5. See my article "Happiness," pp. 143–146; *Augustine's Early Theory,* pp.
214–216.
    6. Solignac's Introduction and notes are especially remarkable, particularly
for outlining the latest scholarly positions on the host of questions involved.
    7. I schematize somewhat the lines of Solignac's treatment, pp. 9–200. See
also, Courcelle, pp. 13–40, and Pellegrino, pp. 21–51, 247–266.

(with special reference to the question of Augustine's conversion) , and finally the sense and unity of the work.

Sources

In the pivotal section of the work (VII, 13–26) the Saint spins out the vision of reality that paved the way for his decision to accept baptism. He found that vision, he informs us, substantially in certain "Platonic books" (*libri platonicorum*) translated from Greek into Latin—at least in part by Marius Victorinus Afer. But does this mean Plotinus, his disciple Porphyry, or both? Scholars are still at odds on the question of whether readings in Porphyry, in addition to the readings in Plotinus that are now generally admitted, may and need be invoked at this juncture of Augustine's career.

Historicity and Conversion

Far from being an hors d'oeuvre for academic ivory-tower dwellers, the source-question intimately affects the more crucial question of the Saint's conversion. Was he really converted to Christianity in A.D. 386? Or is the Bishop, writing his *Confessions* some ten years later, adjusting the facts? Some initially extreme positions in this debate have long since been discarded. But it is no accident that Pierre Courcelle's recent efforts [8] to show that Augustine was introduced to Plotinianism by Ambrose himself, are partially designed to show that conversions to Plotinianism and to Ambrosian Christianity must not starkly be opposed to each other. J. J. O'Meara's attempts to establish Porphyrian influence, on the other hand, bring him naturally to analogous conclusions on the conversion issue. His corollary is that Augustine had already surmounted certain of Porphyry's anti-Christian theses, a finding that would authenticate beyond further question the sincerity of his preference for the "Catholic faith" as the norm of his new-found Platonic "understanding." [9]

Whatever one may think of such proposals, they do make one thing clear: the little game once in vogue, which consisted in playing off the earlier accounts of his conversion against the

8. *Recherches sur les Confessions*, esp. pp. 136–138; also, more recently, *Les Confessions . . . dans la tradition littéraire* (Paris, 1963) .

9. See his edition of *Against the Academics*, Ancient Christian Writers series, 12 (Westminster Md., 1950) , pp. 19–23; more recently, *Porphyry's Philosophy from Oracles in Augustine* (Paris, 1959) , esp. pp. 2–3.

one presented in the *Confessions,* was encouraged by the somewhat facile supposition that both accounts were substantially
understood—and that despite innumerable obscurities of language of the sort instanced above. But the problem of language
brings us once again to the question of sources: for Augustine's
vocabulary is drawn from the intellectual world he had made
his own, a world whose key figures are the Manichees, Cicero,
Ambrose, the Bible, Plotinus, and perhaps Porphyry as well. To
understand his language we must have some notion of the
extent to which it was theirs, or molded in opposition to theirs.

Meaning, and Unity

The danger with all such source-research is, however, that
of deforming the author being studied. One may see so much
Plotinus, Porphyry, or Cicero in Augustine that one fails to see
Augustine himself. Looking for the message of one or other
book or author deemed decisive, one may miss the meaning of
the *Confessions* as Augustine himself intended it. Having
missed that meaning, one may rest content with what is really
an obtuse understanding of Augustine's entire intellectual and
spiritual orientation. Any effort of source-research must, accordingly, measure itself against Augustine's text as he wrote it,
illuminate that text as it stands, help us to understand what its
peculiar meaning is.

This brings us to the heart of our problem, to the challenge I hope to face in this essay: that of showing what the
Confessions "means," and showing further that the meaning
proposed may solve once and for all the nettling question of the
unity of the work. Once this is settled, the comparison with
Augustine's own earlier accounts of his conversion can be
placed on a fresh basis, with far more satisfactory results. The
solution here proposed will both test and confirm previous
suggestions that the Plotinian sources active in the Saint's
earlier works are still exerting their influence in the *Confessions,* and that, in their light, the sense and structural unity of
the work is laid bare.

The Problem of "Meaning": Its Structure

No new solution may be proposed for the twin-problems of
the unity and meaning of the *Confessions* without at least a
mention of attempts that have already been made in this direc-

tion. Before noting these attempts, however, the various aspects
of the problem itself need recalling.[10]

One of the major stumbling-blocks is the apparent lack of
unity between what often passes for the "autobiographical"
portion (Books I–IX) and the final four books. The first portion of the work can be interpreted as an autobiographical
account of sin and conversion; in this view, the "story" may be
said to culminate—more or less naturally—with Augustine's
examination of his present state of soul in Book X. But then,
why preface that examination with an interminable discussion
of "memory"? And why does the Bishop examine his conscience
under the headings of those three sins, concupiscence, curiosity,
and pride?

It is understandable that certain authors look upon Book X
as a later interpolation, without organic link to the first nine
books. But Books XI–XIII only pose an even more nettling set
of problems. Apart for the moment from all the questions concerning *how* he interprets his work, *why* should Augustine feel
obliged or entitled to terminate it with three books devoted to
an interpretation of Genesis 1–2:2?

But the question of *how* he interprets that portion of
Scripture may well hold the key to his purpose. Here the questions only come thicker. Why, for example, his laborious insistence on clarifying the nature of "time" (XI, 17–39) ? Why
the switch to Psalm 113 and the lengthy inquiry into the
"heaven of heaven" of which it speaks (XII, 2–16), particularly when this provokes the embarrassed defense of his interpretation in the face of objections coming from Catholic
exegetes (XII, 17–43) ? What is the purpose of the "prophetic"
explanation of this same portion of Genesis to which Book XIII
is largely addressed?

Again, one can understand why some contend the *Confessions* is a badly unified work—for what bearing can all this have
on what has gone before? The question is styled to suggest the
very conditions for a satisfactory answer: once the meaning of
the last three books is disclosed, their bearing on the preceding
books may become clear, and the unity of the *Confessions*
thereby assured. The problem of the work's unity may well be
one with the problem of its meaning.

But this implies we must at least call into question the

10. See Solignac, pp. 9–44, for much of this material, as well as for more
ample bibliographical data.

conceivably superficial notion which would have it that the first nine books of the *Confessions* are "understandable" and only the last four "obscure." If Augustine's work is a unity, if its sense must be uncovered in terms of that unity, then it may be that we have not *really* understood the earlier books *until* we have understood these last.

PREVIOUS SOLUTIONS

This basic solidarity between the problem of unity and the problem of meaning is implicitly acknowledged by the direction most research on these questions has taken.

The unity sought for, it has been suggested, is provided more or less satisfactorily by the various interlocking senses of the very term *confessio*.[11] Augustine has already "confessed" his past sins, and by the same token (an even more properly Christian sense of the term) "confessed" God's marvelous works in converting him (Books I–IX). Book X represents a "confession" of his present state of soul, whereas Books XI–XIII lead him to "confess"—now in the sense of bearing witness to—the scriptural faith that is typified by his interpretation of genesis. Even if not a "profession" in the sense most consonant with the new convert's action at public baptism,[12] this last *confessio*, apostolic in intention, was meant to culminate the effort of "edification," even of "conversion" his readers were ideally intended to experience in following the story of his own conversion.[13] Perhaps this final portion was also meant to authenticate Augustine's progress from the "old" to the "new, spiritual man," from the *vetus* to the *novus homo spiritalis*, stripped of pride, curiosity, and concupiscence and equipped with their trinitarian opposites (humility, charity, and wisdom) [14] which make him capable of a foretaste of God

11. An excellent recent treatment of the term comes from Joseph Ratzinger, "Originalität und Überlieferung in Augustins Begriff der *Confessio*," *Revue des Études Augustiniennes*, 3:375–392 (1957) . For other bibliography see his article, and Solignac, pp. 9–12, 19–26. Note that Ratzinger's aims are far more modest than those of Heinrich Boehmer, Melchior Verheijen, and Max Wundt, who seem to claim far more unifying power for this multiple-sense title.

12. As Max Wundt's theory would suggest. See his "Augustins Konfessionen," *Zeitschrift für Neutestamentliche Wissenschaft*, 29:161–206 (1923) .

13. Most authors admit to this purpose of "edification"; see pp. 7–9, below.

14. See Horst Kusch, "Studien über Augustinus," in *Festschrift Franz Dornseiff* (Leipzig, 1953) , pp. 124–200. Kusch draws more from this important triad than I am convinced it will yield. Augustine's structural view includes it, but as one key element along with others.

whose presence to man forms the fundamental and mystical theme of the entire work.[15]

Or, put in other terms, after the memory (*memoria*) of Books I–IX, the present "regard" (*contuitus*) of Book X, Augustine now leans on Scripture for an *exspectatio* of that eternal "rest" (*quies*) for which he longs.[16] In still another way, the providentially guided "quest for truth" (*quaerere veritatem*) of Books I–VI results in a providential "finding" (*inventio veritatis*), the "vision" in a "glass, darkly" of Book VII; this in turn leads to the so-called "moral conversion" of Book VIII, and the baptism that bears fruit in the foretaste-vision of Ostia of Book IX. At that point Augustine would wish to illustrate the "enjoyment of truth" (*frui veritate*) at which he has arrived in meditating Scripture.[17]

Thus, in the fundamental image of another theory, the "pilgrimage of his soul" (*peregrinatio animae*) away from God has at last come full circle to provisional term in the anticipated enjoyment of the eternal Sabbath, that "rest" for which the "restless heart" yearns. This, G. N. Knauer's fecund suggestion,[18] coheres admirably with Ilse Freyer's proposal[19] that the work, even in its "autobiographical" portion, interweaves "lived" experience and an imposed systematic (*erlebte* and *systematische Gestaltung*) with the constant possibility that

15. See Fulbert Cayré, "Le sens et l'unité des Confessions," *Année Théologique Augustinienne* (1953), pp. 13–32. Cayré has stressed the importance of presence and omnipresence in his many writings on Augustine, and André Mandouze, in "L'extase d'Ostie," *Augustinus Magister* (Paris, 1954), I, 83ff, firmly agrees. See also my "*Ennead* VI, 4–5," and *Augustine's Early Theory*, pp. 32–35.

16. This is P. L. Landsberg's structural principle; see "La conversion de saint Augustin," *Supplément de la Vie Spirituelle* (1936), pp. [31]–[46]. It is adopted by J. M. LeBlond in *Les conversions de saint Augustin* (Paris: Aubier, 1950), see esp. p. 17. One immediate difficulty is that to lend this structure any *unifying* power, both authors must lay stress on *memoria* as bearing on the temporal past (Books I–IX), *contuitus* as focusing Augustine's present state of soul (Book X), *exspectatio* as bearing on the temporal future (Books XI–XIII). We shall have to question whether this is the real sense of the *memoria* analysis from which this triad is drawn.

17. This insight is common to several, but is stressed particularly by J. J. O'Meara, *The Young Augustine* (London, 1954), p. 17. The passage from *quaerere* to *invenire veritatem* would then be providentially aided, another theme O'Meara stresses, and rightly.

18. G. N. Knauer, "*Peregrinatio Animae*: zur Frage der Einheit der Konfessionmen," *Hermes*, 85:216–248 (1957); hereafter cited as *Peregrinatio*. This article works out some fecund lines of research outlined in his *Psalmenzitate in Augustins Konfessionen* (Göttingen, 1955). The author agrees notably with the suggestions referred to in n. 17, above.

19. In her *Erlebte und Systematische Gestaltung in Augustins Konfessionen* (Berlin, 1937).

Augustine's experience has already to some extent been "systematically" formed in the very review and account of it. This suggestion leads naturally into J. J. O'Meara's penetrating observation that the *Confessions* was at no point meant as a "purely personal history," but as one which is in part at least "typical." Augustine selects his details in accordance with a pattern; he "wishes to illustrate a theory, which he believes to have been verified in his own life," but which amounts to a "theory about life in general." In short, the "story of Augustine's own conversion . . . is to some extent the story of a typical conversion . . . the story of Everyman." [20]

JUDGMENTS ON THE FOREGOING SOLUTIONS

Counsels of Despair

These various answers have been presented in concatenated fashion designed to show they are neither mutually exclusive nor individually devoid of some truth. Any attentive reader of the Confessions will have recognized in each of these solutions some more or less crucial aspect which is undoubtedly characteristic of Augustine's work. He may be led to ask why the addition of them all, as we have done here, does not *eo ipso* solve the problem? Why should so astute and learned a student of the *Confessions* as Aimé Solignac, S.J. eventually despair of such attempts at finding the thematic unity of this masterpiece, and fall back wearily on an appeal to a certain unity of "spirit," of "intention," the intention of "confession"? [21]

The answer may lie in the conviction once expressed by a great Augustinian scholar, that *Augustin compose mal:* Augustine composes poorly. That phrase, we know, came back to haunt its author, H. I. Marrou, as his "retractation" shows.[22] But O'Meara's estimate is not much different from Marrou's earlier view: the *Confessions,* he would have us believe, like so many of the Saint's works, is a "badly composed book." Scholars, he continues, who remain incredulous toward this possibility simply "deny the evidence of their senses and forget that Augustine had no expectation of producing . . . a masterpiece

20. *The Young Augustine,* pp. 5, 17, 18, 13.
21. Solignac, p. 25.
22. H. I. Marrou, *Saint Augustin et la fin de la culture antique* (Paris: Boccard, 1938) , p. 61; *Retractatio,* vol. II of above (1949) , pp. 665–672. Marrou's observations here are excellent, and his remarks on Augustine's "musical" mode of composition especially perceptive.

. . . [but] a work of edification." Hence his own unhesitating agreement with Eduard Williger and Pierre Courcelle that Book X is a later interpolation "with some inevitable derangement of the material"; hence also his assertion that the tenuous connection between Books XI–XIII and the earlier books is explained by the fact that Augustine "combines all these various parts rather awkwardly, merely placing them one after the other." [23] There is, then, no solution to the problem of the unity of the *Confessions,* because the supposition that the work is a unity is false to begin with.

Voices of Hope

And yet, not all scholars will agree with O'Meara. Marrou himself has made some exceedingly apt remarks on the "musical" kind of unity that subtly binds Augustine's works together, and more recently Knauer has concluded that the presence of *peregrinatio* themes in Books XI–XIII is inexplicable unless the entire work shows a unity of conception.[24] But his case is somewhat weakened by the fact that his treatment of Augustine's "memory" meditation in Book X does little justice to the text as it stands, and by his avoidance of the challenge presented by the anomalous meditation on "time" in Book XI.[25]

And yet, the search for unity goes on. That fact alone should give pause. It may betray the lurking suspicion that Augustine composes neither badly nor just middling well. *Ars,* the model of the ancient *rhetor* warned, *est celare artem.* Augustine may actually have composed his work too well for us to detect the traces of his composition. And that failure on our part may signify a mildly ironic triumph on his.

Unity Still Possible

In any event it would be premature to close the debate at this point. We cannot positively exclude the possibility that the *Confessions* may yet disclose some unifying structure, some hidden principle of sense more subtle and elusive than the ones

23. *The Young Augustine,* pp. 13, 16.
24. *Peregrinatio,* p. 248.
25. *Ibid.,* pp. 234–237, 241. One can sympathize initially with Knauer's feeling that the Time-meditation *darf hier übergangen werden* (p. 241) but our analysis will show this is not permissible if the structural unity of the work is to be preserved.

proposed above, which quickens these seemingly disparate
themes, like branches from a single root, with the sap of a single
import.

ELEMENTS OF A HYPOTHESIS

That root-structure, I submit, not only exists but has,
paradoxically, already been found, not once but twice. What
alone remains to be explained is why the discoverers were not
fully alive to the ramifications of their discovery, and therefore
failed to present it in compelling form to the scholarly world.

For O'Meara is perfectly correct in affirming that Augustine is illustrating a theory of man that he felt was verified in his
own life. And that theory of man is none other than the
peregrinatio animae, but taken far more literally than Knauer
suspected: the wandering of the *soul* away from its beatific
contemplation of God in the "heaven of heaven," into a universe of body and space and time, till eventually (O'Meara's
insight again) providentially "admonished" of its true condition, it turns back to Him.[26]

Knauer has presented the rich variety of scriptural *Wort-
und-Bildmaterial* in which this dominant theme is vested.[27] Yet
he remains unable to bridge the gap that separates a dominant
theme from a unifying formal structure. And the reason is, I
suggest, that the Bible itself does not furnish us the unifying
formal structure of the *Confessions*—unless, that is, its materials
are informed, restructured by a Neo-Platonic theory of man, or
more precisely, by Augustine's adaptation of the Plotinian
theory of the soul's fall and return.

This Neo-Platonic view O'Meara himself has consistently
accented, but with almost unique stress on Porphyry. Significantly, however, he has advised us that the view of life contained in the *Confessions* is in substantial harmony with that
presented in the Cassiciacum Dialogues.[28] More specifically, he

---

26. Knauer, *ibid.*, p. 219, seems to have entertained this meaning as a
possibility, only to reject it. Cf. *ibid.*, p. 248, *"der irdische Lebensweg Augustins
fuhrte in der Vergangenheit,"* etc. What the Time-meditation means to make
clear is that Augustine's *peregrinatio animae* was by no means exclusively
"earthly"; it began in Eternity, in the Heaven of Heaven (cf. Book XII).

27. Knauer's own expression, *ibid.*, p. 218.

28. See his edition of *Against the Academics*, esp. pp. 22–23 and note-refer-
ences to *Confessions*. Also *"Arripui, aperui, et legi," Augustinus Magister* (Paris,
1954), I, 59–65.

has admitted that the Providence theme he finds so important occurs in those Dialogues in identifiable relation to Plotinus' treatise On Providence, *Ennead* III, 2–3.[29] He also has pointed to the fact that the "way" image, so crucial to Knauer's *peregrinatio* structure, is expressed in both *Confessions* and Dialogues in terms of the odyssey image—an ancient-world commonplace for the "wandering soul" (*anima peregrinans*)—familiar to Augustine from *Ennead* I, 6.[30]

Far less prominent in either of the above treatments is the omnipresence theme whose importance both Cayré and Mandouze have underlined,[31] and which Knauer rightly but inadequately explains by tracing it to Psalm 138.[32]

Now if Augustine's intellectual evolution can be envisaged as an effort to adapt Plotinianism to "understand" the faith of Christianity, then the challenges of the *Confessions* may bring out a critical confirmation of that view. Hesitantly elaborated, complicated by a series of corrections to Plotinus as Augustine's growing knowledge of Christianity forced them upon him, but, finally, employed as a background view to guide his interpretation of Scripture, this may be the finished view he wished to incorporate in his *Confessions*. But does the hypothesis here advanced yield satisfactory answers to the questions this perplexing work has raised? respect the detail as well as the major contours of the work? take into account what is evidently sound in the work of previous scholarship? Each of these queries must be answered in the affirmative before we can be content that it helps us understand Augustine, what he said, and what he meant by what he said.

The Addressees of the *Confessions*

It may safely be supposed that in writing his *Confessions* Augustine had a certain set of audiences in view, and that he shaped his message to respond to what he thought were their needs. The theory of man he proposed, accordingly, would be meant to confront those problems of human existence which those addressees took most to heart, and correct at need the solutions they brought to those problems.

29. *Against the Academics*, pp. 161, 170.
30. *Ibid.*, p. 186.
31. See n. 15, above.
32. *Peregrinatio*, p. 222. Psalms 138 is unquestionably operative, but inside a formal structure lent by *Ennead* VI, 4–5. See my article on the subject, pp. 32–33, and *Augustine's Early Theory*, pp. 40–42, 66–68.

The Manichees

Now the principal addressees of the Saint's early works are plainly the adherents of the heretical sect of which he himself had so long been a member. In fact, they represent his dominating concern up to and including the year 400, when he publishes his *Contra Faustum*. His sights are shifting slowly about this time, training more and more on the Donatists; some time later the Pelagians will occupy the center of his attention. But it should occasion no surprise that the principal (though by no means the only) polemic of his *Confessions* is still against the Manichees. A brief summary of their teaching may make this plainer.[33]

The Manichees and the teaching of Genesis

The Manichees first of all interpreted man's fallen experience in terms of a dualism which set them outside of the *Catholica*. From the viewpoint of their dualism, the Old Testament generally was to be rejected as an entirely "carnal and temporal" view of the human condition. Most objectionable was the Jewish confidence that a good God could be the creator of this detestable visible world and could have placed His first blessing on the marriage act; for Manichee dogma held matter, *Hulê*, to be identical with the "race of darkness" (*gens tenebrarum*), and thereby linked with the principle of concupiscence which would perpetuate the material imprisonment of souls, divine light-particles all, by inciting men to sexual generation. For these connected reasons, the book of Genesis was, in their eyes, not only a tissue of absurdities (what, for example, was God doing in those vast stretches of time preceding the "beginning" of creation?), it was worse than that: it was the manifest work of the devil, and a very special target for their scorn and criticism. This is why Augustine's first venture into exegesis was the *De Genesi contra Manichaeos;* it is, besides, one reason why he *must* terminate the *Confessions* with an exegesis of Genesis' account of creation. And in both instances his exegesis of Genesis calls forth the fullest and most outspoken presentation of his entire view of human life.

33. For what follows, see H. C. Puech, *Le Manichéisme, son fondateur, sa doctrine* (Paris, 1949). The many references to Augustine's works assure that this was Manichaeism as he knew it.

Faith, the quest for truth, and the problem of evil

But Manichaeism presented a positive program as well. Contemptuous of the "simple faith" in such anthropomorphic absurdities as the *Catholica* allegedly exacted of her children (if man, for example, was made "to His image," then God Himself must have human form, ears and feet and hair!), they lured their proselytes out on a quest for reasoned truth. Their primary question hit directly at man's universal experience of evil: if the one good God made all, then "whence is evil" (*unde est malum*)? Their dualism promised understanding of this situation; but that promise they failed to fulfill. Their "explanation" of human experience generally, and evil particularly, turned out to be a mythical tangle of absurdities, in which, ultimately, they too demanded "faith" of their adherents.

Adrift, as we know, at Rome and at Milan, Augustine was tempted to despair: Can the "seeker" for truth eventually hope to "find" it? Can man hope to glimpse, embrace, "possess" the Truth for which his restless heart longs? No, answered the Academics,[34] and Augustine was tempted to agree with them. Until he read Plotinus.

For Plotinus' answer was affirmative, and it not only made sense to Augustine, it seemed to rhyme with the answer given in Ambrose's spiritual exegesis of Scripture: the mass of mankind must "seek" in order to "find," "believe" before reaching "understanding," follow the indication of "one who points the way" which leads to vision and eventual enjoyment of supernal Truth.

Hence the Saint's first work, the *Contra Academicos*. Dedicated, significantly, to his Manichee friend Romanianus, it attempts to show that the apparently skeptical Academics are really crypto-Platonists speaking a riddle-language which makes sense in the light of Plotinus' revival of purest Platonism. If one but add the Christian fact that Truth Itself has "become Way," then Cicero's Academicism, Plotinus' Platonism, and the Catholic Scriptures (spiritually interpreted) are saying fundamentally the same thing: *quaerite et invenietis:* "seek and you shall find"; *nisi credideritis, non intelligetis:* "unless you [first]

---

34. *Conf* V, 19. Augustine is careful to warn us this was only the *common understanding* of their doctrine; his personal theory has it they were crypto-Platonists (*Acad* III, 37–43). This is part of a preoccupation we shall not go into here, namely, showing that, properly understood, Roman and Greek philosophy agree both with each other and with Christianity. See *Augustine's Early Theory*, pp. 193–196.

believe, you will not [come to] understand." [35] That much
assured, Augustine feels confident he can answer the Manichees'
objections more satisfactorily than they themselves could.

Exercitatio animi *and the return to "vision"*

The *De Beata Vita* stresses this same consonance between
Christianity and Plotinianism, adding that happiness consists in
the beatifying embrace of Truth, the Son of God, and that this
is possible to man. The *De Ordine* moves directly to the question "whence is evil?" If Providence is universal, as the *Catholica* believes and *Ennead* III, 2–3 demonstrates, then whence
indeed does evil come? The solution demands more of Augustine than he can at this time furnish. He backs away from the
central issue not once but twice,[36] and leaves us with the
message found in the *Soliloquies* as well: the clouded eye of the
fallen soul must be "exercised" by an ordered series of studies,
purified and strengthened before it can gaze squarely at the Sun
of Truth.[37] *Exercitatio animi*—the "exercising of the mind"—
Marrou has well underlined the importance of this technique in
Augustine's writings.[38] The Manichees, Augustine insists
throughout his early works and in the *Confessions* as well, do
not realize that their efforts at thinking out the human condition are little more than a tissue of "vain imaginings," shot
through with the corporeal phantasms Plotinus attempts to
exorcise in his Omnipresence treatise, *Ennead* VI, 4–5.[39]

The *exercitatio animi* is, however, a technique with certain
anthropological suppositions; these Augustine has progressively
disclosed in the series of his early works.

Man's real, authentic self is "soul," and soul characterized
as substantial thirst for the vision of Truth *(Sol I)*. Its immortality is evidenced by the fact that it is "subject" in which dwells
immortal Truth—and that, despite its immersion in a bodily
world of mendacious imitations of that Truth, immersion

---

35. See my article, "Happiness," esp. pp. 152–160; *Augustine's Early Theory*,
pp. 223–257.
36. Compare the brutal statement of the problem in *Ord* I, 1 with the
point the argument has reached in *Ord* II, 13 and 22. In both instances
Augustine retreats into an exposition of how much his students need an *ordo
studiorum* before they can face this question with adequate preparation. See
my "The Plotinian Fall of the Soul in St. Augustine," *Traditio*, 19:1–35 (1963),
hereafter cited as "Plotinian Fall"; and *Augustine's Early Theory*, pp. 169–173.
37. *Sol* II, 23.
38. *Culture antique*, pp. 299–327.
39. See "*Ennead* VI, 4–5," pp. 13–14.

which accounts for the (partial) "forgetfulness" of Truth particularly manifest in those incapable of studying the liberal
disciplines (*Sol* II). That immortality makes it impossible that
the soul be thought of as a body, or a "harmony" of the body;
soul can neither perish, nor die, nor be changed into some
inferior species of being (*Immort*). It must not be conceived of
as "great" in any quantified sense. Its true "greatness" can be
grasped only by studying the seven ascending, and progressively
disincarnate, levels of its activity—levels which show that its
true status must be situated well above the human, that nothing
but God is superior to the soul. It is, in fact, the equal of the
angel (*par angelo*), with any (temporary) inferiority to the
angel being accounted for by its having sinned (*Quant*).

How is this "sin" to be conceived of? It must be the soul's
own free act—and yet (the question of the *De Ordine* has returned) not understood in such a way as to make God blame-
worthy for it. To this nettling issue Augustine devotes the first
two books of the *De Libero Arbitrio,* eventually concluding
that the primal sin responsible for the soul's immersion in the
world of bodies, in a "life" that is "death" when compared to
what it once enjoyed, consists in its having "turned away" from
the contemplative embrace of God, the highest and unchangeable good, to find its delight in lower, changeable goods (*Lib*
II, 53). That "aversion," finally, because it is an essentially evil
and defective movement, is in itself a "nothing" (*nihil*) and
therefore cannot be attributed to God whose creative power
always produces something positive and good (*Lib* II, 54).

Immersed in body now, and sunk in sense, the vast major-
ity of souls are unable to arrive at genuine understanding.
Their spiritual "eye" must be cleansed and at the same time
strengthened before it can penetrate to, and bear, the radiance
of the Light whose vision it once enjoyed: thus the need for the
exercitatio animi.

From this point of view, the *Confessions* in its entirety represents one extended *exercitatio,* designed to reawaken the soul
to knowledge of both itself and God: for the Plotinian, the
knowledge of the Archetype is always implied in the knowledge
of the image.[40]

Moral purification, faith, confessio

To arrive at this insight into its quality as image of God, a
stringent moral purification is necessary—not only for Augus-

40. See "Happiness," esp. pp. 153–154.

tine, but for Plotinus as well.[41] And the fundamental supposition underlying the "morals of the Church" and (one side at least of) the Neo-Platonic view is that the soul is fallen partially through its own fault: it is being "chastised" for its own "iniquity." [42] Such admission of fault as rooting the soul's miserable condition in this life is entirely absent from the Manichaean view. The Manichees claim their souls are particles of the Divine Light, taken off into captivity by the jealous hordes of the "race of darkness," but without the slightest fault on their part.

This blasphemous claim to be—not image, but—equal to God, and its related refusal to "confess" their primal sin, is the central instance of that "presumption" (*praesumptio*) which keeps their minds in merited darkness. Here we have the recommendation implicit in still another, and this time properly Augustinian, sense of the term *confessio*.[43] Were the Manichees to abandon this *praesumptio*, humble themselves under God's "powerful hand," don the yoke and admit "the usefulness of belief," submit to the salutary precepts of the *Catholica*, accept the temporal misfortunes entailed in fallen, bodily existence as God's providential means of detaching the heart from this lower world—were they, in short, to "confess" that "none is like unto God"—then their mind's eye might be cleansed and they might arrive at a true understanding of their state and eventual vision of the Divine Light.[44]

But this requires that they become *parvuli*, "little" enough to accept in faith and trust the maternal care of the Church, realizing that the faith initially exacted of them leads eventually to understanding and to vision. For just as charity, the precept central to "morals of the Church," directs the soul to desire nothing above the splendor of that vision, so in all her teaching the Church claims to be doing what all words, all sensible realities are geared to do: "admonishing" the soul, directing its gaze inward (and upward) to the Light which is the Eternal Christ, unique "teacher" of all Christians (*Mag*) .

41. *Ibid.*, pp. 155–156.
42. *Ibid.*, pp. 163–164. This is part of the burden of the *De Libero Arbitrio*, and an important issue in the *De Genesi contra Manichaeos*, both of which endeavor to prove that reason and Scripture coincide in tracing the evils of human existence to original sin, understood in Plotinian fashion. See also *Augustine's Early Theory*, pp. 155–183.
43. See *Conf* VII, 26 and Solignac's remarks, p. 15. Also, *Augustine's Early Theory*, pp. 108–109.
44. See "*Ennead* VI, 4–5," pp. 13–14, and *Augustine's Early Theory*, pp. 43–45.

The Neo-Platonists, Another Set of Addressees

But *praesumptio,* Augustine progressively discovered, was
not characteristic solely of the Manichees. It affected the Neo-
Platonists as well. For they too, despite all the kinship between
their doctrines and those of the *Catholica,* refused to humble
themselves and accept the humble Christ; despite the liminal
function of belief which Plotinus himself had stressed, they refused to believe that the Truth to which he "pointed" could
become the "way" of which he spoke. The consonance between
Plotinianism and Christianity spiritually understood is the positive burden of Augustine's early work; in the *De Vera Religione* he shows pained awareness that the Neo-Platonists themselves do not seem to have appreciated his thesis.[45] The
Confessions represents, therefore, his heroic attempt to show that
consonance again. They could not miss the fact that his
interpretation of human existence from infancy forward was
substantially identical with theirs. His final books are designed
to make clear that their own kind of exegesis, applied to the
Bible, brings out that consonance from another angle. The faith
of the *Catholica* is at one with the "understanding" of the
platonici: why, then, do they still hang back?

"Conservative" Catholics

The tensions of Neo-Platonic Christianity
Between Plotinianism and Christianity, however, there
were a number of major discrepancies.[46] Plotinus' suggestions
that the soul might be "divine," immovable, and centrally
unaffected by the sin that made it "fall," Augustine has in time
eliminated. And still, Plotinianism is manifestly a way for the
intellectual "few" who can arise to philosophic and mystical
heights. Further, it counsels that elect "few" to leave the world
of action and charitable concern for others and flee to the
Plotinopolis of undisturbed contemplation. Christianity, on the
other hand, claims that Christ is the "universal way" (*via uni-*

45. *Ver* 6.
46. We pass over for the moment those Neo-Platonic suggestions of the
soul's enjoying a "divine" status, and their resolute rejection of prayer in any
meaningful Christian sense. It is hard to see how Augustine could have missed
them (see *Enn* III, 2–3 and IV, 3–5, passim) in his earlier readings, but he
does not stress these discrepancies, at least until his later polemic against Neo-
Platonism in the *De Civitate.* On the soul's "divinity," see *Augustine's Early
Theory,* pp. 31–64, 112–131.

versalis) , that He left His Church as mother and capacious bosom for the many, the *turba*. Unable to rise above simple faith to any recondite "spiritual understanding" of the imaged language Scripture employs, these "little ones" can nonetheless live the life of brotherly charity which is the whole of Christ's law.

We have elsewhere observed Augustine's determined effort to iron out these discrepancies. An initial "faith" was in the logic of Neo-Platonism itself, the exigency for passing on toward "understanding" and "vision" part of Christianity's message. That passage, which at first he felt required a full course in the "liberal disciplines," he now believes will be assured by the purifying fire of "charity"—a charity interpreted as the soul's native Eros-desire for contemplative bliss. He will later go so far as to maintain that the "universal way" was the implicit desideratum not only of Plato but even of that Porphyry whose polemic *Against the Christians* raised such difficulties against the faith. That work must only have heaped fuel on the smoldering suspicion, distrust, and opposition that Augustine's writings seem to have met in certain "conservative" Catholic circles.

Opposition from "conservative" Catholics

There are good grounds for thinking that the Saint encountered such opposition quite early in his writing career, and from inside the *Catholica* itself. African Christianity especially seems to have been conservative in tendency, suspicious on principle of any such flights toward philosophic *intellectus* of the faith.[47] In the opening of the second book of the *De Libero Arbitrio*, Augustine seems to have meant to deal with complaints from this quarter: Christ's promise of eternal life implies we must begin with faith, but then pass on to "knowledge" of Him (*Lib* II, 6) . By the time of the *Confessions*, however, his successive triumphs over the Manichees may largely have persuaded the opposition that his quest for understanding was not only legitimate but necessary and salutary. Yet in the *Confessions* the opposition is still present, and from those "lovers of the sacred books" who say that although the Genesis-

47. Cyprian's admiration for the Tertullian he never mentioned, and his dominance in the minds of African Christians, are both uncontested. But there is more than a hint of this anti-intellectual attitude in Augustine's review of his youthful experience for the benefit of Honoratus in *De Utilitate Credendi*, esp. 13–17. Cf. *Conf* XI, 14 where, treating of a Manichee objection, Augustine rejects a kind of anti-intellectual response that may well have had a historical counterpart. See *Augustine's Early Theory*, pp. 232–235.

interpretation Augustine presents may be true and very inspir-
ing, it is not the meaning Moses had in mind.[48]

Again, focus on the Hexaemeron

Augustine therefore had an additional reason for culminat-
ing the *Confessions* with an attempt to show what lights God
had accorded him in interpretation of Scripture—an attempt
designed to prove that the theory of man as fallen soul can be
drawn from the sacred text by "spiritual exegesis." This manner
of interpreting Scripture, he was careful to insist earlier, was
exploited by none other than Ambrose of Milan.[49] His prestige
is beyond question; and with the salutary fruits of his preaching, particularly in Augustine's own case, his readers are by now
familiar.

Until Augustine reaches this portion of his work, in fact,
the Plotinian theory of the fallen soul remains largely implicit.
One could miss it entirely—as indeed scholars seem to have
done for centuries. And part of the reason may be that they
were not profoundly convinced of the unity of the *Confessions*,
and failed in consequence to search these final books for the key
that unlocks the meaning of his experience as Augustine formulated it. Phrases in the earlier books, which there remain
either obscure or ambiguous, recur in the scriptural interpretation later, with most, if not all, their ambiguity removed.

Not only does this opposition from within the *Catholica*
dictate that Augustine demonstrate his theory of human life to
be scriptural. It does more. It virtually dictates the locus of
Scripture he must interpret. And once again the choice falls on
Genesis, but this time precisely on Genesis 1, up to and including the first two verses of Chapter 2.

Augustine's "traditional" view of the Hexaemeron

Put this way, the choice seems utterly arbitrary. But a
glance at the text in any scholarly edition of the Bible will show
that the portion selected is a natural unit, is in fact the
Hexaemeron itself, the work of the "six days" of creation,
terminating in the mention of God's Sabbath of "rest." Immediately we are reminded that the story of creation was, for the
ancient *Hexaemeral* interpreters, a privileged locus for explain-

48. *Conf* XII, 18–43. His adversaries here were quite probably more
competent exegetes than Augustine was. See Maurice Pontet, *L'exégèse de saint
Augustin prédicateur* (Paris, 1944) , ep. pp. 581–587.

49. *Conf* V, 24–25; VI, 3–8. There was obviously a certain advantage in
covering oneself with Ambrose's prestige on this point.

ing the Christian "theory of man." Augustine, therefore, in interpreting this section of Genesis in defense of his central thesis, is following an already well-established tradition. This tradition looked on the *Hexaemeron* as a figured account of the act of creation, granted, but even more important as a symbolic portrayal of man's God-given nature and place in the created order, and further, as a "prophetic" account of the six "days" or ages of the world. Augustine, therefore, was far from exceptional in regarding this "small part of [the] book" as a compendium of all Scripture, enclosing the entire history of humanity, created, fallen, and now wandering under God's providential guidance through the "desert" of this world and back to the promised land, the paradise of eternal "rest" in God.[50] That he shared this view of the *Hexaemeron* is clear from the *De Genesi contra Manichaeos*. No words, he tells us, can do justice to God's manner of creation, "but this exposition in an order of days sets forth a history, as though of things done, in order to concentrate principally on proclaiming things to come": *ut praedicationem futurorum* MAXIME *observet*.[51]

But he betrays the fact that he shares this view still while writing the *Confessions;* the prayer with which he begins his interpretation of it there asks for light to consider the "wonderful things of your Law from the Beginning in Whom you made heaven and earth, even to the everlasting kingdom with you in your holy city" (XI, 3).[52] The same impression is borne out by the fact that, having completed an initial interpretation of them in Books XI–XII, he comes back to extract a "prophetic" explanation of these same verses in Book XIII. Here again, all human history unfolds before us, but under the guise of the soul's *peregrinatio* back to the Sabbath repose in the "city of God" from which it has fallen.

50. See Jean Daniélou, "La typologie millénariste de la semaine dans le christianisme primitif," *Vigiliae Christianae*, 2:1–16 (1948); also Olivier Rousseau, "La typologie augustinienne de l'*Hexaemeron* et la théologie du temps," *Festgabe Joseph Lortz* (Baden-Baden, 1958), II, 47–58.

51. *Gen Man* I, 41. Note that this passage climaxes a "spiritual exegesis" of the seven days of creation as prefiguring the seven ages of human history, I, 35–41, while I, 42 proceeds to find in it the stages of each man's spiritual life. Cf. *ibid.* II, 1: the *Hexaemeron*, though only a *parva pars libri*, deserves nonetheless to be called *liber creaturae coeli et terrae*, since *universi saeculi a capite usque in finem quasi brevis quaedam imago in his diebus septem figurata est.*

52. In the light of the above, I find questionable Courcelle's suggestion that the *Confessions* was originally intended as a prelude to Augustine's interpretation of all Scripture, from Genesis to Apocalypse. See *Recherches sur les Confessions* (Paris, 1950), pp. 22–23.

The Pastor's Flock

No enumeration of the *Confessions'* addressees would be
complete without mention of Augustine's flock at Hippo. His
work is aimed at least in part at urging and helping them to
overcome the temptations which the ambient culture laid in
their path. Frederik Van der Meer has ably catalogued those
temptations as they appear in the Bishop's sermons to his con-
gregation: the cultural unity of the Roman world must have
persuaded Augustine that his parishioners were more or less
typical of Christians more generally, who all had to resist the
attractions of the circus games and gladiatorial contests, astrol-
ogy, the alluring eroticism of the theater, the remnants of
paganism, and the snares of ancient letters.[53] These manifold
temptations were of course known to Augustine from both personal and pastoral experience. His treatment of them could lead
him into a series of edifying digressions which would destroy the
unity of his work; but his theory of man is remarkable at least
for its tremendous power of assimilation. Once uncovered, the
hidden formal structure which is his anthropology places more
than ever beyond doubt that the *Confessions* ranks as one of
the world's great literary masterpieces.

53. F. Van der Meer, *Augustine the Bishop* (New York, 1961), esp. pp.
29–75, 347–360, 471–526. This book is invaluable for understanding Augustine's
diversified pastoral preoccupations.

1 SOUL'S ODYSSEY:
FALL AND RETURN

A number of the elements that form Augustine's theory of man have been alluded to in the Introduction. To clarify what is to follow we should first draw these elements together into a synthetic view.[1]

The Authentic "I": A Fallen Soul

Man, as the Augustine of the *Confessions* depicts him, is a composite of soul and body—"this" body of our experience. But his true identity, the real "I," is soul, soul originally intended for a life spent in blissful contemplation of the divine splendor in the heavenly "City of God." Our souls, then, pre-existed,

1. For justification of the view presented here, the reader may consult *Augustine's Early Theory*. The section titles here closely correspond to the chapter headings of that work, so there will be little difficulty in locating the relevant portions. I shall refer frequently here to the *Notes Complémentaires* which Solignac has appended to the *Bibliothèque Augustinienne* edition of the *Confessions*. Such references are meant to stimulate the reader to compare the interpretation Solignac gives (with ample textual material and bibliographical details) of various key notions from the *Confessions*. The reader will judge whether my perspective leads me to distort the view that emerges from the textual materials Solignac brings together and from the studies he refers to, rather than merely sharpening that view.

"enjoyed" the vision of God's supernal Truth and Beauty, but fell from that blissful state into the life we know as human beings.

Were we in any sense "embodied" there, in the celestial paradise? Augustine, when forced to face that question, admits that we were, but our bodies seem to have been so pure, transparent, and "spiritual" that it becomes difficult to say whether "body" is any longer the appropriate term to describe them. If "bodies" they genuinely are, they are certainly not the sort of bodies we refer to as such from our sense-experience. Heavenly as opposed to earthly, immortal and incorruptible as opposed to the mortal and corruptible bodies our souls now wear like those "tunics" of animal skin the Lord bestowed on Adam and Eve on their dismissal from paradise, the "reformation" which is promised us at the time of the resurrection is described as literally "angelic." We shall, on our "return," be the equal of the angels once again, just as, before our "fall," we were their fellow-citizens in the City of God. It is well to remember in this connection that Platonists, Neo-Platonists, and the early Fathers did not share the widespread contemporary view that the angel is a "pure" spirit, in the strict Thomistic sense.

The ambiguities of this doctrine of the spiritual body, then, permit Augustine to refer to death quite simply as the soul's "release" from the body, a release which (if we have lived well) will issue in the soul's "return" to the "spiritual," to the bliss from which it fell. His later thinking, wherein an early revulsion to the body and sense is compelled steadily to give ground before Christianity's stress on Incarnation, the goodness of the material world, and the eventual resurrection of the body, finds him choosing his expressions far more carefully than in his earlier works; but at the time of the *Confessions*, those pressures have only begun to make themselves felt, and can for our purposes largely be discounted.[2]

> To summarize, then, the real "I" is a soul, fallen into a body, the resulting amalgam being a "man."

2. It is worth noting here how most of the texts adduced by H. I. Marrou in his study of Augustine's resurrection teaching are relatively late texts, almost all, in fact, dating from works subsequent to the *Confessions*. See his "Le dogme de la résurrection des corps et la théologie des valeurs humaines selon l'enseignement de saint Augustin," *Revue des Études Augustiniennes*, 12:111–126 (1966). Also printed as *The Resurrection and St. Augustine's Theology of Human Values* (Villanova, Pa.: Villanova University Press, 1966).

The Mechanism of the Soul's "Fall"

How is one to understand that a soul, blissful, unified, and at rest in a life of contemplation, should choose to leave it for (what Augustine invariably characterizes as) this "miserable" life of being weighed down by a body, and buffeted about among a world of bodies—this life of being torn apart by desires and cares, spilled out in a diversity of activities, stretched out into the succession of time?

The Soul's Triadic "Fault" ◢

This primal iniquitous choice Augustine traces to a triad of vices. The fundamental one is the "pride" (*superbia*) which prompts the soul to reject the "mid-station," intermediate between God and the world of sensible realities, to which the Divine Law inscribed in its very being assigns it. It would seem that without that rebellious pride, the soul would never yield to the second and third of the vices which also help to explain its "immersion" in the sensible, corporeal world: to the "carnal concupiscence" which stirs it to seek bodily delights in place of the spiritual delights of contemplation; and to the restless, inquisitive "curiosity" which goads it to taste of "experience" of every sort, particularly the sense of power that comes with imitating God by acting on and forming the sensible order upon the pattern of the intelligible world.

The Working of Law and the Result of Fault

The soul's "fall" therefore is the result of its own iniquitous fault. But it is, at the same time, in the very nature of things that a soul yielding to the attraction of being independent of God, of tasting bodily delights and the joys of experiencing its own power of action on bodies, should "fall." Its immersion in the world of body and sense is at one and the same time the natural result of its having been drawn downward by the "weight" of its "attachment" to this lower realm, and (because so "natural," so inexorable a result) the effect of the Eternal Law working interiorly to assign to each being the "place" appropriate to its "weight."

"Weights" and Justification of the Fall

Not alone to express, but even to conceive of this inner identity of soul-fault and the working of inexorable law, Augustine employs a daring (and in some respects, disturbing) spiritual analogue of the prevailing image the ancients entertained of the physical world. Each bodily type in the sublunar universe was thought of as containing a dominant portion of one of the four "elements": earth, water, air, or fire. Those elements each had a different "weight," earth being the heaviest, water, air, and fire being progressively "lighter." The relative weight of each element assigned it its natural "place" in the universe of bodies; it tended toward, "sought," its appropriate level, fire traveling upward, earth downward until the former came to "rest" above the air, the latter below the realm of water. In any concrete body, therefore, an admixture of opposing elements (earth with fire, for example) would determine the body's place as somewhere between the places proper to the two opposing elements in their pure state.

The spiritual universe Augustine sees as run on a parallel principle. The soul was meant naturally to enjoy a place on high, just below the Eternal Light itself. By "cleaving" in love to that highest of realities, the soul participated in its quality of lightsomeness, in every sense of that ambiguous term. United to God, it was at "rest." But it turned away from that Light, attached itself, cleaved in love to the inferior (and "heavier") realities of earth; the admixture of earth "weighed" it, drew it "down" to the lower region which it now inhabits. Thanks to God's providential action on its behalf, however, the divine Spirit of love, the "fire" of charity, has been poured into our hearts. The working of that charity-fire is diversely conceived of; it has the effect of "purifying" the soul of earthly alloy, of "lightening" it by detaching it from the earthly accretion which resulted from its having clung to lower realities, "warming" it, "melting" the ice of its sinfulness, kindling it and setting it afire so that it naturally rises again to its place on high. "My weight is my love," Augustine will summarize: *pondus meum, amor meus* (*Conf* XIII, 10).

There is a side-effect to this manner of envisaging the coincidence between the working of Logos and the intrinsically necessary resultant of the soul's "fall": it prevents our complaining against the justice of the decree whereby God "dis-

missed" us to the lower, corporeal world. We ourselves are to
blame; His punishment of us is presented, not as capricious or
arbitrary, but as following inexorably from the innate justice of
things.

But in case this justification of our miserable condition
does not seem adequate, Augustine borrows another consideration from Plotinus to reconcile us with our fallen state. The
experience of evils in this lower world is bound to make us
more keenly appreciate the sweetness of the paradise we left.
Once returned, we shall (Augustine is confident—more confident than Plotinus) be that much firmer in our adherence to
the good: *securior rediturus in coelum* (*Acad* II, 22). One trip
to this underworld, Augustine seems to think, will be enough
for us.

Providence, Admonition, and "Return"

But the same universal Law, the Divine Logos that confers
order on the entire cosmos, works not only to assign to fallen
souls their place in the inferior world of sense; it has set afoot a
thousand devices for bringing the wandering soul back to its
eternal home. All the order of the world is designed to
"admonish," quite literally to "remind" the soul of the higher,
intelligible order on which it is patterned. Even pains, evils,
suffering serve to awaken the soul to the paradise of bliss it once
knew. Providence is not only universal, working in and through
all things without exception; it is also "omnipresent" or, more
correctly (since we are speaking of the utter simplicity of the
divine nature), Omnipresence. It never deserts the soul which
has deserted the Father's house, "turned away" and gone
wandering upon the rugged roads, across the stormy seas and
parched deserts of this world.

From "Un-knower" to "Knower"

One mark of the soul's fallen condition is its blindness, its
ignorance of God's omnipresence working through all the
admonitory created realities that would hasten its return.
Admonished, it is regularly "ignorant," does not "know" the
admonition for what it is, another instance of God's tireless
activity to "convert" it from wandering to homeward pilgrimage. From this point of view, conversion means changing
the un-knower to a "knower."

Incarnation, Symbol, and Authority [3]

In this comprehensive economy of return, the ultimate condescension of Divine Providence is Incarnation: the Logos Himself has been "made flesh" to call us back, "remind" us, make us "know again" the happiness we left.

All the works and words of men perform a similar admonitory function. Their effect is to remind the soul, turn its attention from "outer," sensible realities to "within" itself where it can contact the intelligible Light. The soul in its unfallen state directly intuited not only that Light, but the thoughts and affections of its fellow-souls as well. Now, fallen into body and immersed in sense-realities, it must communicate with other souls through the indirect medium of language, gesture, sign, and symbol; its spiritual eye weakened to the point where that Light is too strong for its gaze, it must begin its reascent to vision by accepting the semiopaque symbolic utterances through which "authorities" point the way back to vision. Both the need for symbolic communication, then, and the soul's initial dependence on "authority," are results of the fall and at the same time instruments for "return."

Toward Reasoned Understanding and Vision

But their value lies in their "usefulness" and is, in consequence, only provisional. Symbol is meant to prompt return to vision without symbolic intermediary; authority is meant to urge the soul to pass upward from initial "belief" toward reasoned understanding, and eventually "arrive" at vision, the permanent "enjoyment" of supernal Truth. This rule holds for all authorities: for the words of a Plotinus, of a Paul, or of a Jesus of Nazareth.

he Man, Christ Jesus [4]

But Jesus holds a special place among authorities. Even Augustine's earliest thinking viewed Him in terms closely resembling those of the Antiochean *homo assumptus* theology: as a "man" (that is, a fully constituted human nature), but

3. Here I group together materials taken from Chaps. 6–10 of *Augustine's Early Theory;* see esp. pp. 161–166, 223–226, 235–257.
4. See *Augustine's Early Theory*, Chap. 10, pp. 259–278.

"participating" in a uniquely special manner in the Divine
Wisdom which is identical with the Divine, Eternal "Christ,"
supernal Truth and unbegotten Son of the Father. The human
words he uttered in the flesh were aimed at turning us within to
where His Eternal Light could be glimpsed; his human works,
on the other hand, were meant both to commend his unique
authority to our belief, and to furnish the most perfect example
of that detachment from earthly goods and freedom from
human fears which the soul's return requires of us.

The Augustine of the *Confessions* scores the inadequacy of
this earlier view; but still, he presents some aspects of Christ's
redemptive work as he did earlier. There has, however, been
one important change. The union of Word and "flesh" he tends
to view in more Alexandrian terms, stressing the closeness of the
union with the danger of confusing the divine and human
natures in Christ: *cibus miscens carni,* "the food [of Truth]
mixed with flesh" is one seriously questionable expression he >
uses (*Conf* VII, 24).

The Lexicon of Happiness

But that expression suggests another image Augustine uses
to portray the soul's situation: as "hungering" for the "food" of
Truth on which it once was fed. The language and imagery first
appears in his earliest work *On the Happy Life,*[5] where he
proves that the soul is "nourished" by thoughts, ideas, and
ultimately on eternal Truth, true food of the mind's "delight"
(*frui*). The implication is that it once enjoyed this spiritual
"banquet" but has fallen into "want" and hunger. What caused ·
it to turn away from the banquet? Augustine suggests (*Vita* 17) ·
it was either weakness, satedness, or "busy-ness," *inbecillitas,* .
saturitas, or *negotium*. The *Confessions* will add another possibility; it might have been a kind of "weariness" (*fastidium*) >
not unconnected, one may think, with a feeling of satiety.[6] The
terms recall Plotinus' own account of "The Soul's Descent into
the Body" (*Enn* IV, 8) where he speaks of the soul's "weary
desire" of leaving the All-Soul and standing on its own (IV, 8,
4). But Augustine almost certainly read that phrase in connection with the Plotinian description of the soul's fall into time
and the "busy-ness" of action. He is thinking of the "unquiet

---

5. *De Beata Vita,* see esp. sections 6–9, 22–32; also, *Augustine's Early Theory,*
Chap. 7, pp. 194–195, and Chap. 8.
6. See *Conf* II, 9; but cf. also VI, 13.

faculty" on account of which the soul, in (what he will regularly term the leisure, *otium* of) contemplative bliss, "could not
bear to retain within itself all the dense fullness of its possession"; like a seed "uncoiling outwards" it makes its way
"toward what seems to it a large life; but . . . fritters its unity
away" and advances into the "weaker greatness" of a temporal
life of action, "busy-ness": *negotium* (*Enn* III, 7, 11) .[7]

Egestas copiosa, "abundant want," is one of Augustine's
favorite paradoxes for characterizing the fallen state. The *De
Beata Vita* furnishes a picture of the fall in language and
imagery which recur frequently in the *Confessions:* it implies
that the soul somehow became "sated" with the food of Truth
which it had in abundance and in which it took delight. It
turned away from the quiet of its contemplation, however, to
seek a more active delight amid the fluid, changing realities of a
lower realm which seemed to it richer, but were really closer to
"nothing"; they proved in the end to be a land of "want"
(*regio egestatis*) . Empty now and famished, the soul is too weak
to find nourishment in the food of Truth itself. It needs to
begin, like a child, by accepting the "milk" of faith, and in
faith, eating that "food mixed with flesh," Truth Incarnate.
The joint has been forged between the lexicon of the happy life
and the way of faith, understanding, and vision.

But there is another (and important) overtone to Augustine's image of happiness: for the soul's delight is often expressed in the frankly erotic imagery of "union" and "embrace"
—"knowledge" in a sense designed to bring the Plotinian Eros
into unison with the Canticle of Canticles.

Splendor of Truth, therefore, in whose Light the soul will
bask in peaceful contemplation; infinite sweetness, food for the
hungry soul; Beauty inviting it to "possession" imagined as
"embrace" and "clinging"—these are Augustine's images of the
God of his desires. They are, as well, the touchstones for
understanding the mission of Incarnate Wisdom: Truth become "way" to lead us back to Truth; "food" mixed with flesh
to prepare us for the heavenly banquet; Beauty peering out
through the "lattices of the flesh," enticing us to run after the
"odor of His ointments."

7. For the connection Augustine's mind has established between these two
descriptions (among others) of the soul's fall, see *Augustine's Early Theory,*
Chap. 6, pp. 173–182.

Memory, Illumination, and the Soul Not
Entirely "Fallen"

But did it not "remember," however dimly, the Truth it once "saw," no "reminder" could ever succeed in prompting the soul to "re-cognize"—quite literally to "know again"—the Truth which it has only partially forgotten.

Or, put another way, the soul is not entirely "fallen." Like a man immersed in water up to the neck, its topmost point still emerges from the world of sense, still remains in contact with the intelligible splendor. "Memory" is not *merely* memory of a past vision, it is also present "illumination": the Light of the "higher" Intelligible World still streams into the soul. This complex way of viewing the soul's situation accounts for the variety of images Augustine uses to depict "conversion." For while "admonitions" all function to "turn" the soul, they can be variously conceived of as turning it *back* to remember again the homeland it left, or turning its gaze to *"within"* itself where the Light still illumines it. It must be kept in mind, however, that this turn "within" is equivalent to raising the soul's eye to what is *above* it, since this interior Light streams down from the superior, spiritual world.

Souls Diversely "Fallen"

Not all souls are, however, equally susceptible to this work of "reminder." The reason is that not all souls are equally "fallen"—their primordial choice sent some of them plunging more deeply than others into the opacities of body and the darkness of fleshly affections. For such as these, the work of "forgetfulness" is more complete; they are, in consequence, more skeptical about this tale of pre-existence. Encouraged, in many instances, by a "carnal" understanding of the Bible, and especially of the creation account in Genesis, they incline to accept the customary evaluation of our condition which thinks that God originally intended us for a "human" life, a life of temporal action with all its attendant getting and begetting, cares and carnal relationships, its dependence on sense, its need to rely on signs and symbols to communicate with other souls. Augustine's view drastically relativizes all the sometimes tragic grandeur of the human situation, and he knows his theory will

not go down too easily with those who take the works of history
and man to be of real and lasting value.

Exercitatio Animi, the "Disciplines," and the
Interpretation of Scripture

What all souls need to some extent, but what these hard-
ened skeptics especially require, is a sharpening of their spiritual vision--*exercitatio animi*--that will promote their coming to
a radically new perspective on the deepest implications of their
experience. Early in his career, impressed by his readings in
Varro, and convinced that Varro's views were basically consonant with Plotinus', Augustine vaunts the "liberal disciplines" (grammar, geometry, music, dialectic, and so forth) as
the appropriate means of training for spiritual insight; he even
goes so far as to try to convince his mother, Monica, that she
should embark on the "order" of studies he traces out for that
purpose.[8] For here, above all other areas of human knowledge,
the mind exhibits a native familiarity with a priori truths; so
contrasted are they in their necessity and universality with the
changing and particular truths provided by sensation, Augustine feels they argue for the soul's having remembered them
from some vision enjoyed in its pre-existent state. Exposing the
mind to them again will sensitize it, he thinks, to truths (and
Truth) still latent in memory. Hence the firm connection
between "memory" and the "disciplines" which runs as a constant through his earlier works.

Even at the time Augustine writes the *Confessions* this
connection has not been entirely repudiated. He would still
have men reflect that the power they have of passing intelligible
judgments shows their souls have come from another realm and
are, to some extent, still "there." But now Augustine widens his
canvas; he wishes to include commoner areas of human experience as well. He would have men reflect on their joys and sad-
nesses, their friendships, ambitions, desires, and doubts, the
delights that attract and the evils that befall them. Each of these
experiences, when scrutinized in depth, points to a life of joy
once lived, desire once totally assuaged, truth once completely
possessed, a life without evil and full of delight. Similarly, the
busy, harried existence amid the successions of time shows up,
under analysis, as a "distention," hinting at a former existence
of perfect leisure, collectedness, and peace.

8. See *Augustine's Early Theory*, Chap. 9, pp. 227–231.

Finally, if they be Christians, men must be assured that this perspective is the one which Scripture, and notably the book of Genesis, assumes on human life. Spiritually and prophetically interpreted, Augustine feels, it tells of the soul's creation in a supra-terrestrial paradise of bliss, of its fall into an earthly human existence, and now, of its providentially guided pilgrimage through history, back to the heavenly Jerusalem, the City of God.

Images of Divine "Care" [9]

That providential guidance of mankind's journey back to paradise finds expression in a series of powerful images, all of them expressing the omnipresent "care" which God, now like a nurse or mother-hen, now like a father or doctor, lavishes unceasingly upon the fallen soul.

At times His care is paternal: like the father of the Prodigal, he awaits our return, but unlike him, He dogs our wandering steps, remains forever present to us, fostering that return at every stage of life's journey. He seasons all our earthly pleasures with disgust and discontent, reminding us that we were made for higher delights than those. He chastises and "disciplines" us as a father should, to bring us into the right way back to Him; He applies (like a doctor) the medicinal pain, sends the tempests of suffering that keep us restless while pursuing the homeward odyssey of human life; He keeps reminding us in a variety of ways that the desert, the storm-tossed sea, is not our haven, our native homeland; He labors in and through all things to "awaken" us from the slumber of the human condition, "convert," quite literally, "turn us around" for the return to Him—or rather, more exactly, twist our head about to face the vile, distorted things we have made of ourselves.

For the action whereby He turns us back to Himself is regularly imaged as of a gentler, more maternal sort. The breasts that nourish infancy really bring us His nurturing bounty; the beauties that attract us are messengers of His supernal beauty calling our hearts home; the wings that enfold us in the nest of the faith are the Church's maternal wings, to be sure, but even more, they are the wings of a God who did not hesitate to figure himself as mother-bird engaged in the patient process of fledging us for flight back to the celestial regions, or

9. See *Augustine's Early Theory*, Chap. 2, for the complex genesis of this image.

send His Son in human guise to strengthen us with the milk of
faith until we should be strong enough to feed upon the food of
eternal, spiritual Truth, Himself.

From Faith, through Understanding, to Vision

For that is the goal of all God's labors, of all life's
journeying: the soul's return to the beatific vision which it once
enjoyed. We must become "little ones," accepting both the
sufferings He sends as sent for our good, and the milk of faith
the Church of His Incarnate Son dispenses to those humble
enough to believe. Purified by the one, strengthened by the
other, and set upon the "way" back to Truth, we can safely
seek, and indeed should seek, a growing spiritual "understanding" of what Scriptures—and philosophers—advise us is our
condition and destiny.

Remedy to Pride, Curiosity, Carnal Concupiscence

Along the "Way," the progressively spiritualized believer
liberates himself from the triadic vice which caused the "fall."
The initial fault of pride remedied by this humble submission
to Divine Authority, the work of purification gradually strips us
of the residues of carnal concupiscence, while the precepts of
the Church invite us to discard our "curious" interest in earthly
matters, to "seek" the understanding of divine realities which
ultimately will flower in "vision." At one time confident that
this vision could be attained in this life, Augustine now has
come to feel that only a foretaste of it is possible to us while in
the body: we can do no more than leave the "first-fruits" of our
spirit there,[10] where eventually we will return to dwell, to
enjoy without end the full splendor of the Divine Beauty.

A Key Word, a Central Image

All these varied images of divine "care" associate with a
single Latin term, *fovere*. I have tried to show elsewhere [11] that
a series of literary coincidences accounts for its remarkably
frequent use throughout Augustine's early works; but it first
occurs in the *Confessions* at the climax moment of God's work

10. See Solignac's measured remarks on this, *BA* 14, pp. 552–555. Read in
the light of the soul's "return" they take on firmer shape.
11. See *Augustine's Early Theory*, Chap. 2, pp. 65–86.

in Augustine's "conversion," to express all the bewildering nuances of the divine action in his behalf. Its root sense is to "warm," so that God is imaged as a warming, melting, sometimes cauterizing, eventually "lightening" Sun "from whose heat no man can hide" (cf. Ps. 19: 6) .

But however the action of the divine Sun is limned, it is always a "fostering," "favoring" action—one of the first transferred senses of *fovere*. God's fostering care is sometimes depicted in the medicinal image of the Omnipresent as "bathing or fomenting" either the wounds of Augustine's sinfulness or the spiritual eyes which need clearing so that he can come to "see." That medicinal care is often accompanied by therapeutic pain, giving it a paternal character. At other times it takes a more maternal form. Then God is like the mother-bird already mentioned, beneath whose wings the chick finds both protection and nourishment to fledge it for mature flight, or like a mother or a nurse, feeding the believing "little one" from what Isaias terms the "breasts of His great consolation," or (in another meaning of the term) "caressing" and "fondling" him, patiently teaching him to walk, then run, along the road of the spiritual life.

But before maternal omnipresence can teach the soul to walk, it must bring it back from wandering; before the fallen soul can be strengthened to run and fly, it must be little enough to "confess" that until now it has been fleeing, running away from where it most profoundly wished to go. Augustine's mother for years had to watch her son pursue life's journey with presumptuous, grown-up confidence, his back to the Light, his eyes upon the empty realities that Light enlightened. She had to listen to him as, sick with sinfulness, he blamed his sores upon a primitive catastrophe for which he claimed to bear no guilt; the sufferings of mortal life he never ceased complaining of, not counting them as salutary, therapeutic chastisement for his own primordial sinful choice, but as the doing of a hostile "race of darkness." He was like a child, tired of her maternal attentions, running off impatiently to seek distraction with his playmates. Playmates, alas, can be cruel; their games can end in loss, frustration, scraped knees, and scalding tears. She could have told him that, but children never listen. Headstrong is the word for them.

But mothers know how to wait their moment. Knees scraped, eyes streaming, even the most headstrong child comes back again, wailing that life has cheated, deluded him, failed to live up to its deceptive promise. Back now he comes, content to climb upon her waiting lap; for one last protest he looks back upon the way on which he ventured forth so hopefully in the morning brightness. This is her moment: with tender maternal hand she caresses his fevered head, gently turns his eyes away from what had been the cause of his complaining, places his head against her breast. Calmed, he sleeps, and wakes, and finds that all is well again.

A hand, a head, a turning motion: *fovisti caput; manu veritate*. How many times Augustine pictures God as putting His divine hand now gently, now almost cruelly, to the head of his sick, proud, querulous runaway, and always with the intent of "turning" that head about. Often paternal, that action is still more often a maternal one: conversion, in the depths of Augustine's imagination, is "returning"—to his mother Monica, to Mother Church, to the heavenly Jerusalem, his "Mother." But in the final instance, conversion is to a God who gathers up all experience had taught him of feminine charm and mildness, of loveliness and care, to a God who answers to his heart's desire for a spiritual fragrance, sweetness, embrace. "Beauty, ever ancient, ever new," Augustine exclaims at the last (*Conf* X, 38), and means that all human mothers and mistresses stand as so many stammering hints of that transcendent beauty.

These were the terms in which Augustine, Bishop of Hippo, viewed his life at the time he composed his *Confessions*. That view defies the ordinary man's way of seeing things, undercuts the normal assumptions he brings to understanding both Christianity and the human experience. This is why Augustine composes his *Confessions* as a single, extended *exercitatio:* to challenge those normal assumptions, overturn the easier view of our condition, bring us in progressive stages to see the mystery of man for what, he is convinced, it is, the odyssey of a soul whose wandering God's ever-present care would convert into a pilgrimage of return.

2 THE PROËMIUM

(BOOK I, 1–6)

Augustine's "musical" mode of composition enables him to launch his work with a masterly prelude, one which announces all the themes of the pages to follow. "Great art Thou, O Lord, and greatly to be praised": the limitless wisdom and power of God is at center-stage from the beginning; the opening bars are a "confession." Even man, "some part of Your creation," wishes to praise God—despite the mortal body (*mortalitas*) which he bears about him (*circumferens*) as "testimony" to the sin of pride, that is, the sin which caused his soul to fall into the changing universe of bodies. *Et tamen:* nonetheless; even this body is God's creation whatever the Manichee may think. Confession is owed Him, not alone because he is infinitely other than the soul, not only because that soul has sinned against Him, but even for the body he has fashioned for its fallen state.

God it is who "arouses" us to praise Him (*tu excitas*), to take "delight" in praising Him; for "You have made us for Yourself, and our heart is restless till it rest in You." Restless and "unquiet," our soul plunged rather into the "delight" of this embodied existence; but having found no rest, its restlessness now is salutary, makes it a "seeker" after that Sabbath "rest" which Augustine lyrically describes in the final pages of

37

his work. There, the restless heart now partially appeased confesses: "From You let it be asked, in You let it be sought, at Your door let us knock for it: thus, thus it is received, thus it is found, thus it is opened to us" (XIII, 38) . The key terms of the *Contra Academicos* are the very ones which sound the closing notes of the *Confessions* and (initial evidence of their unity of conception) preside over their opening phrases. For Augustine immediately asks that God grant him to "know and understand"

which is first, to call upon You or to praise You, and also which is first, to know You or to call upon You? For one who does not know You might call upon another instead of You. Or must You rather be called upon so that You may be known?

The process of dialogue has begun; this series of questions sets the *exercitatio animi* underway. The entire work is meant to answer those questions more adequately. But for the moment Augustine provides the first element of the answer: we call upon God only if we first believe in Him. We must begin with a
> faith which comes, admittedly, through the unassuming "ministry" of God's preacher, a faith which makes us "seek" God; "seeking," we shall "find" Him—"understand" and ultimately, in the densest meaning that word can have, "know" Him. Faith, understanding, and at the last the vision which is mystical embrace, unending "Sabbath rest" in God, these are the steps in the soul's return.

Augustine's "faith" therefore calls upon God: but did he receive that faith from God's minister," Ambrose? [1] Not really; no more than he received help and support in his youth from that other "minister," Romanianus. The omnipresent God "gave" it, "breathed" it into him, through Ambrose's ministering action, through the "humanity" of His own Son.

Faith, then, is only part of the answer. The *Proëmium* is meant to stimulate, and the rest of the *Confessions* to reply to, the original question Augustine asked and inspired Pascal to answer: "you would not have sought Me unless you had already found Me." We could not "seek" God unless "admonished" by ministers like Ambrose, by the humanity of Christ. But

1. Solignac (*BA* 13, p. 275, n. 2) follows Courcelle's suggestion that the *minister* referred to here is Christ himself, not Ambrose; Courcelle's grounds for that opinion I fail to find convincing. After using the term of Romanianus (*Acad* II, 4) , it seems more likely he is referring here to Ambrose who also "nourished" him in the faith (*Conf* VIII, 15; cf. V, 23) .

admonition presupposes we already knew and then somehow
forgot what it "re-minds" us of, else we might indeed "call upon
another" instead of God. Augustine is setting our minds on
edge for the appearance of the memory theme.

"But how shall I call upon my God," that is, "call Him into
myself?" The artful ambiguity of the word *invocare* introduces
an extended meditation on the central theme of omnipresence.
Augustine deliberately teases his reader's mind with the spatial
imagery he will later correct: what "place" (*locus*) is there in
us for God; how shall we, or even heaven and earth entire,
"contain" (*capere*) Him? What is this anomaly, that he should
call God into himself when "I would not even exist were You
not in me"? Here Augustine cannot resist injecting an initial correction: "rather, I would not be unless I were in You"
(I, 2).

But aside from whether there is any "place" in him for
God to "come," there is the deeper question of how the Omnipresent "who made heaven and earth," who claims to "fill
heaven and earth," is to be conceived of as "coming" at all? For
it would surely seem that "whatever exists contains" God
already (2). He already fills all things, and with His "entire
self"—His omnipresence is the integral omnipresence Plotinus
insists upon—yet "all things cannot contain [Him] in [His] entirety" (3). The classic paradox has been stated, but Augustine
does not intend here even to hint at its resolution. He merely
appends a list of other paradoxes—God is "most merciful" and
yet "most just," "most hidden and most present," "unchangeable, yet changing all things, never new and never old, yet
renewing all things . . . ever active, and ever at rest."

To this point Plotinus would agree. But now the properties of the biblical God add to the paradoxes Augustine must
eventually strain to resolve: he addresses God as "jealous, and
yet free from care; You repent, but do not sorrow; You grow
angry, but remain tranquil . . . You take back what You find,
although You never lost it; You are never in want, but You
rejoice in gain . . . Excessive payments are made to You, so
that You may be our debtor—yet who has anything that is not
Yours? You pay debts, although You owe no man anything; You
cancel debts, and lose nothing" (4). All the features of God's
dialogue with mankind have passed in review, each of them
raising the burning question of whether that dialogue can be
made intelligible in terms of a thought that puts the Eternal
absolutely beyond all the change that affects, we are asked to

think, only His human partners in that series of historical encounters narrated in the Bible. The prayer Augustine ends with (5–6), far from hinting at any resolution, only aggravates the difficulty. For how can God respond to man's prayer—help man, show pity, command, speak to him, enlarge his heart and purify it—unless that response somehow follows upon, is timely response to man's petition uttered in time?

The reader is left, then, with a set of unresolved paradoxes, a series of unanswered questions. The effect is an impression of God's breath-taking incomprehensibility, which prompts Augustine to ask who will help him "rest" in that God, "run after" His "voice," and like the bride in the Canticle "catch hold" of Him, "see His face," in a vision that is an "embrace" (5). The years have added to his store of biblical imagery, but for Augustine it still crystallizes about the Eros themes of Plotinian mysticism.

It is doubtful whether Plotinus could fully have subscribed to the "confession" which brings Augustine's *Proëmium* to a close.[2] The house of his soul is narrow, in ruins, contains things that offend God's sight: he will not, as the Manichees do, as Plotinus in certain passages would seem to do, "deceive" himself, lest his "iniquity lie to itself." He is a sinner, and to call upon God is first of all to "confess" one's sinfulness.

Subtly the *Proëmium* has been brought back to the theme of its opening bars, to the sinfulness which ultimately explains that there is "man" at all, "part" of God's creation, but bearing about a "mortal body" as testimony to his pride, plunged into a forgetfulness from which he calls on God, consents to believe and be re-minded, and hopes to pass through an understanding of his condition, returning from the disquiet of time and action to the Sabbath repose of unending contemplation. The entire project of the *Confessions* has been laid out before us.

2. It should be noted that although Plotinus admits a fault of some sort in the soul that falls, it does not seem that fault could be equated with "sin" as the Christian understands that term; nor does it affect the soul in its depths. Similarly, Plotinus' notion of prayer is far from the one which a Christian would recognize. Of the second discrepancy, Augustine may have been keenly aware as early as the *Soliloquies* which he begins with a prayer; of the first, he seems to have become aware by the time of the *De Quantitate Animae*, where all notions of the soul's immutability and quasi-divine status are finally eliminated from his thinking. See *Augustine's Early Theory*, Chaps. 3 and 4, for this latter development.

3 A MEDITATION
ON INFANCY

(BOOK I, 7–31)

"That Time" Before Infancy

The question of "knowing" God has been raised and left unanswered, so Augustine returns to it. The opening sentences of his
"autobiography" set up a series of queries to God, which make
no sense unless the Plotinian connection between knowledge,
memory, and pre-existence is borne in mind.

"I do not know," he confesses, "whence I came into what I
may call a mortal life or a living death. Whence, I know not"
(I, 7). Two paragraphs later the question intrudes once more.
"Tell me," he asks of God, "whether my infancy followed another age of mine already dead." Perhaps, he speculates, it was
"that time I passed within my mother's womb"; but, significantly, he then presses the question further. "What was there
even before this, my joy, my God? Was I anywhere, or anyone?"
(I, 9). The question has been raised, a doubt inserted—the
process of *exercitatio* is again underway. To show us that the
question has been left open, he finishes by praising God "for my
first being (*primordia*) AND my infancy which (*quae:* both of
which!) I do not remember" (I, 10). In his final question on
infancy he seems ready to drop the matter once and for all.

"Conceived in sin," he asks, "where, or when was I innocent? But lo! *that time* I omit: what matters to me that of which I recall no trace?" (I, 12).

But, far from settling the issue, Augustine's question is calculated to keep the question very much alive: for what, the reader inevitably asks, does *illud tempus* mean in this last sentence? Infancy? Or some time of "innocence" before the "time passed in [his] mother's womb"? (I, 9). Could it be that he "was someone" before he entered the womb? Augustine makes as if to brush the question aside: "What matters to me that of which I recall no trace?" But, the alert reader responds, what happened in such a period could make a world of difference! To cite a consideration Augustine never tires of underlining, my own birth is something of which I recall no trace, and yet what happened then, and who my mother was, is of immense importance in any man's life (VI, 7). Without belief in things that we ourselves cannot remember, no human society would be possible.

And, Augustine has taken pains to insinuate, the question of whether or not I pre-existed is an entirely comparable case: in fact, remarkably so in some respects. First, because, like our infancy, it may be lost in "oblivion"—though an oblivion of a different order. Our natural tendency is to reject such pre-existence on the grounds we should remember it; yet on that score we should, as Augustine does, find it annoying (*piget*) to count our infancy as part of our life "in this world" (I, 12). As for whether we were ever infants, who our mother and father were, what happened then, Augustine never tires of reminding us that in such matters we must all "believe" the reports of others: mothers, nurses, "weak women"—and we regularly do! (I, 7-9).

Did we, then, pre-exist? If so, we have forgotten it; having forgotten it, we resist the thought of counting it part of our life in any sense. Understandable, but the same logic would lead us to deny we were ever infants, yet here we have no doubts whatever. Should we then "believe" we pre-existed? Just as we believe what mother and nurse tell us of our infancy? But is there mother or nurse in this case to assure us of it? The *Confessions* are designed to answer that question too: the mother is the Church who nurses us to spiritual adulthood, assures us we were "conceived" in iniquity, points to Paul and Genesis to witness (for those who can understand) that pre-exist we did, were blissful, at "rest," then turned away from the embrace of God our joy in a turning movement that was "iniquity."

Suffice it that for now the question has been raised, and artfully left open. The *exercitatio* continues: Augustine injects a brief consideration of God's unchanging eternity and the relation of our changing times to that eternity (I, 6). The connection is not accidental. For the Platonist, the question of pre-existence is intrinsically linked with that of memory, not with the ordinary sense of memory, the kind that recalls our temporally past experiences of "this life," but with that memory, rather (figured by the former) that puts us in contact with eternal truths, the Eternal Truth which was our joy. The soul's enduring kinship with this intelligible world implies that it has fallen from that world, and does not know itself except in the measure that it recognizes itself as image of the Divine.

The Model of "Conversion"

Our infancy, then, shows that we all "believe" what we cannot "remember"; it raises the question of whether we can get to "know" we pre-existed. But more than that, it presents us with an image of the virtue Augustine finds absolutely crucial to the process of "return": humility. Augustine was—as all of us were—a "little one," suckled on "human milk," the "food of our infancy," given to him through breasts of nurse and mother by the omnipresent God Himself (I, 7). Why did Christ tell us we would not enter the Kingdom unless we be "converted" and become again like these "little ones"? Is it some innocence of theirs that makes them our model? Hardly, for no one is clean of sin, not even the infant of a single day on earth (I, 11). It is their "humility" which brought Our Lord to say that "of such is the Kingdom of Heaven" (I, 30). From the outset of his work Augustine intends that our "conversion" and "return" to God shall take the form of a suckling child returning to the maternal breast.

No child is truly innocent therefore. We are all not only born but "conceived" in iniquity. And yet, Augustine repeatedly suggests, the wrongs a child commits are not so much eradicated as given different form and greater scope when he grows up (I, 11). The theme is carried forward (I, 15, 16, 30) into his treatment of boyhood schooling, as like another Odysseus he sails out over the stormy deeps of human life (I,

13), or treads like any son of Adam the sad and toilsome "ways" of learning (I, 14). We think it right to punish, correct, "discipline" the infant (I, 11), the boy who misbehaves (I, 14), and yet, are adults so very different? Our parents laugh when their children complain of stripes that will do them good, but which, for the child, represent the greatest imaginable evil. The child attempts to elude the master's punishment by earnest prayer to a God Who does not seem to hear, because to hear such prayers would not be a good (I, 14). Could it not be the same, Augustine subtly suggests, for adults who complain of the evils they encounter? (I, 15). The infant image of faith has now become an admonition to bear with evils our sinfulness has merited, and which, if properly borne, may free us from our sin. The "bread" for which all sons of Adam toil and sweat is God, "bread for the inner mouth of the soul"; just so, the bosom which for different reasons attracts both child and man should be the divine "bosom of thoughts" (I, 21); and the "order" which sees to it we suffer when we seek "proud" victories in games or "curious" spectacles at theatre or arena (I, 16) instead of applying ourselves to useful studies (I, 20–22), is a providential order (I, 23) embracing agents who work from evil motives (I, 19) and employing checks that "extend from the schoolmaster's rod to the martyr's ordeal." God's "laws have power to fashion what is bitter but salutary, and to recall us to [Him] from the pestilential pleasure by which we fell away from [Him]" (I, 23).

That fall Augustine limns significantly in terms which blend the image of the Prodigal with Plotinus' observation that return (like fall) is not a journey made "on foot," or with "horses, chariots, or ships"; nor is it a "flight on visible wings." Rather, we depart from God "by darksome affections" (I, 28; cf. Enn I, 6). Even now, the fancied "opposition" between Neo-Platonism and Christianity is subtly set aside. But does Augustine mean to unveil his Plotinian theory of the fall? Not yet; the exercitatio must prepare the reader's mind more fully to accept that difficult truth.

Language and the Human Estate

Was it merely a concern for completeness that brought Augustine at several points in this first book to describe the process whereby he learned to communicate with his fellow-humans? A careful look at the terms he uses creates another impression. The "wants" he wished to communicate to others were, he notes, "inside me" (*intus*), "while those outside (*foris*) could by no sensible means penetrate into my soul." Hence the need of the "signs" he made to them, "similar to [his] wishes" but still "not like the truth" (*veresimilia*) (8).

When finally he learned to speak, it was not because grown people "taught" him by presenting him with words. The process is, rather, the one described in the *De Magistro*. He himself, with his God-given mind, wished to express in signs his "heart's feelings." Noticing when others "named" a certain thing and "at that name, made a gesture toward the object, [he] observed that object and inferred that it was called by the name they uttered when they wished to show (*ostendere*) it" to him. So, little by little, he "inferred" that words, gestures, nods, and all the rest were "signs" of things, signs to which his mouth eventually became accustomed (13). The process is one of slow habituation, and fittingly so, for words have been set up by "that agreement and convention (*pactum et placitum*) by which men have established these characters among themselves" (22). All the apparatus of symbolic communication is, therefore, the work of human custom, making it possible for the soul "within" to express "outwardly" to other embodied souls something of what it knows and feels.

Augustine will later explicitly trace the origin of language to the soul's "fallen" condition. When he does so, it is an invitation to the reader to ask whether the very embodiment of soul, which accounts for this distinction of knowledge "within" and "outward" expression, is not itself a result of that fall. But by that time, the reader's mind will have been better prepared to draw the right conclusion, the same conclusion that underlay the theory of language expressed in the *De Magistro*.

4 THE PRODIGAL'S WANDERING
(BOOK II)

Triple Concupiscence and Omnipresent "Care"

An important step in proving that the soul is "fallen" involves persuading the reader that "the chief kinds of iniquity spring forth from the lust for dominating, gazing at spectacles, or feeling [sensual delight]: *principandi et spectandi et sentiendi libidine,* whether from one of these, or two, or all three together" (III, 16). For this Augustinian adaptation of the *triplex concupiscentia* of St. John's First Epistle (2:16) corresponds to the triad of sins to which Plotinus attributes the soul's fall.[1] Such generalizations must, however, be prepared. Until now Augustine as infant and boy has indulged mainly in the pride of victory over his fellows, the curiosity which displays itself in gazing at gladiatorial contests and in learning what delights the imagination rather than serving some useful purpose for life. Now he arrives at his sixteenth year, and the "concupiscence of the flesh" flares up in him (II, 1–2) with no

1. For a description of the process whereby Augustine accomplished this adaptation, see *Augustine's Early Theory,* Chap. 6, pp. 173–182. Note that he follows this triad in his examination of conscience in *Conf* X, 41ff, showing the systematic importance it still retains for him.

46

one to "stretch forth a gentle hand and soften those thorns that
had no place in [God's] paradise" (II, 3), "root out those briars
of unclean desires spread thick over [his] head" (II, 6). The
image of God's hand put to the head of this son of Adam
immediately evokes all the paradoxes of omnipresence. Farther
and farther Augustine goes from Him (II, 2) but still God
remains "always present" to him (II, 4), His "omnipotence
. . . not far from us, even when we are far" from Him (II, 3).
The pattern formed by exposure to Plotinus' treatise on Omnipresence is still holding together. Nor is the Eros-image absent:
would, Augustine exclaims, he had appreciated Paul's teaching
on virginity, and kept himself for the "greater joy" of God's
"embraces" (II, 3). "Exiled" like the Prodigal "from the delights of [God's] house" (II, 4), Augustine follows his former
"peregrination" to Madaura (in qua . . . coeperam . . . pere-
grinari) with an even more extensive one to Carthage (longi-
quioris apud Carthaginem peregrinationis; II, 5). Thus Patricius plays the role of the Prodigal's father in reverse, giving his
family goods to finance the "wandering" (peregrinatio) through
which his son "deserts" his Heavenly Father, becomes a "desert"
uncultivated by Him, and all to become "cultured" (disertus)
in the ways of men (II, 5). For Patricius too is a fallen soul, in-
toxicated by the wine of that "perverse will, [which] tending
down towards lower things, forgets . . . [the] Creator and loves
[the] creature more than [Him]" (II, 6). To Monica, however,
God is beginning—another Plotinian image—to occupy the
"center." She "feared the crooked ways on which walk those who
turn their back on [God] and not their face toward [Him]"
(II, 6). So, as Augustine wanders "further away" from God, she
"admonishes" her son (monuit) with an admonition
(monitus) which was really God's—tui erant—though he
"knew it not" (nesciebam; II, 7). For "through her [God] did
not remain silent" to him, as Augustine mistakenly thought.
Indeed, "in her [God] was despised" by him, but again, he
"knew it not" (nesciebam; II, 7). So strongly has omnipresence penetrated the "admonition" theme, Monica becomes
almost transparently the maternal presence of God Himself.

Society in Sin

Augustine now passes on to describe the bad companions
he emulated while at Carthage (II, 8), and chooses as a very
paradigm of iniquity the theft of some pears from a nearby

orchard (II, 9ff). The weight he attaches to this incident, it has
often been thought, is exaggerated in the extreme; his view of
infant and childhood sin helps partially to understand it. But
the point he thinks it imperative to make is quite another one:
this boyish adventure will test to the utmost, and eventually
insinuate a needed supplement to his theory of "iniquity."

Augustine here is coping with a classic difficulty in
Neo-Platonic thought, that of explaining how a soul dwelling
in contemplative bliss should ever choose to leave it. Feeding on
the "food" of Truth itself, what desire would prompt it to
"fall" into want? Augustine hints at this problematic by stressing that "want" was not his motive. He had at home, abun-
dantly and better, what he stole; his only "want" was perhaps
a "weariness" (*fastidium*) with justice itself—perhaps that
"weariness" Plotinus also alludes to in his work on The
Descent of the Soul (*Enn* IV, 8). He did not steal in order to
"enjoy" the fruit he stole. *Egestas, abundantia, cibus, frui:* the
De Beata Vita lexicon of misery and happiness is on the scene,
but now in the company of a "tree" whose "fruit" God's "law"
forbids him to eat. The paradisiac situation is the one described
in Genesis as well. "Base in soul was I," he concludes the description of the act, "I leaped down from your *firmamentum*
(support? "firmament"?) even towards complete destruc-
tion . . ." (II, 9) : quite literally, he "fell."

What puzzles him about this act is that the normal motive-
explanation does not seem to work for it. He was "evil without
purpose," stole for the precise reason "that it was forbidden,"
enjoyed not the fruit he stole but the "actual sin of theft" itself
(II, 9). This runs counter to all accepted ways of explaining
such acts. There was neither good to be gained nor evil to be
evaded (II, 10–11) ; no beauty drew him on (II, 12), not even,
it would seem at first, that "shadowy-beauty" to be found in
those "perverse imitations" of God which all the vices represent
(II, 13).

But here he pauses to explain slightly this last concept:

the soul commits fornication when it is turned away (*avertitur*)
from you, and seeks outside of you (*extra te*) what it can find, pure
and limpid, only if it go back to you (*cum redit ad te*). In a
perverse way (*perverse*), all imitate you who put themselves far
from you (*qui longe se a te faciunt*), and rise up in rebellion
against you, [proving thereby] that there is no place where they can
depart entirely from you (*a te . . . recedatur*) (II, 14).

Here the language of *Ennead* VI, 4–5 is at work, along with the "turning-away" which features strongly in that treatise's explanation of the fall.

But Plotinus' *tolma* has since become a stronger thing, a veritable "rebellion" against God. Can such rebellion help to understand the theft of pears? Could this constitute "vicious" and "perverse" imitation of the Most High? Perhaps he wished to "imitate a deformed liberty, by doing with impunity things illicit bearing a shadowy likeness of Your omnipotence" and thus "flee from his Lord and follow after a shadow" (II, 14).

Augustine pauses; he gives thanks to the God whose warmth has "dissolved" his sins "as if they were ice." Like a "physician" God aids some so that they do not fall, others that they fall into lesser ills than Augustine had. Two variants on the *fovere*-image enter and fade away (II, 15).

But now he resumes his question: did he really love "the theft and nothing else (*nihil aliud*)?" But the theft itself was "nothing" (*nihil*): how could that be? "Alone, by myself, I would not have done it," he now remembers, and the crucial final touch is in the picture. This "association" with his evil companions was also what he loved, and still, it too was "nothing" (*nihil*)! Yet his "pleasure lay . . . in the evil deed itself, which a group of us joined to do"—something doubly difficult to understand (16). Is it like laughing, which we generally do only in company? Not quite, because laughing, though seldom, we can do alone: "but that deed I would not have done alone; alone I would never have done it." Companionship, therefore, "friendship too unfriendly," is an indispensable element in explaining such a sin (II, 17), such a "twisted and intricate mass of knots." [2]

But now Augustine has but one desire: his "highest good," the just, innocent, and beautiful God whom he desires "unto a satiety that can never be satiated." From him he "flowed away" (*defluxi*), "went astray" (*erravi*), and "became unto myself a region of want" (*regio egestatis;* II, 18).

The theme of God as "food of the soul," the allusions to

---

2. Gibb and Montgomery in their notes, pp. 42–50, show clearly that Augustine is pointing up the inadequacy of various other motivation-schemes to explain this theft. To say, though, that joy in this evil companionship was the "motive" that finally explains the act is stretching the evidence. Even when this essential element is taken into consideration, it turns out to be another *nihil*, forcing Augustine to ask: *delicta quis intellegit?* (II, 17). Sin in its purest form, Augustine is suggesting, remains essentially mysterious.

"nothing" (*nihil*) suggestively connected with this notion of "flowing" downward—the lexicon of the *De Beata Vita* is, at this point, present in full array. Only one crucial implication has been changed. The early work suggests that God "never ceases offering" such "banquets" as they enjoyed the previous day. "It is we who leave off eating, whether from weakness, or satiety, or business": *vel inbecillitate vel saturitate vel negotio* (*Vita* 17). *Saturitas:* can this alone explain our "fall"? The early Augustine might have thought it did, but the Augustine of the *Confessions* wishes quite unambiguously to stress the inadequacy of that suggestion. The "fall" is not something which can be explained by the motivation of an individual soul, but something requiring a mutual "Let's do it!" (II, 17), a "rubbing together of accomplice spirits (*consciorum animorum*) to inflame the itch of desire" (*accenderem pruritum cupiditatis meae;* II, 16). He is preparing our minds to see that the story of individual sin is ultimately the story of humanity itself.

5 FIRST CONVERSION:
CICERO, THE MANICHEES
(BOOK III)

Joy in Dido's Sorrow

Augustine's arrival at Carthage inspires another meditation on the triadic sin which has him under its sway: the "filth of concupiscence" (III, 1), the "curious" delight he found in drinking in the "vain" imaginary spectacles the theater afforded his "itching eyes" (III, 2–4), the pride in being the leading student that puffed him up (III, 6).

But now he returns to a theme already announced in Book I (20–22): the puzzling phenomenon of joy in unreal sorrow. Why did he delight in sorrowing with the fictional Dido? Can any man love grief, want to be unhappy? Whatever the Stoic may say, a certain kind of sorrow, the kind that leads to acts of mercy and compassion, "is to be commended, but none can be loved" (III, 3). Augustine's explanation of his own paradoxical search for stage sorrows is that, "an unhappy sheep straying from [God's] flock," he was "infected with loathsome sores" and enjoyed being "scratched lightly" (III, 4). But the theme will return.

First Conversion: The *Hortensius*

"Proud of neck" he loved a "fugitive's freedom" which
brought him to "wander" and "depart far" from God (III, 5).
And yet, a "turning" point is not far off. Compared to the
wanton deeds he did with his companions earlier, it is significant to read of the abhorrence in which he held similar wanton
acts performed by the "over-turners" (*eversores*) at Carthage.
Their very lack of "modesty" seems to have provoked in him a
needed sense of measure. The variants on the word for "turn"
should warn us something is afoot: *eversores, eversiones, eversi,
perversi*—Augustine is preparing us for his "first conversion."
Peregrinatio: that central term is about to change its meaning.
From "wanderer" away from God, Augustine will become a
"pilgrim" back to God.

For with the reading of Cicero's *Hotensius* the prodigal
"began to rise up" (III, 7), fired with the new desire for Wisdom, a Wisdom not to be found among visible "elements of this
world." [1] The name of Christ which he drank in with his
"mother's milk" was not there (III, 8). His persistent attachment to Christ makes him turn to reading Scripture; but he is not
yet "little one" (*parvulus*) enough to drink in faith the message
it conveys (III, 9). And so, in search of Christ, he is ensnared by
those pretended Christians, the Manichees.

Manichaeism [2]

Augustine's portrait of Manichaeism here is more a critique than an exposé; it concentrates on three main features.
They fed his soul, he says, not on the food of God Himself,
though they pretended to, but on imaginative fantasies which
shatter against the problem of omnipresence (10–11). They
failed to solve the problem of evil, fundamentally because they
were unable to distinguish unchanging eternal law from changing temporal customs (12–17). And finally, having repudiated
the *Catholica*'s demand for an initial "faith," they themselves
finished by believing the most ridiculous absurdities (18).

1. For more on this "first conversion" see Courcelle, pp. 49–60, and Pellegrino, pp. 83–93. When Augustine eventually goes to Cassiciacum, having finally
consummated his "conversion to philosophy" (as Courcelle describes the invitation of the *Hortensius*), that conversion will have all the intense religious overtones Pellegrino finds in the events of his nineteenth year.

2. On this conversion to Manichaeism, see Courcelle, pp. 60–78, and Pellegrino, pp. 95–112.

But his critique of the Manichees should not blind us to the genuine progress this phase of Augustine's life represented. He was awakened to the desire for Wisdom; he is seeking Christ in the only way that seems to him reasonable at the time. Whereas each of the preceding books has ended with a description of the "fall," the Third Book terminates on a different note entirely, with two consoling and encouraging "admonitions" to Monica, and, indirectly, to Augustine himself. She sees Christ in a dream assuring her that her son will soon stand on the same "rule" (*regula*) as she; she hears from a bishop of the Church —but "as if it sounded forth from heaven"—that it cannot be the "son of these tears should perish." Augustine's return to the rule of the faith is now but a matter of time.

To understand the story of that return, however, it must be borne in mind that to the young Augustine, as to many others of his time, Manichaeism represented a form of "enlightened" and "purified" Christianity. "Truth" was what they promised, and the name of Christ was forever on their lips. The austerity of their moral ideal, moreover, was similar in appeal to the break with the world demanded by the "conversion to philosophy" Cicero's *Hortensius* recommended. At no point in his story, then, does Augustine portray himself as a "pagan." He sees himself as never having been other than a Christian, but already he envisages the Christian ideal as entailing, *for him*, a radical break with the world of action, the undivided pursuit of Truth in a life of contemplation. This is the burden of that phase of his conversion he relates in Book VIII. It is followed by the contemplative interlude at Cassiciacum, and is eventually crowned by the vision at Ostia with which his autobiography terminates.

Augustine, then, envisages his "return" as tending toward the ideal form of life he found haltingly orchestrated in his nineteenth year both by Cicero and the Manichees. Along the way, he will discover that the *Catholica* was far from being so insensitive, as he had once imagined, to the respect for intelligence that life-ideal supposes. But his return is not portrayed as precisely a return to the *Catholica*. Rather, he depicts himself moving back to and through the *Catholica* to the realization of this ideal form of Christian life. This will account, in part, for an anomaly that has occasioned no little controversy:[3] Augus-

3. For a relatively recent discussion of this confused question, see Gérard Mathon, "Quand faut-il placer le retour d'Augustin a la foi catholique?" *Revue des Études Augustiniennes*, 1:107–127 (1955). Compare Pellegrino's judicious observations, pp. 161–162, and *Saint Augustine's Early Theory*, pp. 232–257.

tine never made unambiguously clear in the *Confessions* at
what precise point he considered himself as having returned to
the Catholic Church. At the end of Book V, he informs us
disconcertingly that he "determined to continue as a
catechumen in the Catholic Church commended to me by my
parents" (V, 25). *Tamdiu esse catachumenus.* John Gibb and
William Montgomery rightly note that the "natural implication" of the phrasing is that "Augustine considered himself to
be still a catechumen" [4]—still, despite all the intervening years
of Manichaeism, in some real sense a "Catholic." And yet, there
are numerous texts that seem to support a contrary view of the
matter: what of them? They will, I suggest, make sense if the
reader remembers who wrote them: an Augustine whose eye
was peering always toward the philosophic haven of Cassiciacum, and past it, to the soaring heights of Ostia. From a
voyager that single-minded, the intervening ports receive only
passing, almost casual, notice; for a stare that concentrated on
the distant hill, the landscape in middle-distance tends to blur.

4. Gibb and Montgomery, p. 135n. The authors point to the analogous language used in this same connection in *Conf* VI, 18: "I will fix my feet on that
step where my parents placed me as a child."

6 TO BECOME A
"LITTLE ONE" AGAIN
(BOOKS IV AND V, 1–2)

Fovisti Caput

We have to some extent already examined the content of Book IV, which ends with the *confessio* beginning Book V (1–2 inclusively); the whole is dominated by variants of the *fovere*-image.[1] Augustine pictures himself at the time of writing his *Confessions* as a *parvulus,* sucking from God's breasts the milk of faith (1). Far from being ashamed at this childish posture, he asks "what man is any kind of man while he be a man?"—by which he means us to infer that only when we become disembodied "souls" again will we be "grown-ups" in the truest sense (IV, 1). The proconsul, skilled in medicine, puts hand to his head, but not to "cure" him (5). A dying friend "admonishes" him (8) and Augustine's sorrow following upon his death turns everything to punishment and sadness. Weeping alone is sweet to him. He has again become a great "question" to himself (9).

1. See above, pp. 33–36.

Sweet Sadness

Why, he asks again, are tears alone sweet to the unhappy man? The same question he had asked before, but then about the unreal sorrows of the theater (I, 20–22; III, 3–4). Now that the sorrow is real—and he more prepared to see its import—he comes closer to the answer: sorrow indicates we have "lost something," have in fact "lost [our] joy" (10). Sorrow, he means to intimate, is itself an inverse reminder of joy. It prods us dimly into realizing that we are lost in a land of "death." In love with "mortal things" (11), we can find no rest in all the delights that beckon to us here; we can "flee" from our native place on earth but can never flee the "heart," the "self" which sorrows (12).

One Soul

In his *Retractations* Augustine found but one phrase of the *Confessions* that displeased him: citing his use of the poet's saying that his friend was "half my soul" (IV, 11), he finds the suggestion simply silly. Yet there are grounds for thinking it meant something to him at the time of writing the *Confessions.* If our individual souls are in fact "one" with the World-soul, then the death of a friend quite literally liberates, and separates us from, a part of our very "soul." The suggestion is reinforced by the paragraphs following that phrase, which exploit the "warming" aspect of the ambivalent *fovere*-image by comparing friendship to a "fervor," a "fuel" which melts us, many as we are, into one (13).

Punishment and Particularity

Yet even friendships cannot take the sting out of death: partial, sensible beauties necessarily pass away with the flow of time, like words making up a single phrase. In God's "Word, by which they are created, they hear these words: 'From here, and unto there!'" (15)—or, as Plotinus put it, "so much" and no further (*Enn* VI, 5, 7, and 12). Even the Plotinian notion of time is penetrated now with omnipresential themes. We must love all our friends "in" God, the One who makes all things and "fills" all things He makes; we can but flee from Him "well-pleased" (*placido*) to Him "wrathful" (*iratum*). But the same thing Augustine now sees is true of Plotinus' Providence. The "law" of punishment for sin is "omnipresent"—omnipresent Truth (14).

"Convert us," Augustine prays to God. Indeed, Book IV, 15–18 is a marvelously orchestrated plea for the soul to "return" to the "happiness" it left when it "turned away" from God in pursuit of some "part" of the bodily universe, when it left the Eternal in quest of the temporal, when it "deserted" God and found itself confined, in punishment, to part-icularity. As though to assure us that it still fits neatly into the Plotinian scheme of fall and return, the Incarnation is invoked at the end of this effusion (19) —our Life came down to bid us "go back," "return," "ascend" once more through the fire of charity to the God from Whom we fell.

Love, My Weight

The "fire of charity": lightest of the four elements, a preponderance of "fire" in anything forces it to seek its natural place "on high." That theory of "weights," as we have observed, presides over Augustine's—and Plotinus'—theories of the soul's fall. Now it stimulates the question where those "weights" are situated in that mysterious being, man, whereby he is "secretly governed" by God's will for him (IV, 21–23).

Adam and Infant

That little meditation concerns Augustine's having dedicated his book *On the Beautiful and the Fitting* to the rhetorician Hierius. It introduces a critique of that work, which turns principally on his persistent inability properly to envisage the "spiritual" beauty of God from Whom all beauties derive (IV, 20, 24–27). What profit was it to him, then, to read the *Categories* of Aristotle, when they only led him into wrong ideas of God? He was still under Adam's curse; the earth brought forth "thorns and thistles" to him; with "labor" he still strives to earn the "bread" of Truth (29). But he is sunk "under the weight of pride down into the depths" (27), still determined to keep his "substance under [his] own power" (30), not yet a "little one" content to "grow wings safe within the nest that is [God's] Church," strengthening those "wings of charity on the food of a

sound faith" (IV, 31). The moving confession, which begins
here, ends only at Book V, paragraph 2, with the anticipated
image of Augustine, like a child, weary at last and come back to
the bosom of maternal Omnipresence: as he will put it later
(VII, 20), *fovisti caput nescientis.*

7 FAUSTUS, AMBROSE,
AND THE "ONE TEACHER"
(BOOK V)

Faustus and the Glitter of Words

Again, the insistent variants on the Latin term *vertere*—
"because we have turned away from you *(aversi)* we have
become perverted *(perversi)*; now let us return *(revertamur)*
O Lord, so that we be not overturned *(ut non evertamur)*"
(IV, 31)—along with the profusion of *fovere*-images, artis-
tically prepares for a decisive new step in God's work of "converting" Augustine.[1] Despite his recent strictures on his reading of Aristotle, moreover, it is significant that he takes this step
with the aid of physical "philosophers" who furnished him with

---

1. For detailed substantiation of this "profusion" see *Augustine's Early Theory*, Chap. 2, pp. 83–84. Augustine has earlier alerted us by the "suckling" image
of IV, and the hand-to-head "healing" image of IV, 4–5. Now he evokes the
"care" associations involved in "food" and "milk" dispensed in a "nest" for
young "fledglings" who (the image shifts from little birds to infant children)
need a maternal hand to "carry" them before they can learn to "run" (IV, 31;
cf. VI, 26). He returns to the notion of "healing" accomplished by a "warming"
care; this results in the convert's "mouth" being "turned back" to God for "refreshment and true strength" (V, 1). Paragraph V, 2 climaxes the exercise with
references to God's maternal "gentleness" *(lenitas)* portrayed as a "breast" *(sinu
tuo)* on which converted souls *(convertantur)* cast themselves *(proicientium se
in te)* and find both "re-creation and consolation" *(reficis et consolaris)*.

difficulties against the Manichaean astronomy (V, 3–9). Those difficulties, it had long been promised him, could be resolved by the Manichaean bishop, Faustus, who was at that time about to visit Carthage. Though prepared to "believe" the doctrines of the "master" (*magister*), Mani, on account of the "authority" lent him by his holiness, Augustine is troubled by the apparent impossibility of "understanding" that belief (V, 9).

The terms are another reminder that Augustine's previous descriptions of his infant and boyish efforts at learning language have all been couched in terms of the theory embodied in the *De Magistro*. The association of words with objects is the creation of convention, hence the business of sheer authority. There is, however, a decisive difference between learning such authority-appointed words and understanding "the truth of realities" (*veritas rerum*), a difference that Augustine insinuates he had at least partially learned by the time he met Faustus (V, 3). Faith, authority, and language, then, are still (as in the *De Genesi contra Manichaeos*) associated with the fallen state; understanding, reason, and "realities," on the other hand, still refer to that "inner" and "higher" world where God alone is "Teacher" (*magister;* V, 10).

Skilled in words, Faustus is a disappointment when it comes to conveying understanding. But even in him, God's secret providential "hand" is at work to "re-make" Augustine (V, 13); He has used this heretical bishop as an instrument. In a subtle anticipation of the later head-image, He has "turned [Augustine's] shameful errors before [his] face, so that [he] might see them and detest them" (V, 11). "Neither willing it nor knowing it," Faustus has become—though the word does not occur—an "admonition," warning Augustine, dulling his former Manichaean zeal to the point where he despairs of "learning anything from the rest of their teachers" (V, 13).

Goaded to Rome

Never more will Manichaeism have quite the grip it formerly had upon him. All his determined efforts to "advance" from auditor to the inner circle of the "elect" quite literally "collapse." And yet, he did not then "break completely with them, but as if unable to find anything better than what [he] had in some way stumbled upon, [he] resolved to be content with it for the time being, unless something preferable should chance to appear" (V, 13). The language of "chance" betrays the "un-knower" Augustine then was. At this juncture two equally "unknowing" groups of friends combine with his own perverse desires, those "goads" by which God "works within" the soul; they prevail on him to take a teaching post at Rome (V, 14). So blind is Monica herself to God's providential designs in all that happens, she weeps, "unknowing." Her carnal affection for Augustine is a "remnant of Eve within her" (V, 15), just as Augustine's sins were added to the sin "in which we all die in Adam" (V, 16). But "turned about" (*conversa;* V, 15), she prays for her distant son to the God who is "present in all places" (V, 16), "present to help her" (V, 17).

The Sick One

Seriously ill at Rome, Augustine attributes his "healing" to that same omnipresent Divine Physician. God means to give him even better and more certain health of soul (V, 18). His pride, however, still persuades him to blame his sins on some "other nature"; he carries on relations with the Manichee elect despite the "more loose and careless manner" in which he held those "tenets with which, if [he] came upon nothing better, [he] had resolved to be content" (V, 18). In this seizure of doubt, he is attracted by the Academic philosophers whose "meaning [he] did not yet understand," thinking what was "commonly held" of them, that they were teaching total skepticism (V, 19).

Truth and the *Catholica*

But his profoundest desire remains the one inspired by Cicero's *Hortensius* years before, that of finding and embracing Truth and Wisdom. Had the Manichees not caricatured the *Catholica's* teaching—her "faith was not such as [he] thought it to be" (V, 20)—he would have sought Truth there. But in addition, his corporeal manner of thinking binds him still to a dualist solution to the problem of evil, so that despite his gnawing difficulties with Manichaeism, its residual effects still keep him away from the Church (V, 21). And the key defect is his inability to transcend corporeal imagery, really to "think" in a way that will yield genuine understanding.

Goaded to Milan

The Roman students' trick of evading payment for their schooling angers him (V, 22). Again, unknowing instruments of Providence, his Manichee connections come to his assistance.

They help him gain appointment as municipal *rhetor* in Milan,
where Ambrose dispensed the food of God's oil and wheat and
wine to such as hungered for it. "All unknowing," Augustine
notes, "I was led to him by you, so that through him I might be
led, knowing, to you" (V, 23).

To Become a "Knower"

That passing phrase alerts the reader to the nature of the
"pilgrimage" (*peregrinatio*) Augustine is describing, a pilgrimage which ultimately brings him to revere the Bishop of Milan
as "teacher of truth" (*doctor*—not *magister*—*veri*), less prized
for the "words" he spoke than for the "realities" those words
conveyed (V, 23). Again, the theme of language and its relation
to realities is on the scene. Unsurprisingly, it calls for comparison of Ambrose and Faustus. Inevitably, as we shall see, authority's relation to reason, faith's relation to understanding, will
move into sharper focus. For the "food" Augustine longs for is
not just the oil and wheat and wine of faith; it is the food of
Truth itself, one whose attainment requires that faith give way
to understanding, that from "unknower" Augustine become a
"knower."

8 THE MEDICINE OF
FAITH AND SUFFERING
(BOOK VI)

In Quest of Understanding

In scrutinizing the sections we are about to examine, the classic
question is: did Augustine read the *Enneads* with the "eyes of a
Christian"? To resolve that question, it has often been supposed, we must resolve another: when did he "return" to the
Catholic Church?[1] Was it, for instance, at the moment (which
he is about to relate) when he left the Manichees and again
became a catechumen? Put this way, the reply must be in the
negative; in his own terms, Monica's arrival at Milan finds him
not yet a "Catholic Christian," but still in that "wavering and
doubtful state" to which Ambrose had brought him (VI, 1).

But the terms are carefully chosen: the Manichees were, at
least in pretense, "Christians," though not "Catholic Christians."[2] Augustine, too, has refused to commit his soul's health
to "philosophers" who "were without the saving name of
Christ" (VI, 25). The "conversion," then, whose final stages he

---

1. For an excellent and select bibliography on this aspect of Augustine's
"conversion," see Solignac, *BA* 13, pp. 250–252.
2. J. J. O'Meara's treatment of this issue is excellent; see *The Young Augustine* (London, 1954), pp. 33–60, 87–88.

is about to sketch, is not, to his mind at least, to "Christianity"
pure and simple.

Nor will he give much satisfaction if asked when he returned to "Catholic" Christianity, to the Catholic Church. This
we would find an important, even primary point, but for
Augustine it is not the point of what he is about to tell us. He is,
at last, "rescued from falsehood," but what bothers him is that
he has "not yet attained to truth." He must pass through some
paroxysmic "crisis" before emerging into health (VI, 1), and
that crisis, his entire account makes clear, is marked primarily
by his tormented efforts to arrive at "understanding."

The Ministry of Ambrose

What, then, was Ambrose's function in this passage to
"understanding"? Along with his "words," the "realities" those
words conveyed, the "truths" he spoke, seep into Augustine's
"heart." He begins to see that the Manichee portrayal of Catholic doctrine was a caricature. The Church's teaching as Ambrose
presents it "could be defended," the "spiritual" interpretation
he gave of the Old Testament "could be maintained without
being ashamed of it" (V, 24). Ambrose's Catholicism was
tenable, *possibly* true; but his preaching does not persuade
Augustine this was the "way [that] *must* be held to," nor that
Manichaeism was to be "condemned." Both parties in contention "seemed to be equal in their defenses." The Catholic position, he repeats, seemed neither "overthrown" nor "victor."
Ambrose has brought Augustine to a perfect equilibrium.
Something more is needed to tip the scales, and this requires
that Augustine himself "earnestly apply [his] mind (*animum*)
to see if it were possible, by means of sure arguments (*certis
aliquibus documentis*) to convict the Manichees of falsity"—
something that requires the ability to "conceive of a spiritual
substance," which he is "unable to do."

The "philosophers," he feels, held "much more probable
opinions" on the structure and nature of the material world.
Despite his leanings toward what generally is "supposed" as
Academic skepticism, therefore, he is brought to the resolve
"that the Manichaeans must be abandoned," and determines
"to continue as a catechumen in the Catholic Church. . . .
until something certain would enlighten [him]" (*donec aliquid
certi eluceret;* V, 25) .[3]

3. On this curious phrase, *tamdiu esse catachumenus,* which seems to imply
Augustine regarded himself as *still* a catechumen, see above. Chap. V, n. 4.

Philosophers, certainty, conviction, arguments that illumine the mind and enable it to conceive of spiritual reality: such terms compose the vocabulary, not of faith, but of "understanding." In modern dress, Augustine finds Ambrose's religion "credible" but not "certainly true."

In Quest of Certainty

The Bishop makes him "certain" that the Manichee indictments of Catholic teaching are "uncertain." Augustine is, therefore, in process of being "refuted and converted" (VI, 5). He is delighted that the religion of his infancy is far from infantile. And still, Ambrose "would state things which I did not yet know to be true: *utrum vera essent adhuc ignorarem*." Consequently, he "held back [his] heart from all assent, fearing to fall headlong . . ." (VI, 6). He is still looking for that "something certain" to convince him. Now he lays down the conditions that certainty must fulfill:

I wished to be made just as certain of things that I could not see, as I was certain that seven and three makes ten. I was not so mad [despite the seriousness of his Academic temptation to skepticism] as to think that even this last could not be known, but I wanted other things to be known with the same certainty, whether bodily things that were not present to my senses, or spiritual things, which I did not know how to conceive except in a corporeal way. By believing I could have been healed, so that my mind's clearer sight would be directed in some way to your truth, which endures forever and is lacking in nothing. But as often happens, just as a man who has had trouble with a poor physician fears to entrust himself even to a good one, so it was with my soul's health. In truth, it could never be healed except by believing, but lest it believe what was false, it refused to be cured and it resisted the hands of you who have compounded the remedies of faith, and have applied them to the diseases of the whole world, and to them you have given great efficacy (VI, 6).

Once burned, twice wary: Augustine is demanding evidence of a sort that no "belief" can furnish. The ideal of certainty he proposes, furthermore, is an interesting one. He does not ask to be certain of the things he could not see as he is of the things he could see. Ideal certainty for him is couched in the analytic terms that presided over the *Contra Academicos*. He wishes to be as certain of both visible and invisible realities as he is of the necessary connection between seven, three, and ten.

Faith and Mother Church

And yet, he assures us, belief could have helped clear his vision for arrival at such certainty; more than that, the inability to see which accompanies his soul's unhealth "could never be healed except by believing."

God he portrays as all this while applying remedies as a physician would: first, he applies the remedies of faith. Succeeding chapters subtly sketch an increasing "preference" for Catholic teaching, a growing realization of how reasonable it is to believe, how indispensible belief is to all human life, how unthinkable it would be that Scriptures should have amassed such universal authority among men did God, to whom Augustine believes the governance of human affairs belongs, not sanction their authority. The *Catholica* is "moderate" therefore, more moderate than the Manichees, not only in requiring belief, but in the reasonableness of what she asks her children to accept on faith. The function of Scripture is limned in the familiar dichotomy of authority and reason: "we are too weak to find Truth by pure reason, and for that cause needed the authority of Holy Scripture"; God must then have willed that He "be believed in *through* it (*per ipsam*) and *through* it sought." The maternal image now brings on the distinction of the many and the few. The lowly style in which Scripture couches hidden heights and depths of meaning permits it to "receive all men into its generous bosom (*populari sinu*), and by narrow passages lead a small number (*paucos*) of them on to [God]." These "few," Augustine is quick to observe, "are more numerous than if it did not stand out with such lofty authority and had not attracted the multitudes (*turbas*) into the bosom (*gremium*) of its holy humility" (VI, 8)

Augustine's language shows his earlier theory of faith and reason still substantially intact. Through authority we are strengthened for eventual possession of God by "pure reason"; once Scripture's lowly language has admonished us to "believe in" God, entrust ourselves to Him, "seek" Him, then we can entertain the hope, though the term is absent, of "finding" Him, that is, attaining to some "vision" of His splendor. Only a few are capable of this "finding," however: Augustine means the achievement of a mystical union with God even during this life. These few would be even fewer, though, were the authority of the Church's Scriptures not held up for "the many," the "multitudes," indeed, "all men." The Church is then the "universal" way, but quite explicitly not in the sense of being the exclusive way by which men may come to "find" God. Without her, the few would be fewer, but there would still be some who could—one thinks of Plato, of Plotinus—who did "arrive." So, at least for now, the matter would seem to stand. But Augustine still has not said his final word on the question.

Triple Concupiscence: Pride and Curiosity

The point is to arrive, to "find" the God in whom we "believe" and believing, "seek." Life without "possessing" God in the sense Augustine means is, he constantly reminds his readers, torment and misery. It leaves him prey to the first of those three concupiscences, the ambitious scheming and proud longing for honors and the praise of men, "no true glory" because it does not come from God. By means of eloquent lies he "sought the satisfaction of [his] pride." Even a drunken beggar is an admonition how miserable his life is (VI, 9–10).

Paulinus of Nola had requested some account of Alypius' life and conversion. Augustine turns it to an illustration of the second of his triad of sins, "curiosity." Alypius' passion when first they met was for watching games, races, and gladiatorial contests. Unknowingly (*nesciens*) Augustine becomes the instrument of that God Who makes "use of all men, both the knowing and the unknowing, in the order" that He knows. At first he "had no opportunity to warn (*monere*) [Alypius] or to recall (*revocare*) him" from his attachment to these senseless "spectacles"; but then, his friend begins to frequent his rhetoric classes, and a chance remark one day succeeds in "correcting" him of his weakness, at least for a time (VI, 11–12). Later, at Rome, he is dragged to the games again—as Augustine had been to the theft of pears—by evil companions who, Augustine archly notes, were returning from a "banquet." Too trustful in himself, Alypius thinks by closing his eyes he can escape their attraction. But suddenly, a kill is made; a "clamor" arises from the crowd; Alypius becomes "companion" (*socius*) of the rest. One of the maddened crowd (*turba*), he is "overcome by curiosity" (VI, 13).

Dream of Plotinopolis

Now Augustine pauses to describe the torment born of his alternating hope and despair of "finding Truth," the food for which he, Alypius, and their friend Nebridius "sigh," "ardently search," hunger like three gaping "mouths" till God "give them meat in due season." [4] Groaning, bitterness, and suffering is their fare, because they did not give up the "worldly ways" that brought them only torment; "as yet there shone forth nothing certain, which, such ways forsaken, we might reach out to and grasp" (VI, 17). Eleven years have passed since the Hortensius fired him for Wisdom's embrace. Although once again fixed "on the step where [his] parents placed [him] as a child," his restless longing is not assuaged—indeed, it seems redoubled. He yearns to discover "the clear light of Truth" itself (VI, 18) and yet cannot resolve to "put away his vain and empty concerns," "turn only to a search for Truth," devote himself "wholly to seeking God and the life of happiness" (VI, 19–20). He entertains the possibility of pursuing the "quest of Wisdom" in the married state (VI, 21), but Alypius repeats "over and over again" that if Augustine marries they "would in no wise live together in unbroken leisure in love of Wisdom, as [they] had long desired." The nature of Alypius' dream is shortly afterwards brought out even more clearly. Augustine and his friends are planning escape from all the "turmoils and troubles of man's life" by living a life of "retreat," of "quiet, apart from the crowd." Their goods pooled in common, two of them would administer them, "the others being left at rest" (VI, 24). Freed from the disquieting life of action, these could devote themselves entirely to contemplation, the undivided "love of Wisdom."

From Action to Contemplation

Now it becomes plainer why Augustine's story does not intend primarily to sketch his return to the *Catholica*. Complete conversion terminates, for him, in abandoning the life of action and of temporal concerns, and taking up a life of contemplation; quitting the "life of man" to achieve, as much as may be, the life of "soul"; leaving the arena of "turmoils and troubles" consequent upon the soul's fall, and attaining, even now, to "rest," "leisure," uninterrupted "love of Wisdom." In the *Confessions*, as in the *De Beata Vita*, this is the "life of happiness."

4. They "sigh" and "hunger," as Pellegrino has pointed out (pp. 154–156), for the "happy life," the life-style that will guarantee them the contemplative possession of the Truth for whose "embrace" the *Hortensius* had inflamed Augustine years before.

Triple Concupiscence: Pride and Carnal Lust

Plainer, too, is the root of Augustine's inability to embrace this form of life. Alypius insists it can only be lived in celibacy (VI, 21), and subsequent discussion among the group bears out his point. The whole plan shatters on the problem of what they are to do with the wives some have, and the wife Augustine hopes to obtain (VI, 24). He cannot, he assures Alypius, even dream of living without a woman.

Book VI ends on a lengthy treatment of the first member of the sin-triad that dominates Augustine's theory of the fallen soul: the concupiscence of the flesh. Though proud and anxious for high position, he has insinuated this is not his most serious attachment. Alypius he has sketched as prey to a "curiosity" so strong it now invites him to experience again the sexual delights Augustine finds insuperably attractive; the chains that bind him tightest are the charms of womanly embraces. This is the "insatiable appetite" which most grievously torments him (VI, 22), drives him with "sighs and groans" to "following the broad and beaten ways of the world" (VI, 24) in quest of both position and activity that will assure continuance of his pleasures.

Can it be, then, that pride is not the root of all sin? No: Augustine makes it clear that even his unwillingness to try the celibate life was pride. He "believed that continence lay within a man's own powers." In his folly, he does not realize that "no man can be continent unless [God] grant it to him." He has not yet become humble enough to "cast all [his] cares" on God (VI, 20).

Suffering and Divine Care

Throughout all this, Augustine conceives of God as exercising "therapeutic" action on his behalf. To this point he has stressed the "medicine" of growing faith. Now he begins to stress another side of that therapy: the purifying cautery of suffering.

He finds himself torn between two kinds of "embrace": the love of woman keeps him from the love of Wisdom, keeps him from achieving the dream he has had since Cicero's *Hortensius* inflamed him. Monica schemes happily to arrange a suitable marriage for him (VI, 23). His long-time companion, the mother of his son, is ripped from him and sent back to Africa.

His torment promises to reach its paroxysm, but though the wound goes deep, it slowly festers and grows "cold" again. He finds himself (*procuravi*) another woman (VI, 25). The fear of death and judgment haunts him; but for this, he tells his friends, he would gladly follow Epicurus' theory of the happy life. In the measure that his wretchedness increases, though, God draws closer to him, ever "present," his "right hand ready to help," to deliver him from mire and error. Typically, Augustine thinks of God as a mother tenderly engaged in training her child to walk: "You put us on our way and you console us; you say to us, 'Run forward! I will bear you up, and I will bring you to the end, and there also will I bear you up!' " (VI, 26).

Trust and Vision

Augustine lacks this child-like confidence in God. Despite his growing faith in what the Church teaches, the kind of faith that issues in this humble trust in God's maternal care is wanting.

His failure to cut away the attachments that bind him is, however, intimately connected with an inability to "see"; "this very fact belonged to [his] misery, that being drowned and blinded, [he] could not conceive the light of a virtue and beauty that must freely (*gratis*) be embraced. For this the body's eye does not see: it is seen only from within" (VI, 26). The final step in faith, he still insists, requires a glimpse, however momentary, of the higher beauty we desire, a moment of intense "understanding." When he has become such a man that ∠ no earthly thing delights him, Reason had assured him in the *Soliloquies*, then, at that very moment, he will behold what he desires. Augustine's answer, given then, still holds: it underlies the structure and movement of conversion as he sees it still. "I do not think," he says, "that these things can become for me objects of utter contempt until I shall have seen that in comparison with which these things grow vile" (*Sol* I, 24).

9 PAROXYSM AND ADVANCING CURE

(BOOK VII, 1-12)

As we approach Book VII that crucial glimpse of the supernal beauty is not far off. Augustine's growth in understanding aids him in discarding several unacceptable notions of God, of His nature and relation to—more specifically his omnipresence to—the world (VII, 1-2). Satisfying solutions to such questions still elude him, however; so too, the problem of evil and the freedom of the will manage to defy his groping efforts to make sense of them (VII, 3-7).

Growing Faith

Yet God's work continues. His faith and suffering have not abated—on the contrary:

Such things I turned over within my unhappy breast, overladen with gnawing cares that came from the fear of death and from not finding the truth. Yet the faith of your Christ, our Lord and Savior, the faith that is in the Catholic Church, was firmly fixed within my heart. In many ways I was as yet unformed and I wavered from the rule of doctrine, but my mind did not depart from it, nay rather, from day to day it drank in (*imbibebat*) more of it (VII, 7).

His astrological superstitions collapse about this time—
another triumph of "understanding"—so that one more obstacle
is cleared away (VII, 8–10). And still the key questions remain
unanswered. His hunger for understanding remains unsatisfied;
he cannot *see* what he insists on seeing. Whence, for example,
does evil come, if the Manichee dualism is to be definitively
rejected? No answer dawns on him, yet

in none of those wavering thoughts did you let me be carried away
from that faith in which I believed both that you exist, and that
your substance is unchangeable, and that you have care over men
and pass judgment upon them, and that in Christ, your Son, Our
Lord, and in the Holy Scriptures, which the authority of your Catholic Church approves, you have placed the way of man's salvation
unto that life which is to be after this death. These truths being
made safe and fixed immovably in my mind, I asked uncertainly,
"Whence is evil?" What torments there were in my heart in its time
of labor, O my God, what groans! . . . When I sought an answer . . . the unspoken sufferings of my soul were mighty cries for
your mercy. You know what I suffered . . . all that "I roared with
the groaning of my heart" went into your ears, and "my desire was
before you, but the light of my eyes was not with me" (VII, 11).

If compared to the catalogue presented a few paragraphs
earlier, it is clear Augustine has somewhat extended his list of
beliefs. Ever since the end of Book V, in fact, his growth in faith,
whether we consider the firmness of his commitment or the
range of truths to which he is committed, appears to advance in
a series of insensible steps, a continuum unmarked by any really
dramatic leaps, crises, or victories. Hence the difficulties encountered in answering the usual question posed to this portion
of his *Confessions:* he just does not mean to make it clear at
what moment he may be considered a Catholic "believer" in
the sense we moderns accord to that term. This is not the question the text is composed to answer. He alludes to his growth in
faith in what the context reveals as a series of parenthetical
asides: the main thread of his narration centers rather on the
problems, both speculative and existential, some of which he
gradually overcomes while others still nag at him, defying his
desperate efforts to achieve some understanding of them. For
the moment, at least, the steps in his advance in understanding
represent the main burden of his story.

Growing Torment

The same insensible gradation of intensity characterizes the suffering that marks this period of his life. One would think his growing faith would issue in a sense of peace, but his message seems to stress the exact opposite. No sooner does he assure us that those truths were "safe and fixed immovably" in his mind, but he turns immediately to the growing torment of uncertainty that marks his grappling with the problem of evil. That torment makes him labor, groan, seek with unspoken suffering—and set before God his burning desire to pass beyond faith and *see*.

Faith and Vision

This peculiarity of Augustine's conversion story is rooted, I suggest, in the notion of "faith" which dominates his mind throughout the description. He knows of faith as making the believer a member of a visible believing community, the *Catholica;* he speaks of it as assent to propositions offered on the authority of Church and Scriptures. More crucially, the final step in faith becomes an act of childlike trust in God's maternal care. All these elements are here, and they have their importance, but the conception of faith that dominates and structures his account of this period is slightly different from any of them. It is the propaedeutic notion of faith he speaks of in the *Soliloquies,* and has spoken of in the *Confessions:* faith is envisaged ⸾ primarily as "healing" the mind's eye so that its "clearer sight ⸾ would *be directed (dirigeretur)* in some way to [God's] Truth."⸾ Hence the coordinate growth in heaven-sent suffering. Its providential function is to dissolve the attachments that keep the soul from the embrace of Truth, weighing it down with earthly desires, tearing it to pieces with disquieting temporal cares. Only when these two remedies have done their work will Augustine become at last "just as certain of things that [he] could not see, as [he] was certain that seven and three makes ten" (VI, 6). Only then will he come to "see."

Understanding

This access to understanding—not his return to the *Catholica* nor his becoming a "believer" again—is what Augustine's story highlights as the next dramatic moment in the process of conversion. God's work has succeeded in reforming most of his deformities. By "inner goads," Augustine relates, "You aroused me so that I did not rest until you stood plain before my inner sight. By the secret hand of your Physician my swelling wound subsided, and day by day my mind's afflicted and darkened eyes grew sounder under the healing salve of sorrow" (VII, 12).

He means to insinuate by this that he is ready for the decisive "admonition." It is mediated with providential irony by "a certain man puffed up with the most unnatural pride" who put into his hands the very books from which he gleaned his understanding of the faith: the *Enneads* (VII, 13).

10 THE DECISIVE
ADMONITION:
LIBRI PLATONICORUM

(BOOK VII, 13–27)

Inde admonitus: Augustine wishes it clearly recognized that he
considers the Platonic books a pivotal "admonition," coming
from God himself, Truth and font of all that is true whether in
Scripture or philosophy. But he does not guarantee to tell us
what he read there exactly as he read it: "I entered into myself,
and saw." He is going to relate what, profiting from that
"admonition," he came in time to "know," to "understand." He
is about to unfold the view of reality and of man's place in it
which became "certain" for him because "manifest" to his
mind's "inner eye."

It is the view of reality that answers all the questions which
he has advanced in the *exercitatio animi* of the preceding books.
More than that, it is the view which presided over the very way
he has framed those questions, diagnosed and accounted for the
difficulties he had in solving them, selected and formed the
episodes that illustrate them.

In short, he is about to present his view of reality at the
time he conceived and composed the *Confessions,* a view that
weaves biblical and Plotinian themes together into an amalgam
resulting from a creative process which it took him years to
bring to term.[1]

---

1. Along with the vision at Ostia, this section has had scores of studies devoted to it, in whole or part. See Courcelle, pp. 157–167; Pellegrino, pp. 162–169;

This accounts for the correspondences between sections of
Confessions VII, 16–23, and certain of his earlier works. The
beatifying Light he saw (later, he will characterize that vision as
"through a glass, darkly" [VIII, 1]), of whose existence he became more certain than of his very own, is the "Eternal Truth,
True Love, Beloved Eternity" toward which the *Contra
Academicos* and *De Beata Vita* both aspired (VII, 16–17).

This, too, is the Supreme and hence absolutely incorruptible Good alongside which all inferior realities both "are and
are not." But, though inferior to God, they do exist in some
fashion and commend themselves to him as "good," "so long as
they exist"; corruptible, they could not be corrupted, that is,
deprived of good, unless they already possessed, from God, the
goodness they could lose (18). The Manichee theory of substantial evil must, therefore, be rejected: no existent can be totally
evil.

Good in themselves, even things which clash in discord with
certain of their fellow-beings nonetheless accord with, are good
for, other members of the world-order. Even the "viper and the
worm" (VII, 22) on which the Manichee objections harped, are
"in keeping with the lower part of reality, which we call earth"
(VII, 19, 22). Like the Manichees, and like the Gnostics
Plotinus had to contend with, we might wish that this "lower
reality" of visible, corporeal things did not exist at all. If we
"considered them alone" we might, as Augustine admits he was
tempted once to do, "desire" that only the "better things" of
the higher, spiritual realm should exist. Augustine's correction
of this desire parallels Plotinus' rejoinder to the Gnostics: he
"thought of *all* things," "higher and lower," and judged that
"all things together"—invisible archetypes along with visible
copies—"are better than the higher things alone" (VII, 19).
Such is the harmonious order of the universe that everything,
whether archetype or image, is in its "place," a place befitting it
and which it, in turn, befits.

Whence, then, does evil come? Now at least the necessary
preliminary question—"what is evil?"—has been answered.
Evil is the "corruption" whereby a limited changeable good
becomes "deprived" of some good features. It is neither positive
substance nor inferior status as "imitation" of the higher world.
The plaints Augustine once uttered about any "part" of God's

---

and Solignac, *BA* 13, pp. 679–693 for some good observations and ample bibliography. My own treatment of the matter will be found in *Augustine's Early Theory*, Chap. 1, pp. 43–51, Chap. 8, and Chap. 10.

creation were symptomatic, rather, of his own moral "ill health": for "bread that pleases a healthy appetite is offensive to one that is not healthy" and even that beneficent element, light, can become "hateful to sick eyes" (VII, 22). On the intellectual side, moreover, that "madness" plunges its victim into the misconceptions of God and created universe which he had previously entertained.

The intellectual key to the problem of evil supposes a "vision" not derived from the "flesh," from its bodily senses and "vain imaginings"—a vision of God as infinite, but in a "different way" from what corporeal, spatial thinking can represent. What is required is a vision of all things in God's "Truth-Hand." Derived from the Infinite Good all things are good and "in place." But now the same rule holds for their "truth." Derived from Truth Eternal, "all things are true insofar as they have being"; they are, accordingly, "in harmony not only with their proper places, but also with their [temporal] seasons." The moment of their appearance and departure from the changing temporal world corresponds to the "activity and unfailing presence" of the God Who alone is Eternal (VII, 21).

This vision once attained, it follows that it is really God's "justice" which "offends the wicked." They complain of certain features that are perfectly "in keeping with the lower parts of [God's] creation," as a sick man would complain of bread and light. They fail to perceive that they themselves, the "wicked," are "adapted" to those same lower parts of creation, "in harmony with those lower things insofar as they are unlike [God]." The irony of their position is that "insofar as they become liker to [God]" they would by that very fact become more "in harmony with the higher things" they yearn for (VII, 22). What they are in effect bewailing is their presence and confinement to the lower, visible world: they feel out of place in it, hanker after the higher world, languish like Augustine in this "region of unlikeness" (VII, 16). Yet their very wickedness makes that lower world the "proper place" for them.

But, like Augustine, they can still "make sound judgments," by which he means they retain the insight to give "approval to the beauty of bodies," saying that "this should be thus and so, and that not" (VII, 23). Let them search into the grounds which enable them to pass such judgments. They will find, as he did, that there still remains in them some "remembrance" of God, a loving and longing memory "of that immutable, true, and eternal Truth which exists above [the] changeable mind" (VII, 23). Their very power to make normative "judgments" of this sort shows they still have some residual vision of the transcendent norm according to which they judge.

But can that residual vision properly be termed a "memory"? Augustine tosses out the bait, and once again as quickly snaps it back. The question teases his reader's mind, but he gives only a sybilline reply in terms of another, connected theme: "iniquity."

"Whence does evil come?" was the Manichee's repeated question. The answer to that is the answer to the other question Augustine has now inserted in his reader's mind. What accounts for our presence in a world of images when we yearn still for "reality"? The cause of that situation can be put in that single term: "iniquity." It took Augustine years to come to a satisfactory resolution of that problem. The *De Ordine, De Libero Arbitrio, De Moribus Ecclesiae* each contribute to the answer he first elaborates in the *De Genesi contra Manichaeos,* then refines in the *De Vera Religione* and subsequent works. But the root of our human situation can eventually be expressed in that one word. For our presence in the world of bodies is a result of our having fallen, is testimony to God's having leveled punishment on our "iniquity."

Augustine has alluded a number of times to the soul's fall. Patricius, Alypius, and on numerous occasions he himself have all been characterized as "fallen," but in terms that were veiled enough to leave the reader puzzled on what those terms might mean. All this was in keeping with the intention of "exercising" the reader's "mind," goading it gradually to realize the paradox that is the human situation. Now he is ready to be more outspoken, though still not perfectly plain. The remainder of the Confessions will illumine the language he uses here: that man finds himself in this "region of unlikeness" because God has made his "soul waste away like a spider" (VII, 16), "corrected" him "for his iniquity," that is to say, for that "perversity of will, twisted away from the supreme substance," God, "towards lower things" (VII, 22). The will's primordial "free decision" is the "cause of our doing evil." It has as its inevitable result in God's "just judgment" that man suffers evil (VII, 5).

Augustine's own descent from the contemplative heights he has momentarily attained is paradigm of the original fall. His soul is "borne down from" God, not by some extrinsic divine decree, but "by its own weight"; he is "plunged into the midst of these lower things" (VII, 23) by the weight of the "corruptible body" which is a "load upon the soul," an "earthly habitation [which] presses down upon the mind" (VII, 23). And yet, in spite of its infidelity, the soul still "sighs for God" day and night (VII, 16), aspires to "cleave" to Him (VII, 17).

For it retains a residual contact with the realm of beatifying, unchanging Truth—a "memory" which polarizes its longing, but at the same time provides it with the ladder for passing inward and upward, as now Augustine does, "from bodies to the soul . . . and thence to its interior power . . . to its own understanding," eventually to "find that Light by which it [is] sprinkled" when it makes its normative "judgments." At last, in a "flash of trembling sight" it glimpses the "immutable being," "that which is," the Being from which once it turned away, and turning, fell (VII, 23).

If it be of Augustine's caliber, the soul at this point of its ascent will find itself "unable to fix [its] gaze" on God's "invisible realities, understood by the things that are made" (VII, 23); because of its "infirmity," its "feeble sight" (VII, 16) will be "struck back" by the very radiance of the vision (VII, 23). To "gain sufficient strength to enjoy" what it has only glimpsed, it must seek for a "way of gaining strength" (VII, 24), a "way that leads not only to beholding our blessed fatherland but also to dwelling therein" (VII, 26). It is not enough "only to see" God; the soul must be "made strong to hold fast" to Him (VII, 27).

Christ and "Return"

Christ's function in this "return" to the blessed fatherland Augustine conceives as twofold. First, he contemplates the case of the man less intellectually endowed, "who cannot see from afar off" as he has done. For such a one Christ constitutes the "way" upon which he may "walk . . . come to . . . see . . . and hold fast to [God]" (VII, 27). For the Monicas of this world, then, Christ now provides an alternative to the intellectualist way of the "disciplines."

But secondly, even for the intellectually endowed, there is a difference between glimpsing the fatherland and being strong enough to dwell therein, enjoy, endure the vision's splendor. Food of Truth mixed with flesh, Christ provides the "strength" which makes the difference between a momentary glimpse and continued enjoyment of God.

He has made some severe remarks about the Platonists who either reject or fail to recognize Christ—"all this the writings of the Platonists do not have" (VII, 27). He stresses the dangers of striving "in vain toward [the land of peace] by unpassable ways, ambushed and beset by fugitives and deserters" and the contrasted security of keeping "to that way . . . guarded by the protection of the heavenly commander, where no deserters from the heavenly army lie in wait like bandits." Yet Augustine never once overstates his case. Never once does he say or imply that it is flatly impossible for such as Plato and Plotinus to "arrive" at vision. "They scorn to learn of [Christ] because he is meek and humble of heart"; they "shun that way, like a torture"; these things have been hid from them, "wise and prudent" though they are, and revealed to "little ones" (VII, 27). And yet, they seem still capable at least of "beholding our blessed fatherland" though not of permanently "dwelling therein" (VII, 26). The reason for that latter inability he expresses later in the semi-juridical terms familiar from the *De Utilitate Credendi* (24): speaking of baptism, he avers that "there is no other entrance into the kingdom of heaven from the time that [God] decreed that such [i.e. Christ] should be the entrance" (XIII, 29). What features of the soul's situation in reality ground the appropriateness of that divine decree? The radical spirituality of Augustine's anthropology seems to offer none. Why should a sacramental rite like baptism, or a temporal, bodily reality like the Incarnation, be the universal and necessary way for the soul's return to its eternal home? Plotinus himself lived after that decree had been issued; his philosophic activity took place at Rome, the very heart of Christianity. What of him? One can understand Augustine's discretion on that nettling issue. And yet, it is one he cannot leave totally in abeyance. His answer comes only with his discussion of the sacramental economy in Book XIII.[2]

2. In *Conf* XIII, 29 Augustine confesses that "there is no other entrance into the kingdom of heaven from the time that God decreed that such should be the entrance": *ex illo, quo instituisti, ut sic intretur*. Again, the *instituisti* has a peculiarly juridical ring, all the more so in the context of the "spiritual" Christianity Augustine is exposing throughout this portion of Book XIII.

11 A CENTRAL DIFFICULTY: EMANATION AND OMNIPRESENCE

Augustine seems on the whole content that the series of reflections (done for the most part in his early writings) through which he attempted to elaborate a Plotinian synthesis of the biblical faith has, by the time of the *Confessions,* issued in a satisfactory view of the soul, its origin, destiny, and place in the universe. A modern would be less inclined to grant him that satisfaction, for a variety of reasons.

Fundamental among those reasons is the difficulty I have alluded to elsewhere.[1] Augustine does not seem to have sensed the gigantic problem involved in bringing an emanation style of thought into genuine coherence with the insights of omnipresence. This is partially because of his ignorance of the Platonic tradition whose varied strands went into Plotinus' developing thought.

The emanation image predominates in Plotinus' earlier thinking, making its presence felt particularly in *Enneads* I, 6, and V, 1. There, inferior reality is imaged as "cascading" downward (or "radiating outwards") from the One, the Font and

---

1. See, on this same question, *Augustine's Early Theory,* Chap. 4, pp. 117–121. Compare the many places in which Solignac handles cognate questions, *Notes Complémentaires* 7, 10, 23, 26, in *BA* 13 and in *BA* 14, Notes 9, 20, 23.

Source of all the rest. Each level of reality, therefore, can be imaged as distinct from, and subordinate to, the level above it. Between the higher, spiritual world of the Three Hypotases (the One, the *Noûs*, the All-Soul) and the lower world of sense and bodies there cuts a radical differentiation. This makes it necessary for Plotinus to explain the individual soul's presence in the sensible world of bodies by a "fall." Its downward motion of procession has been prolonged beyond the point where it should have stopped. It has become immersed in body and sense more deeply than it should have.

In virtually all his appeals to this emanation image, Plotinus reverts, in a second moment of his thinking, to stressing, along with the differentiation between the various levels, their inner unity and continuity as well. But the primary service this image renders is to allow for that differentiation, not only between the "two worlds," but interior to each of them as well. Here the imagination comes to his aid. Each level risks being "pictured" as "below" and at some "distance" from the level above it. The lowest region can therefore be named a "region of unlikeness," as we have seen both Plotinus and Augustine name it; the soul is pictured as "down here," exiled and alienated from the divine realm "up there." Hence the appropriateness of speaking of an upward "journey" or "flight", involved in its return.

To what extent were both thinkers duped by this imaginative form of thought? The question is difficult to settle. It seems quite clear, however, that Plotinus feels the need, in his treatise on Omnipresence, of warning his readers against misapprehensions that might come from such misuse of the imagination. Far more than in his earlier works, he makes use now of the rich resources of a Stoic monism which permits him to think out the integral presence of the higher to the lower worlds, presence that demands elimination of all such notions as space and "distance" between the two. Here the primary drive of this thought is unitive rather than differentiating. There is, apparently, no difference in the way the higher is present to the various strata and members of the lower world, it being integrally present to all and each. The problem then becomes the one of accounting for the differentiations between various levels of being in the sense-world, or between the various rational souls who find access to and recognition of the Omnipresent diversely possible to them.

Now he must account for that differentiation in terms of

the diverse "competence" of members of the lower world to "receive" the Omnipresent which, from its side, is both unchangeable and totally, integrally present to each. This diversity of competence arises, he tells us, from their having "turned away," "absented themselves" from the Ever-Present, allowed an addition from the realm of non-being to parcel them off from Being (and from each other) such that they ignore the unity whereby they are all "one being." This in turn brings him to re-explain the soul's alienation from the higher world as resulting, not so much from a "downward" motion of soul itself, as from an upsurge of the "rabble" of non-being, become unruly in its hunger after higher form and being. Though he admits this upsurge is possible in virtue of matter's already having been enhanced by the influence of soul, the aggressive dualism involved is an important feature in this explanation of the soul's alienation. It does not, however, totally eliminate the notion of the soul's "turning away," a notion far more proper to the emanation register. The "turning" image frequently occurs in connection with omnipresence language, despite the fact that it actually owes its origin to the "cascade" image of procession-and-conversion, and seems to be intelligible only in function of that image. How, on the face of it, is a "turning away" any longer possible, when every turn will also be "towards" the Omnipresent?

Now our question here, as always, is not so much whether Plotinus manages to overcome this difficulty. The question is whether Augustine shows a sensitivity to it, and overcomes it. In these reflections on the *libri platonicorum* he has evidently intended to sketch, in terms more unmistakable than heretofore, the soul's "fallen" position in reality—a view which is more easily expressed in emanation-terms—and yet, the whole account is held together by a constant reversion to omnipresence themes. Again and again he moves from one register to the other, manfully attempting to bring them into unison. Does he succeed?

The answer is, I think, that each time these two modes of thought come into clear collision, the emanation style wins out because Augustine's focus is primarily anthropological, only secondarily metaphysical. First in his intention is the concern to limn the soul's situation in reality: its native habitat in the other, upper world, its fall and fallen state, its residual memory of the divine, its consequent capacity to mount back upward in the movement of return—all notions calling for emanation imagery and emanation metaphysic. The fall, accordingly, is regularly imaged by a "downward" movement, never once in terms of the upward "intrusion" of matter Plotinus felt it necessary to invoke in the Omnipresence treatise. The fact that matter is clearly (in Augustine's view) God's creation may have dissuaded him from explicitly portraying it with the inimical aggressiveness Plotinus' modified dualism permitted him to attribute to it. The difficulty is to some extent obviated in that Augustine need no longer be disturbed at introducing changeability into the soul, even while it inhabits the upper regions. He can therefore accord to soul an initiative in its downward movement which Plotinus saw he had to avoid, or at least persuade himself he had avoided it.

Be all that as it may, this much is certain: each time Augustine sketches the soul as fallen or mounting back upward, the spatial images of place, distance, and direction become vital for the expression of that view. Yet his awareness of omnipresence canons of thought constantly intrudes, forcing him to counter such spatial imagery not only with respect to God, but also with respect to the creature's relation to God. But then, at the final moment of his thought, the metaphors of space and distance must recur again, to re-express the sense of fall and alienation which remains, in spite of everything, the central burden of his account.

Fall and Emanation

Thus, to set the scene for the soul's fall, he finds himself compelled to locate the "light" he glimpsed "above" the mind, "above" the soul, and himself "beneath it." God "took [him] up" from the "region of unlikeness" where he formerly was "far" from Him; he hears the divine voice "from on high" (16). He returns to behold the "other things below" God (17), finds creation disposed in an "order" boasting "lower parts" and "high places," "lower" and "higher things" (19), all of them being in their "proper places" (21), including the wicked who are "adapted" to the "lower parts of [God's] creation" on account of their "unlikeness" to Him. For their sin consisted precisely in twisting away from the "supreme substance" and "toward lower things" (22). "Borne up" to God, attracted by His beauty, Augustine finds himself soon "borne down" again by his own "weight," and "plunged into the midst of these lower things." And yet he has found that changeless Truth exists "above" the changing mind. In its light his soul succeeds in "raising itself up" along the ladder of its powers to the immutable its insight sets "above" the mutable, to the light which once again "struck back" his trembling sight (23).

Omnipresence and Image-Correction

Nevertheless, as we have noted repeatedly before, Augustine knows he must correct this imagery. The light he saw was not "above" him in any local sense, but in the way what "makes" is above whatever is "made by it." That light is Truth, "diffused neither through finite nor infinite space" (16). Abiding "in" Him allows one to abide "in" one's self, but not in any spatial sense, because He spacelessly "abides in himself and renews all things" in space (17). His infinity must be conceived not extensively, but "in a different way." All things must be conceived of as "in" Him, "not as though in a place," but rather, as in His omnipresent, because spaceless and space-transcending, "truth-hand" (21). The corrections are, therefore, dutifully entered.

Tensions Unresolved

But the question is, do they genuinely "correct" the emanation imagery with all the spatial connotations it furnishes for picturing the soul as "fallen"? Despite Augustine's excellent intentions, I do not think they do. He shifts from one register to the other, sometimes within the same sentence, but the registers are really juxtaposed, not synthesized.[2]

Consider, for example, his central description of "inquity." The will is said to "twist itself away" from God. Now in Plotinus' treatise on Omnipresence, God is initially imaged at the "center," the soul's "turn" is to the peripheral "oppo-

2. In fairness to Augustine, it should be remarked that this is simply one of various angles of approach to the profound philosophical problem of relating Divine Immanence to Transcendence. A. H. Armstrong observes that even Plotinus, as powerful a thinker as he was, did not entirely succeed in "synthesizing" the emanationist and omnipresence styles of thinking; see his article, "Emanation in Plotinus," *Mind* 46:61–66 (1937). Indeed, one wonders whether the most heroic efforts of subsequent philosophers have been significantly more successful. Perhaps the best human thought can hope for here is to locate that horizon point where the mind succumbs to a species of metaphysical "double-vision," seeing *that* two apparently antinomic propositions are to be respected, not quite seeing *how*, but somehow seeing *why* (God being and remaining God) that *docta ignorantia* is to be expected and accepted.

sites"; there is an initial suggestion of the "radiation" rather than the "cascade" form of the emanation image. But the entire context is a strenuous attempt to eliminate such unpurified "radiation" corollaries as would imply that the divine light traveled through "distance," got weaker and dimmer as it traveled outward, till at last it reached the darkling "region of unlikeness," "far" from the central source. Hence the difficulty again: if the light is omnipresent, then a turn in one direction will be toward the light in as pure and genuine a form as in any other direction. One can turn away from a central "source," but once thought has "eliminated" the localized source by the process of dynamic image-correction [3]—once the light has been imagined as "throughout the entire sphere" and the image of localized source entirely dropped—then no "turn away" from the Omnipresent is genuinely imaginable. Plotinus must, therefore, go to considerable lengths in order to furnish a more sophisticated explanation of the "fall" than unpurified emanation-imagery required.

In this central description of the "fall," however, Augustine fails to live up to this demand for greater sophistication. He has begun with a series of images involving downward and upward movements of the soul away from and back toward God, and then has reminded us that things must not be imagined as "far" from God, nor God imagined as "in" them—they are all inescapably "in" God, but not "as in a place." One looks for an account of the fall, then, embodying that correction. Instead, Augustine not only fails to purify the emanation imagery, he actually compounds the difficulty. He slides from the unpurified image of God as "center" (from whom the soul twists "away") directly into the image of God as "highest," so that the soul's "fall" is, quite literally, imagined as propelling it downward toward "lower things" which, following the logic of the "center" image, must be "peripheral" realities as well. Had he remained with the "center" image solely, he might well have worked a correction something like Plotinus' own, but he has tried to combine what seems to have been initially an omnipresence element with the classic "cascade" of emanation and

3. For this (in Bréhier's term) "dynamic image" see *Ennead* VI, 4, 7. The Omnipresent is originally imagined as a corporeal light-source, then (by process of image-correction) de-localized entirely so that the Light is understood as equally present throughout the "sphere" of the real. Compare *Augustine's Early Theory*, Chap. 1, pp. 58–59, and (for its use by Augustine) Chap. 2 entire, but esp. pp. 65–68, 80–86.

thereby lost all chance of preserving whatever intelligibility)
might possibly have been salvaged.

The same defect vitiates all his allusions to the "fall." The
imagery that allows him to describe the soul as "fallen" is invariably drawn from the register of emanation, taken in its
baldest, uncorrected form. Often enough, there occurs side by
side with such imagery a reminder, for example, that "not on
foot, and not by distance of place do we depart from you or
return to you," not by "horses, or chariots, or ships" or by
"visible wings." The soul's departure is effected by "lustful
affections," and must be understood in terms appropriate to
express that moral alienation. But how, then, understand such
an expression, in the immediate context, as "I was *far* from your
face in the *darkness* of my passions," or the observation that "to
be *far* from your face" is tantamount to yielding to *"darksome
affections"*? (I, 28). At this point Augustine regularly shifts
back to an emanation image wherein "darkness" symbolizes the
"region of unlikeness" at some imaginative "distance" from the
central, highest source of being, while the vice in his "affections" is depicted as "turning" him from God to the beings in
this region of "darkness." He never, to my knowledge, manages
to respect the controlling insights of omnipresence theory while
still, *in the same act of thought,* successfully depicting the soul
as "fallen." He more than once presents us with an initial statement of the case in emanation terms, then inserts a corrective
from the omnipresence side. I know of no instance where he
passes on to what Plotinus' dynamic imagery indicated was the
vital third step called for in this dialectic, that of at least
attempting a formulation which assumes both previous steps in
the very act of transcending them.

Augustine's adaptation of Plotinus' "light"-correction is
particularly instructive. It points to what may have been the
underlying metaphysical difficulty which, left unresolved,
forced him to resort to the indecisive shifts we have been
examining here. Working again on the hypothesis that *Confessions* VII, 16–17 embodies "interferences" between the light-
images presented in *Enneads* V, 8 and VI, 4, one can understand why Augustine begins by situating this light "above" him,
why he then goes on to warn us it was not a material light ("of
the same kind"), even were that light (as in Plotinus' second-
stage correction) to "shine many, many times more bright, and
by its great power fill the whole universe." "Different" in

kind, therefore, this light must be (not imagined now, but) understood as being "above" the mind as archetype is above its created image: "above my mind, because it made me."

Is this the third stage of Plotinus' dynamic image? No, it is, rather, an attempt to shift out of the image register entirely, quite probably encouraged by Plotinus' own attempt, later in the Omnipresence treatise, to explain the "priority" of Idea to copy in more conceptual terms.[4] Significantly missing is Plotinus' step of "shattering" the image he has begun with, a masterful stroke (given his suppositions) which aims at "untracking" the offending imagination entirely, thereby (hopefully) preventing it from exerting any further influence on the thinking process. This Augustine clearly fails to do; his imagination remains still "in gear" and running powerfully under the surface of his thought. Carried "upward" by an enthusiastic situation of the "light" as *aliud, aliud valde*—"other, entirely other"—its surreptitious working can bypass the momentary shift into the more conceptual causality-categories, gain strength from the sense of alienating distance implied in Augustine's "sighing" for his God, then reassert itself in bold uncorrected terms when he passes on to picture God as "taking him up," "beating back" his feeble sight, then pictures himself as "far" from God in the "region of unlikeness." Imagination and emanation-thinking have taken their revenge. The "light" is no longer omnipresent, but "up there." Exactly where it must be, if the soul is to be thought of as "down here," fallen into a "region of unlikeness."

Thought, Image, and Man

The foregoing analysis supposes, as both Plotinus and Augustine do, that "imagination" and genuine "thought" may be distinguished in the manner they insist those operations must, that "imagination" can, therefore, be utterly "untracked," completely transcended when thinking on such matters as the divine omnipresence.

The supposition was, for purposes of this analysis, merely a methodological one. I doubt quite seriously that such a disincarnate performance is accessible to the human intelligence. In any case it can, I think, be shown that neither Plotinus nor Augustine succeeded in doing so.

The irony involved is a nice one. The thesis that imagina-

4. See above, pp. 11–12, and *Augustine's Early Theory,* Chap. 4, pp. 117–121.

tion could be left behind was corollary of the theory of man whose coherent expression regularly meets with shipwreck because its proponents fail to accomplish what their theory claims can be accomplished: they never really manage to leave imagination behind.

12 THE PEARL
IS PURCHASED
(BOOK VIII)

Choosing a "Way": Marriage or Celibacy

"Admonished" by his platonic readings, Augustine is sure that God is eternal life, although, he observes, he "saw it only 'in a glass, darkly'" (VIII, 1). He is certain now; all his "doubts concerning incorruptible substance . . . had been removed." Yet certainty is not enough. "To be more steadfast in [God]" is what he still desires.

The question facing him concerns the disposition of his "temporal life" (VIII, 1). For in the Church, he saw, "one went this way, another that," some being "eunuchs who made themselves such for the kingdom of heaven," while others, aware that Paul did not forbid them to do so, chose the "softer place," married life (VIII, 2).

Though freed from the desires of honor and of wealth, Augustine is still "tightly bound by love of women." Weaker, he too feels inclined to "choose the softer place." "For this one thing [he is] tossed all about in other ways . . . faint and wasted away with withering cares," forced "in other matters . . . to adapt [himself] to the conjugal life." For marriage means one must make money, strive for position, compete amid the "withering cares" of the world of action. He has "found the good pearl," has fallen in love with the "beauty of God's house," but hesitates to abandon all his hopes for married bliss in order to pursue, possess, embrace that supernal Beauty. Still faithful to the conviction voiced in the *Soliloquies* (I, 22), Augustine feels that the Beauty he longs for demands an undivided love. And for him, now, that implies a life of celibacy.

The Terminus of Conversion

The burden of what he is about to tell us will inevitably be misconstrued if approached with the wrong suppositions. One such supposition would have it that Augustine has been recounting a conversion precisely to "Christianity," and, moreover, one which occurred in an "intellectual" stage described in Book VII, and a "moral" stage which he is about to recount here. Such a view forgets that he very likely considered himself an enlightened sort of "Christian" while a Manichee. Ambrose has persuaded him that the Manichaean charges against the *Catholica* were puerile caricatures, but still left his mind in suspense. Having at length attained a glimpse of that "something certain" which positively proved the falsity of Manichaeism, he has compared the certainties of the Neo-Platonists with the Catholic understanding of St. Paul and found them in substantial agreement. He now considers himself as having returned to a specific type of Christianity, as a "Catholic Christian." The question which confronts him now is that of choosing one of the several ways he finds men treading *inside* the *Catholica*. Both the married life and the life of celibacy, he is assured by St. Paul, are legitimate and permissible for Catholics *in general;* the question is, which one is appropriate for one "affected" like himself?

The Question of Baptism

His situation is complicated to our modern eyes by the fact that he has not yet been baptized. He has earlier explained Monica's refusal to have him baptized. She feared he would afterwards fall into serious sin, a relapse that would be graver than his sinning before receiving the sacrament (I, 17). Her eagerness to see him settled in the married state he attributes to the same motives: she thought that, married, he would be out of serious danger, he could be baptized without the risks he would

run if exposed to sexual temptation while single (VI, 23). The
ancient penitential practice, which included adultery among
the "irremissible sins," may well have had much to do with
Monica's decision.[1] But at all events it is clear that in the fourth
century a man could in a quite real sense consider himself a
"Catholic Christian" even before baptism.

Augustine the Bishop did not approve of such delayed
baptism. He tries to make the reader understand Monica's
error, but he does not justify it. On the contrary, to be a Catholic in the *fullest* sense meant being a baptized Catholic. But it is
easy to see why now he feels that before taking that irreversible
step the risks must prudently be weighed.

The Life of Contemplation

But the questions of celibacy and baptism are closely
interwoven with a third. The fundamental reason Augustine is
tormented by the celibacy issue lies in the decisive choice he
feels himself faced with, a choice between the "active" and the
"contemplative" lives. His reading of the *Hortensius,* years before, had fired him with the "desire to fly away from earthly
things and upwards" to God. "Enkindled and set aflame" he
longed then to "love, and pursue, and attain, and catch hold of,
and strongly embrace . . . Wisdom Itself," the "undying
Wisdom" of which, he thought, Cicero was speaking (III,
7–8). And Cicero, it should be remembered, was speaking as
one who had retired from the troubling arena of political action
to the peace of philosophic meditation. "Philosophy," for him,
was not just an intellectual discipline, it implied a definite way
of life.

The dream inspired by the *Hortensius* never really left
Augustine. It continues to bother him, but when it surfaces
again in Book VI it has acquired firmer contour. He remembers
his half-formed resolution, eleven years before, to abandon all
other hopes and desires in his "zeal for Wisdom" (VI, 18). He
agonizes over his long delay in surrendering all worldly ambi-

1. See Gustave Bardy's note (#18) in vol. 6 of the *Bibliothèque Augustinienne* series of *Oeuvres de saint Augustin* (Paris, 1952), pp. 504–506. He gives
good reason to suspect that the three sins Augustine refers to in the *De Libero
Arbitrio* (I, 6) reflect this "irremissible sins" practice known from the early
Church. One of them was adultery. Gibb and Montgomery, p. 18 quote Adolf
von Harnack's observation that, in practice, many fourth-century Christians
treated baptism more as the "completion" of than as an "initiation" to the
Christian life. See his *History of Dogma,* Eng. ed. (New York, 1961), IV, 284.

tions and devoting himself "wholly to seeking God and a life of happiness" (20), a life which even now he dimly perceives would require "continence" of him, keep him "from a woman's arms" (20).

For were Augustine to marry, Alypius argues compellingly, they could "in no wise live together in unbroken leisure in love of Wisdom, as [they] had long desired" (21). Augustine tries to argue that marriage might conceivably be combined with this life of pursuing Wisdom (21; cf. *Sol* I, 17) but when he and his friends discuss the concrete conditions of such a life, his hopes are smashed.

They deliberated, he tells us, about a "life of quiet apart from the crowd," an idyllic philosophic community. Certain of its members would, by turns, discharge the necessary administrative duties, but the others, meanwhile, would be "left at rest." The language of the *Confessions* and the regime observed at Cassiciacum lead one to suppose that this "rest" (*otium*) would be devoted to study, discussion, and contemplation, the *exercitatio* whereby the mind at length "attains," "catches hold of," "embraces" Wisdom in mystical union.

But what would they do about the wives some of them had and those that others planned to marry? On this question, the whole project collapses (24). The contemplative life of "quiet," "rest," of "wholly seeking God and a life of happiness," requires that one leave behind all "dis-quiet," and "busy-ness" (*negotium*), all the cares of the active life that distract the soul from "wholly" seeking God. It therefore required, as its indispensable condition, that its devotee free himself from the need to support wife and children.

"Conversion to Philosophy"

This spiritual quandary brings Augustine to Simplicianus. He no longer seeks intellectual illumination, he desires spiritual counsel on the style of life he should adopt as a Catholic. The reason the issue of celibacy has come so sharply to the fore is that Augustine views it as a necessary condition for accomplishing, now, after all these years, the "conversion to philosophy" to which the *Hortensius* had so powerfully, but inefficaciously, solicited him. Even then, he had envisaged that "conversion to philosophy" [2] as a life given over to pursuing the

2. On "conversion to philosophy" in the ancient world, see Arthur Darby Nock, *Conversion* (London: Oxford, 1933), pp. 164–186; Marrou, *Culture an-*

Truth and Wisdom his faith identified with the Eternal Christ.
Now, he still sees his faith as a step toward "understanding,"
understanding as the "pursuit" of vision. He thinks of conversion to "philosophy" as having distinctly religious, mystical, and
Christian overtones. Dare he make the break with the world required for living the "philosophic" life that promises he may
"attain, and catch hold of, and strongly embrace" (III, 7–8)
the Wisdom he has glimpsed? For one "affected" as he was
toward women, the celibate cast of that life held obvious dangers; marriage, even with the cares of the active life that at-
tended it, was both a "softer" and a safer place.

The phase of his conversion he is about to relate deals with
how God "broke the bonds" that still held him to the love of
women, and therefore to the active life. God will accord him the
strength to "sell all he had" and acquire the "pearl of great
price," the life of happiness in contemplation, its requisite celibacy included. The "second stage" of his conversion, then, is
not to Catholic Christianity as such, but to the contemplative—
and therefore celibate—"way" of Catholic Christian life.

Victorinus and the Conquest of Pride

Simplicianus receives Augustine graciously. He congratu-
lates him on having read the Neo-Platonists, for like Augustine
he feels they are the philosophers who came closest to the Christian truth. But what Simplicianus chiefly brings to the process
already (and still) underway is the story of Marius Victorinus'
celebrated conversion. Like Augustine, Victorinus had much to
lose; like Augustine, a famous *rhetor,* he was unlike him in that
the principal attachment which held him back was pride. Already voted a statue in the Roman forum, devotee of the idol-
worship with which Romans were "inflated," eloquent defender
of such pagan rites as he had "proudly imitated and accepted,"
his conversion is chiefly marked by the uncompromising refusal
to "blush to become a child" of Christ, a "newborn infant,"

---

tique, pp. 161–186, shows the richness of the concept as it applies to Augustine's
conversion. Pellegrino, pp. 187–188 tends to underestimate the religious reso-
nances of the phenomenon and the break with the world it entailed (though
compare his remarks earlier, pp. 83–93). This may be part of his reason for
thinking of Augustine's conversion to "philosophy" as already consummated in
his nineteenth year (cf. Courcelle in a similar vein, pp. 49–60). I find little support in the text for Courcelle's interpretation (pp. 168–174) of these conversa-
tions with Simplicianus as a series of relatively speculative discussions on the
consonance between Neo-Platonism and the Prologue of St. John's Gospel. Cf.
Pellegrino, pp. 175–179.

publicly bending his neck "under the yoke of humility" (VIII, 3–4).

Society in Joy

Just as before the phenomena of grief and societal malice had prompted him to reflect on their meaning, now Augustine asks why it is men rejoice more over the lost sheep that returns than over the lambs who had never strayed; why the Father rejoiced at the prodigal's return rather than over his other son's long fidelity; why the neighbors rejoiced more with the lady of the parable over the drachma she had lost and found than over coins never lost (VIII, 6)? Such questions now shift slightly to introduce another: why does the soul itself "take greater delight if things it loves are found . . . than if it had always possessed them"? Why does the sailor rejoice so especially over the calm that succeeds the storm? Eating gives more pleasure when it follows hunger; the bride is dearer for having been for a time withheld (VIII, 7). Sheep, drachma, stormy passage and safe harbor, prodigal and bride, food and drink after protracted hunger and thirst, these are the familiar images of the soul's fall and return. They move Augustine to pray that God "arouse us, and call us back" (VIII, 9), but they illustrate as well Plotinus' assurance that the soul which has fallen and experienced evil will return with keener appreciation of the good which it left in falling.[3]

Still in Bondage

Augustine finds the story of Victorinus paradigmatic of his own situation. "On fire to imitate him," he envies him the good fortune brought him by the Emperor Julian's edict forbidding Christians to teach literature and oratory, because it gave him "opportunity to devote himself to [God] alone" in a life of contemplation, the "very thing" for which Augustine "sighs" (VIII, 10). Stripped of the excuse that made him formerly "unable to despise the world and to serve [God] because knowledge of the Truth was still uncertain," he finds himself still slave to the habit of lust he has freely allowed to enchain him. "Still bound to the earth, I refused to become your soldier" (VIII, 11).

3. See *Augustine's Early Theory*, Chap. 6, pp. 160–161.

Two Soldiers: "Agents" Become Contemplatives

That final image evokes the light-armed infantryman who travels best when freed of cumbersome extra baggage, but it also leads into the next example from which Augustine drew inspiration at this time. Ponticianus, a servant of the emperor, recounts the conversion of some fellow "agents" in the service. [4] Again, the choice of active and contemplative life is prominently to the fore. His story opens with allusions to Anthony of Egypt (VIII, 14), passes to the "flocks within the monasteries and to their way of life"—one such was near Milan, under the "fostering care of Ambrose," *sub Ambrosio nutritore* (15). But whereas pride was the dominant note in Victorinus' story, here the talk turns to certain "agents" (*agentes in rebus*) in the "secular militia," imbued with "worldly hopes" for which they undertake all sorts of "labors" and "dangers." They wander in a garden while the emperor is enjoying the "spectacle of the circus." The reader begins to note that the entire account has subtly been punctuated with allusions to "curiosity," that disquieting tendency which keeps the soul active and "busy about many things," away from rest in peaceful contemplation (VIII, 15). These "agents," Ponticianus' story goes, chancing on a book recounting the life of Anthony, leave the emperor's service to enter God's : they embrace the monastic life.

The Two Wills in Man

How is it that these "agents" could leave behind them all worldly cares to imitate St. Anthony, while still Augustine hesitates? Finally God has forced him to acknowledge the compromise in his present position. The *Hortensius* had long since made it clear that worldly pursuits were nothing beside the undivided "pursuit" of Wisdom; now, his doubts at last erased, the possibility has presented itself of "finding" her. Even the "unlearned" (*indocti*), such as these soldiers, "rise up and take

4. Following Courcelle (pp. 181–182), Solignac (*BA* 14, p. 38, n. 1) observes that *agentes in rebus* were inspectors of the imperial administration. I use Ryan's literal translation, "agents," because of the other language in this context suggesting that Augustine was subtly playing on the word to orchestrate the opposition between the "active" and "contemplative" lives. See Gibb and Montgomery's note, p. 218, referring to Epictetus' depiction (*Dissertationes* IV, I, 42–50) of the "unrest and anxiety" involved in the kind of position that these "agents" dreamt of attaining. See also Courcelle, pp. 175–187, and Pellegrino, pp. 179–182.

heaven by storm" while he and Alypius with "all [their] erudition . . . wallow in flesh and blood" (VIII, 19) .

Not Victorinus' pride, nor the curiosity of a worldly "agent," but the concupiscence of the flesh holds Augustine back. In a torment of self-disgust, he plunges into the garden, symbolic setting for aversion and conversion, to set out on the final stages of a journey "not by ships or in chariots or on foot." Complete conversion requires only "the will to go, to will firmly and finally" (VIII, 19) .

Yet though it is easy for his bodily limbs to "obey the soul's most feeble command," his soul refuses "to obey itself and to accomplish its own high will" (20) —a "monstrous" state that faces him with the Manichee theory of divided man. But that, he sees, is no solution. The root of this inner division is a "sickness of the mind" which, though "supported by Truth, does not wholly rise up since it is heavily encumbered by habit" (VIII, 21) and therefore neither "wills completely nor . . . refrains completely from willing" (22) . There are no grounds for supposing "the nature of a different mind within" the person. This division of the self is "rather the punishment" of the self's own nature.

And yet, Augustine immediately explains, "it [was] no more I that did [evil], but sin that dwells in me, sin that issues from punishment of a more voluntary sin, for I was Adam's son"; *de supplicio liberioris peccati, quia eram filius Adam* (VIII, 22) .[5] That dense and puzzling sentence will bear close examination: the Manichaean dualism has been rejected, but it would appear that something very like another dualism has replaced it—attenuated, perhaps, but still a dualism.

Augustine condemns the "horrid pride" that holds the "soul's nature to be that which God is" (VIII, 22) , blaming another nature for the opposition that accounts for sin. It is "I,

5. The Latin allows for several interpretations, and translators differ. The *liberioris* could conceivably be construed as modifying an implied *hominis;* in which case the "man" in question could be Adam only. His "freer" sin resulted in the "punishment" Augustine finds himself suffering, a punishment that involved a constriction of his own freedom. Or, "man" still referring to Adam, Augustine could be implying (as he sometimes does) that all men sinned "in" the sin of "man," Adam now being taken almost as a symbolic archetype. This would more easily explain the justice of our being punished by this constriction of our liberty. It seems most natural, however, to construe *liberioris* as modifying *peccati.* Then the question is left open how and why this "freer sin" (Adam's only? or Augustine's—and ours—"in Adam"?) has resulted in the punitive restriction of liberty experienced by all the "sons of Adam." My suggestion is that, having alerted us to this question, Augustine will later resolve it in favor of the second alternative: all of us somehow sinned "in" Adam's sinning.

I myself" who am responsible for sin. When confronted with
the phenomenon of inner division, "when eternity above delights us and the pleasure found in a temporal good holds us fast
from below," the same soul wills "but not with its whole will."
The Manichee dualism is firmly rejected.

Still, that soul is somehow "rent asunder" by the opposing
attractions of higher truth and lower habit (24). Lower habit is a
kind of residue, toward which the soul is looked upon as relatively passive; over against the soul's true aspirations there
stands a "devastation made against [the] will, indeed" (VIII,
22). This division of the self makes it valid for Augustine to say
"it was no more I that did it" (VIII, 22).

The promptings of this "law of the members" fighting
against the "law of the mind" must, he thinks, have some mysterious origin: "perchance man's hidden penalties and the darkest
sufferings of the sons of Adam" may shed some light on their
source (VIII, 21). That suggestion, he finds, is a sound one.
The "sin that dwells in [him] . . . issues from punishment of a
more voluntary sin, for [he is] Adam's son" (VIII, 22). Was this
"original sin," the "sin of Adam," genuinely "voluntary" in the
case of each of us? Augustine ambiguously hints it may have
been both "ours" and "more voluntary" than our succeeding
sins. He has moved another step toward driving home his doctrine of the soul's fall, and of the residual dualism, the two
conflicting loves, it has left in man.

The Beauty of Continence

He goes on to describe the battle between these two loves.
His "lovers of old" pluck at him, whisper to him of all that will
no longer be allowed him if he gives himself to a life of celibate
contemplation. Their appeal is a chain which loads him down
as he strains to attain some imagined height: "I had almost
made it . . . did not make it; still, I did not slip back . . . but
stood my ground and regained my breath. Again I tried . . .
all but reached it and laid hold of it; yet . . . I did not reach
. . . did not catch hold of it" (VIII, 25). The image is a
variant on the soul's desire to "ascend," shuck off the "weights"
which bind it to earthly things, and rise. The "way" in which he
has "set [his] face" (VIII, 27) is an upward way; he would
"shake [himself] free . . . and leap over to that place where [he]
was called to be" (VIII, 26). The work of grace is imaged, ac-

cordingly, as stripping some encumbering weight from him, lightening him, giving him the strength to rise up.

But there is another, psychological scheme for the work of grace. It corresponds to the *Soliloquies'* question of how the drawing power of his lower loves can be broken if he has not first glimpsed the higher beauty. Augustine's answer comes in the form of a vision: at the very height of the struggle in the garden "the chaste dignity of Continence" appears to him, "serene and joyous, but in no wanton fashion, virtuously alluring, so that I would come to her and hesitate no longer. To lift me up and embrace me, she stretched forth her holy hands." His "unclean members upon the earth" may tell him of "delights," but even greater, she assures him, are the delights "of the law of the Lord." Here the notion of grace as "victorious delight" is operative. The soul is drawn by the attraction of a higher, truer beauty than bodily "concupiscence" can aspire to. In this framework Continence appears, like the figure of *Philosophia* at Cassiciacum, as "mistress" of the soul, the object of the higher Eros.[6]

But that is only half her role. Like *Philosophia* she is both maid and "fruitful mother of children, of joys born of [the Lord] her spouse." As mother, she can promise the nourishment and strength Augustine needs; the youths and maidens she points to as examples did not reach their heights of virtue "of themselves, [but] rather in the Lord their God."

Abruptly now, but typically, the image of Continence gives way. It is God Himself who becomes the mother. "Cast yourself on him," Augustine hears, "have no fear. He will not draw back and let you fall. Cast yourself trustfully on him: he will receive you and will heal you" (VIII, 27). This is the third aspect of grace, one that corresponds to the act of "trustful" faith in a personal God, "maternally" solicitous for his erring children.

The Working of Grace

Augustine seems to assume these three aspects of the work of grace are virtually coordinate with one another. One may be pardoned for questioning that assumption. The view of grace as

6. See *Augustine's Early Theory*, Chap. 2, pp. 70–73. For another view of this entire section, see Mary T. Clark, R.S.C.J., *Augustine Philosopher of Freedom* (New York, 1958), pp. 70–81, where the function of this Eros is, to my mind, seriously underplayed.

"lightening" the soul for its upward flight fits neatly into the Neo-Platonic physical world-image where everything is in a "place" determined by its "weight." The second view of grace, as illumining the soul to the attraction of the higher beauty, fits a Platonist psychology in which to know the good is to pursue it. Both views suppose the rationally ordered universe of Hellenism. The Greek preoccupation would be to show they are at root identical with one another: the individual soul's capacity to "see" would both measure and be measured by its spiritual "weight," and the consequent "depth" to which its fall had plunged it.

But the third view introduces a radically interpersonal relationship, an unpredictable element of "care" on God's part and "trust" on the part of the soul. The theme is much more biblical than Greek. It is far from clear that Augustine was sufficiently sensitive to this difference. One may think his theoretical formulation of Christianity too often loses for having been forced into the mold of an inexorable necessitarianism.

Providence and the *Sors Libri*

Even the "admonition" he now receives, through the voice of the child crying "Take and read," [7] is subtly implied as outcome of the secret "order" presiding over all that happens. He likens it to the "admonition" Anthony received from a Gospel read when—as it would appear—he just "chanced to be present" (VIII, 29). The fact that the phrase of Paul's epistle, immediately following the one Augustine reads, serves as appropriate "admonition" for Alypius need hardly surprise (VIII, 30). By just such "chance" as operated in the case of Anthony, Augustine has previously made us understand, the astrologer often predicts what actually will happen; but chance, we know, is a mistaken name for Providence. Augustine's faith in the *sors libri* technique he uses when he takes up St. Paul at the child's behest is founded in his conviction that even in such matters nothing is really chance, all is Providence:

For you, O Lord, most just ruler of the universe, while both those who consult and those who are consulted in this way know nothing of it, by a hidden inspiration bring it about that, according

7. On this *Tolle, lege* episode, see Courcelle, pp. 188–202. For subsequent discussion of his views, see Pellegrino, pp. 182–186, as well as Solignac, *BA* 14, pp. 546–549.

to the secret merits of men's souls, the consultor may hear what he ought to hear out of the depths of your just judgment (VII, 10) .

". . . And make not provision for the flesh in its concupiscences." This admonition came when the book fell open in his hand (VIII, 29) , an admonition coming from God's "secret inspiration" and at the same corresponding to Augustine's "secret merits." It was startlingly apposite for one recoiling before the call to a life of contemplation where, he keenly saw, no such "provision" could be made.

Out of some "deep and hidden pit" Augustine's free will is "called forth in a single moment." His bonds are "burst asunder," he is stripped of the weights that kept him down; he bends his neck to Christ's mild yoke and his shoulders to His "light burden." Grace is triumphant delight indeed. "Things that I once feared to lose it was now joy to put away. You . . . the true and highest sweetness . . . in their stead entered in, sweeter than any pleasure" to free his mind from "the gnawing cares of favor-seeking, of striving for gain, of wallowing in the mire, of scratching lust's itching sore." But grace converts, makes us "little ones." The symbol of true conversion is at last completely realized: "I spoke like a child to you . . . My Lord God" (IX, 1) .

The Unity of Augustine's "Conversions"

It has often been remarked that Augustine's earlier accounts of this period (in the dedications to the *De Beata Vita* and *Contra Academicos*) lay heavy stress on the Neo-Platonic illumination he recounts in Book VII of the *Confessions,* but do not overtly allude to the scene in the garden at Milan. They do not, consequently, convey the impression of the "two-stage" conversion that has often been elicited from the *Confessions* account.

There are more problems involved in this prima facie discrepancy than I wish to handle here, much less pretend to solve. But in the light of everything we have seen, some helpful suggestions may be developed. The first is that there is a profound continuity between the critical "phases" of his conversion as Augustine recounts them in Books III, VII, and VIII, once the terminus of conversion is viewed not as a return to Christianity, nor even to the *Catholica,* but to the contemplative heights of Cassiciacum and Ostia, described in Book IX. His reading of the

Hortensius fired him to a desire to "embrace," "attain" to a
mystical union with Wisdom envisaged as hypostatic Beauty. "Is
there anything we love," he queries apropos of his first literary
effort, "besides Beauty" (IV, 20)? In Books V and VI he recounts his gradually dawning "faith" that such incorporeal Wisdom and Beauty truly exists. In Book VII he describes having at
last arrived at the stage of purification necessary to "see" it
(VII, 23), though only momentarily, and "through a glass,
darkly" (VIII, 1). There is a gap between glimpsing and enjoying that Beauty (VII, 26) in more stable fashion. The work of
grace must continue in him if that gap is to be spanned.

But Augustine insinuates that, however dramatic the moment in the garden when his bonds were "burst asunder," that
moment was already the climax of a protracted work of grace.
God's medicinal hand has been bathing his eye, reducing his
swollen face, turning his head in slow stages from Book III onward. In Book VII, the "ascent of the soul" (VII, 23) that terminates the Neo-Platonic illumination is only momentarily successful, but it is *that* successful: [8] he does gain a glimpse of the
celestial splendor, is "born up" by its attractiveness (VII, 23),
experiences a shiver of delight in the "beauty of [God's] house"
(VIII, 2). More than ever, all other pleasures pale in comparison. The work of grace as "victorious delight" is already far
advanced; it continues through Book VIII and extends to the
end of Book IX.

But the "victorious delight" experienced in this vision of
supernal beauty is already paired, in Augustine's mind, with the
work of grace as "lightening" the soul for ascent. *Tu assumsisti
me,* he confesses (VII, 16); even in Book VII, it was God who
"raised [him] up." Even now, the "bonds" that finally "burst
asunder" in the garden at Milan no longer "weigh him down"
so heavily as they did. His soul's "weakness" has to that extent
been strengthened for the upward flight. However fleeting the
moment of enraptured vision, in that "flash of trembling sight"
he "clearly saw." The "tyranny of habit," the "weight of carnal
custom" has, to that extent, been reduced (VII, 23).

But the same is true for what Augustine imagines as the
third (and, one may think, most crucial) function that grace
performs: that of empowering the soul that no longer relies on
its own efforts, but has "cast its care on God" (VIII, 27). Even

---

8. The "successful" character of this vision Courcelle seems to have under-
estimated, pp. 157–167; compare Pellegrino, pp. 170–171, and Solignac, pp. 698–
703.

in Book VII, he images his conversion as the return of a soul, become a little child again, throwing itself humbly into the lap of maternal omnipresence. *Cessavi de me paululum:* "I turned from myself a little." At the central moment, immediately preluding his glimpse of the Divine Truth-Hand, he alludes to Isaias' exhortation (Isa. 2:22) to put all trust in God. *Paululum:* "a little." But even that "little" has had its effect. When his trust becomes more total, the effect will be even greater. Instead, therefore, of considering Book VII as recounting an "intellectual," Book VIII a "moral" phase in Augustine's conversion, it seems juster to view what occurs in Book VIII as the organic prolongation of the work of grace that has been going on since the reading of the *Hortensius* described in Book III. And that work of grace ought then to be envisaged as moving both on the intellectual and moral levels, or, perhaps, more exactly, as moving at the deep personal level where the intellectual and moral fuse to become indistinguishable.

This does not deny that Book VII describes a climactic moment in that continual process; but a climax is not a terminus, and the events described in Book VII usher in an even more intensive phase in which the work of grace already under way will move even closer to its completion. There is, then, both an intellectual and a moral dimension to Augustine's resolve, in Book VIII, to take up the kind of life that promises him enduring "enjoyment" of the divine splendor he has, until now, only glimpsed. But by the same token, there is a moral and a "graced" dimension to the events described in Book VII: it represents an Augustine already partially "lightened," partially conquered by the divine "delight." He has already, to some extent, cast his cares on God, become the "little one" who dimly, obscurely sees and will only later be able openly to "confess" that the "continence" he yearns for is God's gift, the work of grace, not merely the achievement of his own will. Granted, Book VIII brings him to an even more agonizing recognition of the "weight" and "weakness" that prevented him from feeding on the "bread of grown-ups" (VII, 16). The scene in the garden brings to its fullness the childlike surrender that already, to some degree, characterizes the "return" described in Book VII. Now that this already nascent surrender to grace has become even more complete, he will find it possible to try the experience of the contemplative life that his sojourn at Cassiciacum represents. Having tasted the peace he enjoyed there, his resolve will extend to asking for baptism. And the grace of

baptism, in its turn, will flower into the contemplative delight
of the vision he enjoys at Ostia. The prodigal soul will be that
much closer to the paternal "mansion" (IV, 31) he deserted,
the wandering soul that much closer to "dwelling" in its
"blessed fatherland," departure and arrival point of its restless
odyssey through time (VII, 26; cf. *Vita* 2) .

13 CONTEMPLATION AND THE SOUL'S "FIRST-FRUITS"
(BOOK IX)

The *fovere*-images proliferate once again as Augustine looks back with wondering praise at the way God has accomplished the final phase of this conversion, one which affects his friends as well as himself. The "examples" of God's servants "turned from black to shining bright" He had brought together in the "bosom of [their] thought," had "set fire to [their] torpor and burned it away," had enkindled "so strong a fire" that even calumnies about them would only "inflame [them] more fiercely and not put out that fire" (IX, 3). Augustine pictures his dead friend Nebridius as now living in "Abraham's bosom," where he puts his "spiritual mouth to [God's] fountain, and in accordance with his desire he drinks in wisdom, as much as he can, endlessly happy" (IX, 6).

Cassiciacum: Rest and Peace

A heaven-sent weakness of the lungs provides Augustine with a plausible excuse for setting aside his teaching activity. As the vintage vacation begins he sets out with his friends to Vere-cundus' villa at Cassiciacum. The idyllic dream of a contempla-tive community is briefly fulfilled. Away from the world's tur-

moil (*aestus*) they find "rest in [God]" (IX, 5) , a "season of rest
in that country place" (8) , a "peace in the Self-same" God in
whose unchanging Light "there is rest, forgetful of all labor"
(11). Again and again the terms recur. Augustine cannot
dwell enough on that period when, the busy and disquieting
life of action finally behind him, he enjoyed the contemplative
serenity of "those days of rest" (12) .

Baptism: The Sweetness of the Lord

But it was only a "season," like everything temporal destined to pass away; besides, the sacrament of baptism must complete the work God has brought this far. Augustine resigns his
professorship, informs Ambrose of his intention to continue in
the contemplative way, inscribes himself for baptism at Milan.
Once baptised he finds all "anxiety over [his] past life fled away."
During all this time he cannot "take [his] fill of meditating with
wondrous sweetness on the depths of [God's] counsel concerning the salvation of mankind." He weeps with keen affection at
the hymns and canticles of Milan's "sweet-singing church," (14)
all the more poignant because they recall to him another time
when like the bridegroom in the *Canticle* "the odor of [God's]
ointments was so fragrant" but Augustine failed to run after
Him (IX, 16) .

The erotic imagery is fully intentional; Augustine is describing the lyric time of his spiritual honeymoon, a period in
which the taste of God came to him in everything. The word
for Cassiciacum was "rest" and "peace." Now the recurring
term is "sweetness": *dulcedo*. There is a real advance here, and
Augustine hopes we will detect it. Baptism has borne its fruits.

But—commentary on his mother's fears about having him
baptized earlier—there is greater fruit to come. A variety of
reasons make it fitting that fruit should be tasted in the company
of Monica.

Return to Monica

One of those reasons is psychological: how many times does
it occur that full maturity alone permits eventual reconciliation
with our parents! Augustine's need of this reconciliation is particularly acute, for his portrait of Monica has been fraught with
ambiguities of sentiment. A latent resentment toward his
mother needed resolving. She concurred with Patricius' worldly

hopes and educational plans for him (II, 4, 8), delayed his baptism (I, 17), failed when the outbreak of concupiscence ensnared him to arrange for the remedies of marriage (II, 4, 8). Her simple and uneducated piety must have been a thorn to him when the relatively urbane objections of the Manichees drew him into their sect. At Milan she starts on her rounds of visiting the martyrs' tombs with offerings of food and wine, the remnant of a pagan superstition that Augustine very early combats after ordination. Ambrose manages to wean her from this custom, but Augustine strongly insinuates her attitude toward the bishop had much of the "human" in it: his influence on behalf of her son is what chiefly grounds an affection which, he thinks, facilitated a submission she might not so easily have accorded another (VI, 2). Augustine can now recount her dreams and "revelations" with somewhat more equanimity, but obviously he found her bothersome in those early Manichaean days, with all her fussy prattle about his future conversion (III, 19–21). Importunate, she will not let him be. He flees to Rome and leaves her weeping—poor carnal-minded daughter of Eve— desolate in separation from the brilliant son of whom she is so obviously proud (V, 15). She follows him to Milan and there thinks as much of possible grandchildren as she does of spiritual matters. She engineers a marriage that will forward his worldly career far better than the faithful liaison in which he has for years been living with the mother of his son (VI, 23–25). When, in the least endearing episode Augustine recounts in his book, that unnamed woman is "torn from [his] side" and despatched home to Africa—"vowing that she would never know another man"—the shadow of Monica lies heavy over the scene (VI, 25).

There can be no doubt of Monica's fidelity, her piety, her sturdy and persevering—literally obstinate—love for her son. Augustine's maternal image of God owes much to her. But he can hardly be said to have skimped on the dark side of her character. If anything, his sometimes inhuman moral standards make him more severe with her than we would be. Her prayers and tears had much to do with his conversion, but one may be pardoned for wondering how long her possessive importunities did more to keep him away from the faith.

Even now, as he recalls her life of evident virtue, he dares not say "that from the time [God] regenerated her by baptism no word had issued from her mouth contrary to [God's] commandment" (IX, 34).

All her merits are, after all, God's gifts to her; he must, accordingly, set them aside to "beseech [God] in behalf of [his] mother's sins." May He "forgive her her debts, if she contracted any in so many years after receiving the waters of salvation" (35). "She will not answer that she owes no debt, lest she be convicted and seized by her crafty accuser. She will answer that her sins have been forgiven" by the Christ who died an innocent victim for our sins (36).

And yet, so different here from the Plotinus who, "ashamed of being in the body . . . could never be induced to tell of his ancestry, his parentage, or his birthplace" (*Vita Plotini*, 1), Augustine speaks of his mother, and with a son's affection. He "will not pass over" whatever he can recount of "that handmaiden" of God's, "who brought [him] to birth, both in her flesh, so that [he] was born into this temporal light, and in her heart, so that [he] might be born to light eternal" (17).

There is defiance, but also a measure of discomfort in Augustine's divergence from Plotinus on this point. The latter is surely more consistent with his theory of man as soul, fallen into the body, when he refuses to speak of his parentage. Augustine feels this discrepancy keenly. His discomfort shows in what modern readers must be tempted to consider a wearisome and apparently pointless meditation on the sorrow that tormented him at her death.

A Puzzling Meditation on Tears

"I closed her eyes, and a mighty sorrow welled up . . . and overflowed into tears." By a "powerful command of [his] mind," he staunches the flow of tears; and still, "something childish" in him "which was slipping forth in tears" he must again restrain by the "youthful voice" of his heart (29).

He beguiles his grief by discussing a subject suitable to the occasion with some friends, thus "soothing a torment known to [him] alone"—successfully, it would appear, because the others even thought him "free of all sense of sorrow." And yet, within, his sorrow swells. He "upbraided the weakness of [his] affection and held back the flood of sorrow . . . but again was swept away by its violence, although" he notes for any who value such self-mastery, "not as far as to burst into tears, nor to any change of expression." He himself sets obvious store by such self-mastery. It "distressed [him] greatly that these human occurrences, which necessarily happen in due order and on account of our allotted condition, still had such sway over" him. So distressed did he find himself, he "sorrowed over [his] sorrow" and was therefore "torn by a twofold sadness" (31).

With the faintest note of triumph in his tone he notes that he "went out" to his mother's burial "and returned without tears." Not even during the moving prayers of the service for the departed "did [he] shed tears." "But all day long in secret, heavy was my sorrow, and with a troubled mind I besought you as best I could to heal my anguish. You did not do so" (32). He bathes; it does no good. But then he sleeps, and wakes to find his "sorrow had in no small part been eased" by sleep which, in the words of Ambrose's hymn, God gave to "ease our weary minds, and free our worried hearts from grief" (32).

I took comfort in weeping in your sight over her and for her, over myself and for myself. I gave way to the tears that I had held back . . . for your ears were placed at my heart, not those of a mere man who would interpret with scorn my weeping.

Now, Lord, I confess to you in writing. Let him read it who wants to, let him interpret it as he wants. If he finds a sin in it, that I wept for my mother for the small part of an hour, for that mother . . . who for so many years had wept for me . . . let him not laugh me to scorn. But rather . . . let him weep over my sins before you (33).

At first, one might have been tempted to think Augustine was parading his self-control before those attached to the Stoic ideal of "apathy." Such self-advertisement is hardly his way, and even if it were, this final collapse would deprive such a perfor-mance of its point.

Is he, then, showing his contempt for such philosophic moralities of detachment? This was, after all, his mother, one who loved him with a Christian love and whom in return he loved. He may want to say such Christian love runs counter to the steely indifference so prized in the ancient world. What "grieved [him] so heavily" was, he informs us, "the fresh wound wrought by the sudden rupture of our most sweet and dear way of life together . . . for out of her life and mine one life had been made" (30). What more legitimate cause for tears could be imagined?

But, attractive as this interpretation seems, too many ele-ments in the text militate against it. Why, for example, even in the grip of sorrow, does he "upbraid the weakness of [his] affec-tion"? Why, once his heart was "healed from the wound" of

Monica's departure, does he "afterwards blame" his "merely natural feelings" for the sorrow that overcame him (34)? And what does he imply, in later reflecting on this episode, by saying that "as for other things in this life, so much the less should they be wept over, the more they are wept over; and all the more must they be wept over, the less we weep when among them" (X, 1)?

Monica's True Relation to Augustine

Augustine gives us a clue when describing the "sweet and holy care" Monica had of all of them (IX, 33). One is tempted to catalogue it as "maternal" care until the echo of another phrase gives grounds for hesitation. Monica's relation to Augustine begins subtly to undergo a certain slippage: "Of all of us . . . she took care as though she had been *mother* to us all, and she served us as though she had been *daughter* to all of us" (22).

A mere figure of speech? A parallel from the *De Vera Religione* makes one wonder. Augustine is speaking of the Christian commandment that we love our neighbor like ourself:

All are related who have one God for their Father and who love him and do his will. And all are *fathers* and *sons* to one another, fathers when they take thought for others, sons when they obey, but above all they are *brothers* because one Father by his Testament calls them to one inheritance (*Ver* 89).

Perhaps, in a theory of a man as essentially soul, such contingent relationships are doomed to slide about this easily. Perhaps Augustine means us to guess at this from his final remarks on his parents: let all who read these *Confessions,* he prays, remember Monica, "together with Patricius, *sometime* her husband, by whose flesh [God] brought [Augustine] *into this life*—how [he] know[s] not." These, he admits, were his *"parents* in this passing light"; but a moment later they become his *"brethren* under [God] our Father in our Catholic Mother," and an instant afterward his *"fellow citizens* in that eternal Jerusalem, which your pilgrim people sigh after from their setting out even to their return" (37).

One could pass all this off as overprecious rhetoric, were it not for the peremptory tone of a text from the same *De Vera Religione* context: "sometime" husbands, "parents in this passing light"—even, indeed, "brethren" in the Church—seem surely covered by the admonition that:

> Man is not to be loved by man even as brothers after the flesh are loved, or sons, or wives, or kinsfolk, or relatives, or fellow-citizens. For such love is temporal (*Ver* 88) . . .
> If we are ablaze with love for eternity, we shall hate temporal relationships. Let a man love his neighbor as himself. No one is his own father or son or kinsman or anything of the kind, but is simply a man (*Ver* 89).

The modern reader is inclined to think the point Augustine is making here is dreadfully abstract. His theoretical framework drives him to berate himself that on his mother's death "these human feelings had such sway over [him]" (IX, 31). Is not the ideal he holds out frankly inhuman? The *De Vera Religione* answers that objection with rigorous logic:

> Let no one think that is inhuman. It is more inhuman to love a man because he is your son and not because he is a man, that is, not to love that in him which belongs to God, but to love that which belongs to yourself. What marvel if he who loves his private advantage and not the common good does not obtain the Kingdom (*Ver* 88)?

Initially puzzling, that moral makes sense in the light of the Plotinian theory of the soul as the "real self":

> Whoever loves another as himself ought to love that in him which is his real self. Our real selves are not bodies. . . . Human nature is to be loved . . . without any condition of carnal relationship (*Ver* 89).

But there is a deeper dimension to Augustine's contempt for such "temporal" relationships. They root in the sin that accounts for our present fallen state:

> We should have no such connections as are contingent upon birth and death, if our nature had remained in obedience to the commandments of God and in the likeness of his image. It would not have been relegated to its present corrupt state (*Ver* 88).

The commandment of love was given us to guide our return from the "corrupt state" resulting from our "disobedience." The implications of this Augustine draws as follows:

No one can perfectly love that to which we are called unless he hate that from which we are called. We are called to perfect human nature as God made it before we sinned. We are recalled from love of what we have deserved by sinning. Therefore we must hate that from which we choose to be set free (*Ver* 88).

This, then, is why Christ enjoined that we "hate father and mother"; "Truth himself," He thereby "calls us back to our original and perfect state, bids us resist carnal custom (*consuetudini*), and teaches us that no one is fit for the kingdom of God unless he hates these carnal ties (*necessitudines*)" (*Ver* 88).

When, accordingly, he prayed God to heal his anguish over Monica's death, it is plain why his prayer went unanswered. "It was, I think, to impress upon my memory by this one lesson that all custom (*consuetudinem*) is a chain (*vinculum*), even upon a mind that no longer feeds upon deceptive words" (IX, 32).

Consuetudo: habit, custom. How else can one translate it? Yet the term has such a density of sense in Augustine's theory that no translation fits. It evokes the entire fallen realm, with all its easy suppositions—that the human estate is natural and normal, that human life is our authentic life, that human experiences, achievements, relationships, and loves are truly valuable, as dear in themselves, as dear to God, as they are to us. All this, he means to say, is false and therefore wrong. If man is fallen soul, then such relationships as mother to son are inessential, temporal, evanescent; human achievement is but vanity; human loves can breed attachments which, when broken, leave us bleeding from a wound that should remind us where our love ought to be directed: there, to the higher realm whence we fell, to which we are called to return, where there is neither brother nor sister, wife nor husband, mother nor son, but only "fellow-citizens in that eternal Jerusalem."

Monica's Real Identity

"So" Augustine describes his mother's death, "in the fifty-sixth year of her life . . . this devout and holy soul was set loose from the body" (28). Delivered from the mortal flesh she merited by sin, now she is free. Augustine wept for her: wrongly, because for the wrong reasons. Even then he should have known better. But now he finds more appropriate the "far different kind of tears" he sheds, tears poured out to God on her

behalf, from a "spirit shaken by the thought of the dangers be-
setting every soul that 'dies in Adam' " (34). As fallen souls, we
have all "died in Adam," are all "sons of Adam." There is an
interesting suggestion contained in the phrase. "Daughter of
Eve," Augustine called his mother earlier, but if carnal and
temporal designations like "mother" and "son" mean little, perhaps such others as "man" and "woman" mean no more.

The True Status of Woman

Augustine ended his autobiography on this "return" to his
mother for another reason. The Plato of the *Timaeus* echoes
the ancient world's contempt of women by suggesting they em-
body souls who in an earlier existence sinned by such weaknesses
as cowardice. The Manichee contempt of the *Catholica* regularly expressed itself in accusations about "old wives' tales";
Monica's "admonitions" to her growing son are spurned as coming from a woman; the problem of *mulierculae* was what
wrecked Augustine's dream of Plotinopolis.

But those in Christ, St. Paul warns, are neither Jew nor
Greek, slave nor freeman, male nor female (Gal. 3:28). And
Augustine agrees: "in [God's] spiritual grace" there is, "as to
bodily sex, neither male nor female" (XIII, 33). He feels his
theory of man, and woman, as fallen soul unveils the hidden
meaning of that text. He never to my knowledge accepts that
facet of Plato's, and Plotinus', theory whereby the soul is engaged in a multiplicity of incarnations. Once "returned," he
prefers to think, the soul's rude experience of evil will result in
so keen an appreciation of the good it has regained that it will
rest and rejoice eternally in the heavenly Jerusalem.

No foundation, therefore, can be found in transmigration
theory for the "inferiority" of woman. His own inferiority to
the mother of his son is couched in the ironic phrase that when
she left him, vowing she "would never know another man," he,
for his part, was found incapable of being an "imitator of
woman" (VI, 25). More crucial yet, his desperate attempts at
putting up a manly front at his mother's death manage to high-
light the tears that finally overcome him. Nothing more
womanish could be imagined—he wept.

But Monica on the other hand—*mulier virili pectore*—
showed far more freedom from the bond of "custom" than he.
Her life was, surely, marked by faults, but Augustine's brief
biography of her is designed to show that in the end God's work

in her soul had not been wasted. Her childhood tippling could
have led her into serious trouble, but the providential "admonition" of a quarrelsome maidservant, wounding her "like a sur-
geon's knife," forces her in the typical movement of conversion
to "look about on her own foul state," snap the chain of this
growing "habit" (*consuetudo;* IX, 18). Her life with Patricius
disciplines her to that "subjection" which her parents had failed
to instill; her "admonitions" to other married women preach a
similar humility (19). Docile to the "inward Master teaching"
she lives in peace and spreads its power all about her (20–21).

No other teacher, Augustine subtly suggests, seems ever to
have formed her mind. The God Who created her was responsible for her "education" as well (17). And yet, her lack of
cultivation, her wifely "subjection," were never true inferiority.
Her final victory was to win her lord Patricius to the faith (22).

Throughout all this, the ancient world's view of woman is
undergoing metamorphosis; Augustine's final chapters overturn
it once and for all. Her hopes for grandchildren through her
brilliant son have been thwarted. She comes in time to see those
hopes even more grandly fulfilled in that he has become God's
"servant." She no longer finds "delight" in anything in this
mortal life (IX, 26). Only a final stroke of detachment is required of her. "I recalled," Augustine tells us, "what I already
knew, how concerned she always had felt over her burial place,
which she had arranged and prepared for herself next to her
husband's body. . . . She wished—so little is the human mind
able to grasp the things of God . . . that the earth of the two
wedded ones have a joint covering of earth" (IX, 28).

But when, in her final sickness, Augustine's brother insists
"she should not die in a foreign land but in her own country,"
she stares "reproachfully at him with an anxious countenance"
and chides him for letting care about her body disturb him (IX,
27).

At what time, out of the fullness of your bounty, this vain wish
began to fade from her heart I do not know. I marveled and rejoiced over the fact . . . it did not appear that she wanted to die in
her native land. I also heard . . . that one day while I was absent,
she talked with a mother's confidence about contempt of this life
and the advantages of death. [Those who heard her] were amazed at
the woman's strength, which you had given her (28).

A "mother's confidence," a "woman's strength"—her son
knows where they came from: "I thought of your gifts, O God

unseen, which you instill into the hearts of your faithful, and from which come wonderful fruits; and I rejoiced and gave thanks to you" (28).

When asked by those who listened to her "if she did not fear leaving her body so far from her own city," her reply is worthy of her son's most soaring insight: "Nothing is far from God" (IX, 28). One in heart, they have become one in mind as well. The Augustine of Cassiciacum thought this might eventually come about were his mother only to practice the mental gymnastics of the "liberal disciplines." When she appears in the *De Ordine,* his reflex of self-defense quickly becomes a justification for a mere woman's presence in a philosophic dialogue. A woman, too, can be an intellectual, despite what men may say. Later he assures her she has already attained to the "heights of philosophy," but then his argument is different. Plotinian intellectualism goes unmentioned; Plotinian detachment is the reason he gives.

The intervening years have made him think the latter, informed by Christianity, was sufficient. The goal of life remains what it always was: vision. A fallen soul can be content with nothing less. But the patient fidelity of Christian living can supply, even in a woman, an uneducated woman, for all the baggage of the "disciplines." At Ostia, mother and son together pursue an ascent of the mind whose steps the Plotinian would find familiar, but whose language the Catholic would recognize as the language of the Church, that Mother whose figure Monica represents, just as they both—the Church and Monica—befigure the tender care of the "maternal" God Augustine worships. The discrepancy that once disturbed him was illusion. To return to the one, in the deepest sense, is to return to all three. That indissoluble unity is sealed in intimate "society" at Ostia.

Society of Soul with Soul [1]

For Ostia represents, in miniature, Augustine's estimate of human life, and notably, his model for the "society" of soul with soul. Human custom counts the bonds that link mother to son, husband to wife, friend to friend, as the very cement of society's unity. To mediate the understanding and cooperation needed for the common temporal good, human custom has

1. For valuable bibliography on this "vision" of Ostia and the questions connected with it, see Solignac, *BA* 13, p. 186, n. 2, and pp. 262–263. See also, Courcelle, pp. 222–226, and Pellegrino, pp. 198–199, esp. p. 199, n. 15.

erected a gigantic fabric of signs and language, laws and education, disciplines and arts, held together by the force of authority
and convention. But all of this is proper to the soul in its fallen
state, to sons of Adam, daughters of Eve, wandering unhappily
since the time of that drama played out, as the Bible's imaged
language tells it, in a "garden."

Something of human society's flavor Augustine has tasted:
the adults who laughed at the pains he endured to learn their
conventional ways at school, but were themselves as worthy of
punishment; those childhood companions with whom he joined
in an utterly wanton deed of sin; the "overturners" of Carthage; Alypius' companions, dragging him to the games. Now
and again, however, he stumbled on the presage of something
better: the youthful friend he lost as one would lose the half of
his own soul; his friendships at Milan, bonded by the common
quest of Wisdom; the shared joy of the Church's children at
Victorinus' conversion; monastery life; Ponticianus' fellow-
agents, drawn together to the monastery; the peaceful interlude
at Cassiciacum, until now the closest approximation of his
dream of Plotinopolis.

One should note in passing how often the pivotal episodes
of human life are played out in a "garden": the theft of pears,
the conversion of Ponticianus' companions in the service,
Augustine's final crisis at Milan—the Garden of Eden. And now
they stand, the two of them, leaning from a window, overlooking
another garden. "Far from the crowd," they are "resting" from
the "hardships of the long journey" they have been making;
resting, too, for the "voyage" across the seas which lies ahead of
them. How long, the painful "journey" of human life, how
unforeseen the "voyage" on which, at last, Monica will soon
"depart from this life" (IX, 23). They are about to share the
sweetest moment of their "most sweet and dear way of life together," the moment which more than any other made "out of
her life and [his], one life" (IX, 30). "Conversing together most
tenderly, 'forgetting those things that are behind, and stretching forward to those that are before,'" they question what the
"eternal life of the saints would be like"—a life above eye and
ear and every grasp of sense, "'nor has it entered into the heart
of man.'" Bond of his finest friendships heretofore—at Milan,
Cassiciacum, the dreamt-of Plotinopolis—Augustine wishes to
insinuate that this is the act which binds us closest in true society: the act of together "straining with the heart's mouth for
those supernal streams flowing from [God's] fountain" (IX, 23).

In all Augustine's life that bond was best achieved at Ostia, when these two souls together mounted upward through the world of sense, attaining at last to "the region of abundance which never fails, in which [God] feeds Israel forever upon the food of truth," where "life" is one with "Wisdom" eternal and unchanging. Embodied souls, they must "discourse of it," using the "noise of mouths," the words of temporal human custom which "begin and end" (24). But what if all fell "silent"—tumult of flesh, images of earth, air and waters, silent all dreams and imagined appearances, silent "every tongue and every sign" —if all the "words" whereby created things proclaim their maker were to announce their message and then "become silent"? What if, no longer "mother" or "son" but merely soul with companion soul, at rest after human life's hard journey, breaking clear of all the bonds and symbols that custom sees as knitting the life of men together, what if one were to "raise up [his] ear to him who made" these things until "God alone speaks, not through such things but through himself, so that we hear his Word not uttered by a tongue of flesh" nor by any other created voice "but by himself . . . without their aid"? That moment, if prolonged, that "moment of understanding" for which they "sighed" at Ostia, were only "visions of a far inferior kind . . . withdrawn" and "understanding" brought to vision of that which alone can "ravish, and absorb, and hide away its beholder within its deepest joys": the Catholic would admit that moment must be final "joy in the Lord," and Plotinus, "sempiternal life," the fallen soul's complete return. In this, for both of them, the life that begins in faith must terminate. Past the intermediate exercise of understanding, the seeker must strain to "find," and, understanding, mount to vision (25).

Let the ancient world object, and even Plotinus demur; reformed in the light of Christianity, Augustine thinks, their deepest insights are fulfilled in Monica. No longer does he think unbroken contemplation can be enjoyed by souls while still embodied. At the apex of their ascent they "left behind, bound to it" only the "first fruits of the spirit" (IX, 24). But one day, "as she lay ill, [Monica] lost consciousness and for a little while she was withdrawn from all present things." Coming back to them again, her words imply she is no longer really with them: "after the manner of one seeking something" she gazes at her sons. "Where was I?" she asks them finally (27), and Augustine reads worlds of meaning into the question. Once the most stubborn difficulty, she has now become the very paradigm of his theory

of man. At Ostia, she too, in intimate society with her fellow-
pilgrim, has come to share an ineffable moment of "understanding," come to "see," and on the strength of that vision
pass, for all intents and purposes, from human life to life of soul
"returned."

Memory—and Forgetting

"Forgetful of the things that are behind, stretching forward
to those that are before"—so Augustine depicts his attitude, and
Monica's, in their common ascent of the mind at Ostia. A moment later he deftly hints at the way he is using those terms.
The highest delight of "fleshly senses," the "brightest corporeal
light," when set against the sweetness of the higher life, seem
unworthy "even of remembrance" (24). He means the expressions "behind" (*post*) and "before" (*ante*) neither spatially
nor temporally, but as Plotinus uses them, to indicate the ontological superiority and inferiority of the realities involved. The
wise man will, in Plotinus' theory, be a "good forgetter" of
inferior things which in the order of emanation come "after"
the superior realities from which they proceed. He will set his
mind on the "superior" beings that lie "before" and "above"
the soul when "turned" again for its re-ascent toward the Intel-
ligibles. These are the realities with which Platonic *anamnesis*,
Augustine's "memory," keeps the soul in unbroken contact. To
return whence it fell, the soul must follow the track of memory
in this, not in its customary sense.

To illuminate this distinction, Augustine had to write that
troublesome book which several have suggested does not belong
to the original design of the *Confessions* at all, and write it
exactly as it is written. It constitutes in great part a long
"mental exercise" designed to raise his reader's sights above the
banal sense of "memory." He would jog them into grasping,
and accepting, the notion of a memory that houses, not images,
but "realities," not temporal events or spatial objects but eternal spiritual truths. Such truths, he has already noted (VII, 23)
permit us to "judge" of grades of the real, find some superior to
others, and in this way ascend to the *Summa*, the subsistent
Veritas in Whose Light we judge, Whose supra-sensible existence is implied in all our judging—the God to Whom once we
cleaved in blissful embrace, and even now, despite all appearances to the contrary, dimly remember. How shall the soul
effect return, Plotinus asks—and answers: by taking its "memo-

ries" of the intelligible as its starting point. A careful examination of Book X will show the vital role it plays in the *Confessions,* once Augustine's purpose is firmly grasped.

Concluding this analysis of the ninth book of Augustine's *Confessions,* it is hard to overcome a dispiriting sense of dryness, a feeling of chilling unreality. One need not be a believer to admit that one of western literature's most imperishable tableaux seems here to have been drained of its haunting power. What more touching than the deathless memory of both of them, mother and son, reconciled at last in the tenderest of peaceful intimacies? The traveler especially, roaming meditatively amid the cypresses and sea winds of *Ostia Antiqua,* desperately wants it to be otherwise. Till time has run its course he hopes that men will recall them there, leaning from that window, the silence gathering about them both. The names they bore in time were Monica and Augustine. One feels one never knew them better, loved them more dearly, than at this unforgettable moment.

How horribly theoretical to claim that the man who drew so memorable a tableau was warning us to forget it, warning us that Monica and Augustine were merely names borne by two whom we, enchained by human custom, identify as mother and son. Son and daughter of Adam and Eve: this was their real identity then; or, more exactly, companion souls in a wandering "journey" at last become a "pilgrimage." Now, all this behind them, they are "fellow-citizens" in heaven. We too, he counsels, should put this memory "behind" us, quite literally "forget" it as we "stretch forward to the things that are before," to an eternity where we shall meet a Monica no longer either Monica or mother, an Augustine no longer in any true sense her son.

How horribly theoretical, indeed. But such was Augustine's theory of man, and this was his point in drawing the tableau of Ostia.

14 NOVERIM TE
NOVERIM ME
(BOOK X)

The purpose of Book X is slightly different from the intention that presided over Augustine's composition of the books that preceded. There the "mental exercise" moved from a preliminary stage which sowed each page with questions, to an intermediate phase where more and more boldly the expressions began to insinuate the answer to those questions. From questions he proceeds to hints, until the *Weltanschauung* developed in Book VII unfolds the answers, but in such condensed form that their full import can scarcely be grasped. In Books VIII and IX Augustine is living out "knowingly" the destiny which before he could only blindly follow. The outline of his theory of man is for that very reason more explicitly unveiled, though far from unmistakably uncovered. The interpreter must compare his language and imagery with Plotinus', must search his earlier works for more overt clues on what he means.

Now, however, the single extended "exercise" Augustine's "autobiography" represents may be supposed to have done its work. He has, he feels, told a story in which each of us can recognize himself, thereby giving his theory experiential basis and resonance, but at the same time teasing, with a host of questions, minds that subtly have been attuned to understand and accept the answers he means to present.

The *exercitatio* technique will not, however much our minds have been prepared, be abandoned in the books that follow. If anything, its pace will quicken, its requirements be even more demanding. We shall be asked to follow his mind along tricky paths of thought, but when the path winds finally home, the answer in each case comes in terms we have seen before, terms we are more prepared to understand aright, their former ambiguities removed. The one comprehensive question Augustine's "autobiography" means to pose is answered now, clearly, and unmistakably. What is man, that his experience should be as Augustine has recounted his?

For the single unifying point of Book X is one with the point of the *Confessions:* Augustine would bring his reader to the self-knowledge he claims to possess on himself. *Cognoscam te, cognitor meus, cognoscam, sicut et cognitus sum:* "I shall know you, my knower, I shall know you, 'even as I am known,'" he begins. To know oneself means to know God, and know the self as God knows it (X, 1), for from Him nothing can be hidden (X, 2). In this self-knowledge can man truly "confess," to God in a silence which "cries aloud with love," a cry expressed not with "bodily words and sounds but with words uttered by the soul" (X, 2).

Words, Belief, and Charity

But the confession "of the heart" to God is one thing, that of "the pen" (*stilo;* X, 1) quite another. Why confess to men, desirous though they be to hear his confessions? "Eager to know about another man's life, but slothful to correct their own," they seek to hear from him what he is, but all too often "do not want to hear from [God] what they themselves are" (X, 3).[1] The answer comes couched in the inner-outer distinction, with its attendant relegation of outer, sign-communication, to the realm of fallenness, possible deception, and belief. The men

1. There is reason to think that Augustine is here acknowledging the interest stirred by Books I–IX of his work having already enjoyed considerable diffusion. He may also be manifesting a reflex of self-defense against those (Donatists?) who professed scandal at the darker portions of his youthful past. It *may* be that Books X–XIII were composed after a time-gap had intervened (see Solignac, I, 46–48, and 29–33). The question remains open, however, whether Augustine was able to conceive of Books X–XIII in such terms that a unity of design would be preserved between them and the books that had preceded. The contention here is that he could and did. Cf. Pellegrino, pp. 203–207.

who desire to hear his confession are unable to place their ear
close to his heart "where [he] is whoever (*quicumque*) [he is],"
unable to pierce the secret of his interiority by "their eye or ear
or mind." He finds himself compelled, accordingly, to speak in
the signs of written language, confessing "in such manner as
men may hear" (X, 3–4). On those terms, he cannot "prove to
them" that he confesses truly (X, 3), must trust that they are
"men ready to believe" (X, 4) —that, "sharers in [his] mortality,
fellow citizens and pilgrims with [him] . . . companions on [his]
journey," their charity toward him will make them hear his
confessions as "believing sons of men" (X, 6).

And then, they may get to know him, as he was and is now,
pray for him, and themselves praise God for His marvelous work
on his behalf (X, 5–6). But there is also a hope, half-spoken,
that his work may be an admonition, turn them to "hear about
themselves from [God]" and hearing, come to "know themselves" (X, 3).

Inward and Upward

So, in the now-familiar image of the "little one" taking
refuge "under the wings" of the Selfsame Who is his true Father
—"who begot me and watches over me" (X, 6) —Augustine
reminds his reader once again that only God has comprehensive
knowledge of man: "for there is something further in man
which not even that spirit of man which is in him knows" (X,
7). That "something further" will emerge in due course if we
follow the upward path the soul takes in reaching its knowledge
of God: that non-bodily voice, embrace, aroma, light, and food
Augustine loves when he loves his God (X, 8). That upward
path leads from visible outer realities to the invisible, higher,
"inner man" that "knows such things through the ministry of
the outer man." "I, the inner man, know these things; I, I, the
mind, by means of my bodily senses": *ego interior cognovi haec,
ego, ego animus* (X, 9). Diverse though the operations of sense
may be, "I, who am one single mind, perform [them] through
the senses": *unus ego animus,* the real self (X, 11).

The crucial function of that inner man, the *index ratio*, is
identified as "passing judgment": *judicare*. This function of the
understanding empowers man to pass from the world's beauty
and "see clearly the invisible things of God," provided, that is,
they have not "through love for such things . . . become subject to them, and in subjection they cannot pass judgment on

them," the very language used to account for Augustine's pre-conversion blindness to the spiritual (X, 10; cf. VII, 11). We are, in fact, being invited to ferret out the implicits in that ascent to God he made at Milan (VII, 23), starting from the beauties in the world of sense, and performed through the mind's power of "judging," that is, affirming in the light of eternal truth that certain things *should* be the way they are, and others not.

Augustine insists that a knowledge of God must pass inward and upward, beyond the soul's power to animate the body (X, 10), or use it as an organ of sensation (X, 11), until it reaches those "fields and spacious palaces of memory." [2] Memory is for the present being understood as containing the countless "images" of "objects perceived by sense" (X, 12), not "the realities themselves . . . but images of realities" (13). This same level of memory records our past experiences and affections, "things . . . either experienced by me, or" (the connection with belief is significant) "taken on trust from others" (14). A rapturous expression of wonder follows: the mystery of man would be mystery enough, were the marvelous treasure-house of such memories as these its sole manifestation. But again that insistence: to this point in our consideration not "the realities themselves" are present in memory, "but only their images," images, moreover, impressed on the mind "by each bodily sense" (X, 15). There is more to memory, and to man, than this.

To Realities Remembered

For memory encompasses not only images, but realities also (*res ipsas*) : "all those things learned from the liberal studies"— the connection of "disciplines" and memory in this new sense remains intact. "What literature is, what skill in disputation is, how many kinds of questions there are"—the examples are all in the nature of essential definitions. But the point is repeatedly

2. On the tormented question of "memory" in Augustine, see the remarks and bibliographical indications in Pellegrino, pp. 208–213, and Solignac, *BA* 14, pp. 557–567. The frequent tendency is to interpret this section of the *Confessions* in the light of the theory presented in the *De Trinitate*, Books XI and XII, written nearly twenty years afterwards. There, Augustine seems anxious to eliminate the necessity of a reference to pre-existence that I submit he is actually trying to demonstrate here. Compare Gibb and Montgomery on this entire section, especially pp. 286 and 294. Augustine is exposing the *Meno* view of memory, though he later appears to have rejected or at least modified it.

made that unlike memory operating as described above, "of
these things it is not images that I carry about, but the things
themselves" (*res ipsas,* 16) . The words expressing them I retain
as images, but not the realities, for "I neither attained to them
by any bodily sense nor did I descry them anywhere except in
my mind." Colorless, odorless, tasteless, they entered the mind
through none of the "portals of the flesh," nor were they
learned by giving "credence to another's heart." No, Augustine
insists, "I recognized them within my own [heart], and approved
them as true." He then concludes that "they were there even
before I learned them, but they were not in memory." The
conclusion must immediately be corrected, however, for were
they not in memory, there would be no accounting for the fact
that "when they were uttered" he "acknowledged" them
(*agnovi*) and approved them as true. The correct conclusion
therefore must be this: "they were already in memory, but so
removed and pushed back as it were in more hidden caverns
that, unless they were dug up by some admonition (*nisi
admonente aliquo eruerentur*) I would perhaps have been
unable to conceive them" (17) .

Re-collecting the Scattered

Having gotten his reader to assent (he assumes) that such
knowledge as the liberal disciplines represent is already present
in memory, merely awaiting excitation by some "admonition,"
Augustine is ready to take a crucial step in his *exercitatio.* He
takes it first by suggesting it in a series of images; then he but-
tresses his conclusion by a grammarian's appeal to etymology.
When it concerns such knowledge as was pre-contained in memory, he suggests, "learning" consists in this: "we gather together
and collect" (*colligere atque animadvertendo curare*) items
which "previously lurked scattered and neglected" (*sparsa et
neglecta latitabant*) . Thinking, then, requires that such items be
"brought together again" (*cogenda rursus*) , they must—he repeats the image—"be collected together, as it were, out of a sort
of scattered state" (*velut ex quadam dispersione colligenda*) . A
series of etymological parallels is brought forward to justify this
view. The relation between the terms *cogo* and *cogito* shows
that "to be cogitated" (*cogitari*) means that what is cogitated is
"brought together" (*cogitur*) or "collected together" (*colli-
gitur*) in the mind (18) . He has gone to some lengths to make
his point; having made it, he passes on. But he has left us with a

vague question rattling about in our minds. How did these things become "scattered" in the first place? Does the thesis that all learning is re-collection imply that those same things, before becoming scattered, were once "collected"?

To What Really Exists

Instead of sating our curiosity immediately, he passes on to another stage in his *exercitatio*. Besides such definitional realities as spoken of above, memory also houses the "principles and countless laws of numbers and dimensions": *numerorum dimensionumque rationes et leges innumerabiles*. Bereft of all sense-qualities, perceived "within" the self "without the conception of any body whatsoever," they are neither the words which express them, nor the bodily realities we both number and measure by them, nor images of these latter. And yet, they "truly exist": *valde sunt* (19).

The Food of Joy

Now he passes to the memory of past affections, such as joy and sadness. He compares these two, as if only incidentally, to "food," respectively "sweet and bitter," committed to memory as to the "mind's stomach" (21). But he proceeds to play on the comparison by suggesting that "just as food is brought up from the stomach by rumination, so such things [as joy and sadness, fear and desire] are perhaps brought up from memory by recollection": *recordando proferuntur*. Our understanding of such affections when they are spoken of shows that they must have been in memory before the speaking. They must, therefore, have been committed to memory by the mind which experienced them, or—curious suggestion—"or memory itself retained them for itself, even though they had not been committed to it": *etiam non commendata retinuit* (22). Curious the suggestion is, but important for Augustine's purpose. He is setting the stage for our acknowledgment that we have deep memory of some affections, without that memory being accounted for by past, that is, temporally past, experience.

Forgetfulness

But how can such a thing be? Again Augustine recalls his key distinction: either the image or the reality of the thing recol-

lected must be present in memory for recognition to take place
(23). At this point Augustine takes up the question from another angle. He focuses, as he found he had to do in the *Soliloquies,* on the inverse problem of "forgetfulness": *oblivio.* Rec-
ognizing the meaning of forgetfulness implies its reality must be
in memory, and yet forgetfulness is a "privation of memory": its
presence in memory should wipe out memory! What a set of
paradoxes. "What man will search this out," Augustine exclaims, "Who can comprehend how it is?" (24). "Lord," he
cries, evoking the image of Adam's curse, "I truly labor at this
task, and I labor upon myself. I have become for myself a soil
hard to work and demanding much sweat": *terra difficultatis et
sudoris nimii* (25).

Again, man is become a mystery to himself. "It is I who
remember, I the mind": *ego animus.* Yet the self cannot even
name the self without employing a memory which, it now real-
izes, it cannot fathom in its workings (25). The exclamation
recurs, along with the same identification of the real self: this
"awesome thing" the memory, "boundless and manifold," "this
thing is the mind, and this I am myself: What then am I, O my
God? What is my nature?" (26). Let those turn elsewhere who
would look for neat and obvious answers to the human predica-
ment. The phenomenon of forgetfulness, which "surely was
itself once present so that its image might be acquired," implies
for Augustine the certainty that he "remembered forgetfulness
itself" though it be the very thing "whereby what we remember
is destroyed." A dazzling paradox, one that suggests we must
remember it somehow, but in a manner both "incomprehen-
sible and inexplicable" (25).

To the Lost God Found Again

An impasse has been reached; the answer must be sought
on another level. "I will pass," Augustine decides, "beyond
even this power of mine which is called memory, desiring to
reach You . . . and cling to You," pass "even beyond memory"
with its vast reaches, "so that I may find you . . . O truly good
and certain delight." But then, the question twice repeated,
"where?" (26).

Where indeed: for "If I find you apart from memory, I am
unmindful of you. How then shall I find you, if I do not remember you?" (26).

Reach, find, cling; good and certain delight—Augustine is parading his vocabulary of the "happy life," a life consisting, as always, in contemplative union with God. Does "passing beyond" memory really mean passing to the limit of its reach? Is the reach of man the reach of mind, the reach of mind the reach of memory, and God Himself present to memory? "How then shall I find you, if I do not remember you?" The vital Plotinian question, one Augustine will answer as Plotinus did, by showing the soul retains both memory and forgetfulness of God.

Plotinianism, merely? No. The same truth is suggested in Scripture, for those who will understand. "The woman who had lost the drachma and searched for it with a lamp would not have found it unless she had remembered it." The argument reproduces the classic reasoning of the *Meno* and the *Phaedo*: "When it was found, how would she know whether it was the same one if she had not remembered it?" Augustine insists: a series of everyday examples illustrates the conclusion that what is looked for and found must be "interiorly re-cognized" (*intus recognoscitur*). "We do not say that we have found what was lost, unless we recognize it (*agnoscimus*), and we cannot recognize it, if we do not remember it. It was lost to sight but kept in memory" (27). Further examples follow in the same vein. They suggest that forgetting may after all imply "the entire matter had not slipped from us," but part was retained, stimulating memory to "demand the return of what was lacking," setting it off in pursuit of what was lost. "Reminders" may help in this process, but they do not adequately account for it. "If it had been completely wiped out of mind, we would not remember it even when reminded (*admoniti*) of it." We have not therefore "completely forgotten what we still remember to have forgotten." Had we done so, we could not even "look for it if it is lost" (28).

All this may be true of common objects—a drachma, a name, a face. Is it, though, true of God? Augustine is convinced the cases are substantially parallel. The question of the *Proëmium* has returned with renewed urgency: how can we call upon God unless we already know Him somehow? "For one who does not know you might call upon another instead of You" (I, 1). But Augustine's hope is that the long *exercitatio* of the intervening books has prepared us to accept the answer, despite all the difficulties it may create for our habitual thought-ways and evaluations.

Happiness Unforgotten

The next step toward that answer brings him to the question of the "happy life," whose lexicon he has already deftly introduced above. For he himself, and "all men," seek the happy life. How? The abstract possibilities are listed as three: we seek it either as something known through remembrance, or as something unknown, whether because never known, or so completely forgotten that we do not even remember we have forgotten it. But the preceding train of reasoning implies we must have known it: where? "Where have they [i.e. all men] known it, that they in such wise will to possess it? Where have they seen it, so that they love it? Truly, we have it, but how I do not know." Even those who are happy only in hope would not desire its possession "unless they possessed it in some fashion . . . They have known it, but how I do not know, and therefore they have it with I know not what kind of knowledge." Is it a knowledge "in memory"? If so, "then all of us have already been happy at some period (*iam beati fuimus aliquando*), either each of us individually, or all of us together in that man [Adam] who first sinned, in whom we all died, and from whom we are all born in misery."

However our relation to Adam may figure in the picture, we must in some fashion "know" the happy life, or "we would not love it." Name it in any language and the meaning is grasped by one who speaks the language, something which "could not be unless the very thing (*res ipsa*) for which this is the name were retained in their memory" (29). In certain respects, unlike the way we remember Carthage, or numbers, or the arts of speech, could this memory be "like the way we remember joy?" (30). If so, "where, then, and when did I have experience of my happy life, so that I remember it, and love it, and long for it?" Augustine's question is not merely his, it is a universal human question, for "all of us, without exception," and notwithstanding disagreements on what concrete form it will take. All of us "want to be happy", "want to be joyful"; this is the one thing "all strive to attain" which proves that joy, happiness, "is therefore found in memory and re-cognized (*recognoscitur*) when the words 'happy life' are heard" (31).

As for Augustine, he knows the concrete form the happy life must take if it is to be truly happy. "To rejoice over You, to

You, and because of You: this is it, and there is no other." Yet even those who pursue another, untrue joy, do not have their will entirely "turned away from a certain image of joy," and hence they still come under his argument (32). To prove this, ask of any number of men whether they would have joy in truth or falsity, and, no matter how depraved, they will uniformly reply they "prefer to have joy in truth." This, in fact, is the "happy life": *gaudium de veritate*, "joy in the truth . . . joy in You Who are the Truth, O God." This all men desire: "all men desire joy in the truth."

"Where then," the central question recurs, "where then have they known this happy life, except where they knew truth as well?" For "they would not love it unless there were some knowledge of it in their memory," though "they remember [it] so faintly" that their memory does not have power to draw them away from things that presently make them only miserable (33). The faintness of that memory explains that men can even "hate the truth for the sake of that very thing which they have loved instead of the truth." It does not weaken the universality of Augustine's thesis. Even though miserable, man's soul "prefers to have joy in true things rather than in false," and hence dimly longs for "that sole truth by which all things are true" (34), the God Whom Augustine can now confidently say he found nowhere else than in his "memory" (35).

The implication should be clear. It is authentically Plotinian—to the extent, that is, to which Plotinus is content to remain in the central Platonic tradition. We could not long for happiness unless we somehow knew it; but knowing it, in this case, meanns we somehow "remember" it, and *therefore once possessed and enjoyed it*. In the *Proëmium* Augustine had cryptically suggested that there are no traces (*vestigia*) left of "that time" of "innocence." There, it was provisionally classed with infancy as though equally lost to memory. Now that false impression has been decisively corrected. Pre-existence has become something even more certain than our infancy in this life, because we all "judge" in the light of Truth, and hence once knew the Truth we judge by. We pre-existed as happy souls ⁊ before falling into our embodied misery.

That implication will be muddled, however, if this section is read with the half-acknowledged determination of finding Augustine speaking indifferently of any of several forms of epistemological "innatism." The muddle will worsen if it is read through the lens of *De Trinitate* XII, 21 and 24, written nearly twenty years later, during the years 417–418.[3] There, it would appear, Augustine is striving to liberate his conception of "memory" (now become an acknowledgment of God *as present,* rather than God as present-but-object-of-a-*past*-vision [4]) from the implications of Platonic reminiscence and pre-existence. The resulting conception involves an "innatism" of a sort different from that special form of innatism represented by Platonic *anamnesis,* literally understood. Here, however, there is no such preoccupation in evidence; quite the contrary. Although the God we "know" through memory is eternally present (indeed, omnipresent), there was some *past knowledge* of him that grounds the memory that persists in us. Because we quite literally "remember" Him, we can now (like the slave-boy in the *Meno*) "find" and "re-cognize" Him (27); because all men have "known" the happy life, "have seen" it, "have already been happy" they retain a "memory" of it (29; cf. 33); because Augustine himself had some past "experience" of the happy life, it is now "found in memory and re-cognized" (31) . *Memor ejus; memoria tenebatur* (27), *memoria teneretur* (29); it is precisely a "memory"-form of innatism that grounds the possibility of "re-cognizing" (*recognoscitur,* 27) and "recalling" (*recorder,* 31) . *Noverunt, viderunt, iam beati fuimus* (29), *expertus sum* (31), *noverunt* (33) —these verbs are all in the past tense: we knew, saw, were happy, have experienced the happiness we can now recall. But when or where? Clearly not in this life "here." It must, then, have been "There" in Plotinus' sense of the term, where we pre-existed as souls, and whence we fell into this life "here."

3. See the *Bibliothèque Augustinienne* edition of *La Trinité* (*BA* 15 and 16) by M. Mellet and Thomas Camelot (Paris, 1955) , *Note Complémentaire* to vol. 15, p. 559.

4. In *Letter* 7, 2, Augustine endeavors to convince Nebridius that one can speak strictly of "memory" with respect to ever-present eternal truths. The correct usage of the term "memory" requires, he admits, a necessary reference to the "past," but not necessarily to the past-ness of the *objects* remembered. Those who criticize Socrates' *nobilissimum inventum* lose sight of the fact that our seeing of those eternal truths was in the past (*non adtendunt illam visionem esse praeteritam*) ; it is on the basis of the past-ness of our having glimpsed them that we can now remember them. See Johannes Hessen's accurate analysis of this section in *Augustins Metaphysik der Erkenntnis,* 2d ed. rev. (Leiden, 1960) , pp. 53–54. How R. A. Markus interprets Augustine here as trying to show that *"memoria* does not necessarily refer to the past" I am at a loss to understand; see his essay on Augustine in A. H. Armstrong, ed., *The Cambridge History of Later Greek and Mediaeval Philosophy* (Cambridge, Eng.: Cambridge University Press, 1967) , p. 370.

Absence from the Ever-present

Thus far Plotinus as spokesman for Platonism. At this point in his *exercitatio,* Augustine shows he still follows him in what he himself admitted was his personal contribution to the theory of the fall, the contribution that entailed the set of inner tensions that brought him close to contradiction. The soul's forgetfulness is never entire. However faint, some memory persists, and memory, for its part, is not merely memory of possession of Truth in the past, it is testimony to present illumination. The fallen soul is not entirely fallen, it is to some extent still "there."

The omnipresence insight only exaggerates the paradox, for it insists that the fallen soul is never really "far" from God. It may in some sense "absent" itself from Him, but God for his part remains unchangeably present to the soul. By a series of incidental touches Augustine has kept us alert to those paradoxes of omnipresence, even while dealing expressly with memory. God, he has reminded us, was with him even before he was with God (*qui mecum es et priusquam tecum sim,* X, 6). However true it may be that "as long as I journey apart from You, I am more present to myself than to You" (7), still it remains equally true that God's "light, which no place can contain, floods into my soul" (8), and He remains, in Plotinus' ringing phrase, the "life of life," life of the soul which enlivens the body (10).

But "where within my memory do you abide, Lord," "in what part of it do you abide"? The omnipresence insight reminds us the question itself needs correcting. If God abide in memory, and memory be mind and mind incorporeal, "why then do I seek in what place you dwell therein, as if forsooth there were places there?" (36). But even that correction is not enough. God is not so much "in" things as things are in God. "Where then have I found you, if not in yourself and above me?" Are things in God, then, as though in some "place"? Augustine's answer remains firm: *Et nusquam locus,* "There is no place; both backward do we go, and forward, and there is no place" (37). And we are ready for that lyric description of the fallen state, with all the themes of omnipresence fully orchestrated:

Too late have I loved you, O Beauty so ancient and so new, too late have I loved you! Behold, you were within (*intus*) me, while I was outside *(foris)* ; it was there that I sought you, and, a deformed creature *(deformis)*, rushed headlong upon these things of beauty which you have made. You were with me, but I was not with you *(mecum eras et tecum non eram)*. They kept me far *(longe)* from you, those fair things which, if they were not in you, would not exist at all *(si in te non essent, non essent)* . . . When I shall cleave *(inhaesero)* to you . . . my life will be life indeed, filled wholly with you *(tota plena te)*. But now, since you lift up *(sublevas)* him whom you fill with yourself, and since I am not yet filled with you, I am a burden to myself (38–39).

How is it possible that Augustine should propose an extended *exercitatio* on memory in order to suggest we are fallen souls, and yet conclude it with a reminder of God's ineradicable presence to the soul? Just as possible, I suggest, as that he should paradoxically claim God was with him even when he was not with God. For the seeming inconsistency, if such it be, is at bottom the same, and it comes from having thought out, and exacerbated, the paradoxes of the soul's fall in terms of the paradoxes proposed in Plotinus' treatise on Omnipresence. However difficult we may find digesting those paradoxes, however violently they may shock our philosophical and theological a priori judgments, neither shock nor difficulty should blind us to the possibility that this, exactly this, is what Augustine said and meant to say. Imagination may be required to make sense of it and at the same respect it, but the text is there; it is difficult to read it otherwise than as it stands, but (against a Plotinian background) quite possible to understand it as it stands.

Where the "Middle-Place"?

Augustine is far from finished with his task. Memory is by no means the only phenomenon he means to analyse in order to admonish us that we are fallen souls. An eloquent portrait of the misery of human life is climaxed by expression of ardent longing for some "middle-place" *(medius locus)* of peace, where the soul may cleave to God, where the pain and toil and warfare of this life "on earth" will be no more (39). This brief allusion to Plotinus' "mid-rank" station of the soul is followed by a cryptic reference to "continence," the virtue whereby "we are gathered together and brought back to the One, from whom we have flowed downward into the many." *Colligimur, redigimur, defluximus in multa:* language to rejoice Plotinus' heart. It is meant to whet our curiosity for later; but it also serves as transition to the second phase in Augustine's pursuit of self-knowledge, the examination of conscience which occupies most of the remainder of Book X.

Wounds of the Fall

That examination of conscience makes, surely, some of the most depressing reading in all of Christian literature. There is something profoundly saddening about the portrait it presents: the great Bishop of Hippo tormenting himself about the pleasure he cannot avoid while eating (43) or listening to psalmody (49); berating himself that the spectacle of a dog chasing a hare, or of a lizard snaring a fly, can still distract his interest (57). Saddening, too, the estimate of art-activity implicit in these pages (49–50, 53); the condemnation of man's quest "to search out the secrets of nature" and "know the courses of the stars," from which "men desire nothing but the knowing" (55–56). Even more saddening, perhaps, the thought of Christian generations who have been confused and troubled by the dreadful indictment of those wholesome human things, to say nothing of Christians today and tomorrow who, influenced by pages like these and others following their inspiration, will continue to doubt their own healthy acceptance of the world God made "good," indeed, "very good."

It has often been suggested that Augustine still shows the excessive wariness of a man who has been burned by sense-delights. The residues of a Manichaean affectivity have also been invoked to account for some of what he writes here. All of this may be true. But there is more; the question is not merely one of affect. Augustine's undervaluation of man's engagement in the sensible is systematic, and based on an intellectual construct. It remains substantially faithful to his estimate of it in the *De Quantitate Animae:* "great, these things, and altogether human," but only when one leaves them behind in pursuit of the upward way does "goodness begin, and all that is truly worthy of praise" (72–73). For the fallen soul, bent on return, these things are only snares. Its prayer must be Augustine's repeated prayer throughout this section: "Lord, pluck me out."

The first indication of this fallen-soul systematic is the fact that Augustine, still pursuing his quest for self-knowledge, now searches his soul for traces of the triadic sin (concupiscence, curiosity, pride) which—in his variant of the Plotinian theory—caused our fall from cleaving to God, and made us "flow downward" into the multifarious occupations which bring on the toil, sorrow, and warfare of this temporal life. Secondly, he reverts explicitly again and again to that virtue of "continence" (40, 41, 45, 60), not only in its obvious connection with concupiscence, but even as the remedy for pride. In fact, "in this vast forest of snares" which lure men to "acquire new experiences through the flesh" (54), he calls on God to witness "how many of them I have cut away (*praeciderim*) and thrust out of my heart" in the journey toward the "pure and chaste fatherland, Jerusalem" (56). For curiosity, too, the remedy is continence. As for Plotinus, "all is purification." In the flight of the "Alone to the Alone," one who would arrive must "cut away everything."

To be Gathered Again

The examination of conscience is followed by a brief summary of the book to this point (65–66), and a probably anti-Porphyrian meditation on the "false mediator," that fallen angel who has "in common with men that for which he is condemned to death along with them": *unde simul damnetur in mortem* (67). Did the angels, then, fall *simul*, "along with" the souls of men? Raised, the question is left temporarily unanswered. The True Mediator is, however, said to occupy—as God the *Summum* cannot—a *medius locus* in a sense recalling, though quite possibly different from, the *medius locus* which is the soul's ideal state.

But Augustine's fall is limned in terms which suggest what is to come: "In my greed, I did not want to lose you, but together with you I wanted to possess a lie . . . Thus did I lose you, because you disdain to be possessed together with a lie" (66). He pleads that in God his "scattered longings be gathered together," that God be sweet to him in a way that "will not belong to this life"; he expresses nostalgic longing for those contemplative delights his episcopal duties deprive him of enjoying (70; cf. 65); and he concludes with the resolution now to "consider the wondrous things of your Law" (70). A Plotinian would have caught the hints, for contemplation of the Eternal is beatitude, "re-collecting" the soul from the "scattering" effects of its fall from the One into the multiplicities of time, action, and fabrication of a sense-realm which, to some extent at least, is "lying" image of the True, Intelligible World. Augustine means to pass now to the fall considered as from eternity into time,

15 ETERNITY AND
THE FALL INTO TIME
(BOOK XI) [1]

Contemplation of Eternal Law

Eternity is God's, but it does not prevent him from hearing and answering man's prayer in time (1). Indeed, Augustine's life is sown with His "exhortations, warnings, consolations and acts of governance," acts which have brought him to the episcopacy with all its demands of service toward other men, to the busy life of apostolic action.

Yet the contemplative yearning has never left him. He still burns to "meditate upon [God's] law," finds those "drops of time precious" which he can let "flow away" in this contemplative activity (2). Now he begs God to bestow on him "time for meditation" on the "wonderful things of your law," by which he seems for the moment to mean the *Hexaemeron,* which recounts God's activity "from that beginning, wherein you made heaven and earth, even to an everlasting kingdom together with you in your holy city" (3).

1. It is remarkable how many interpretations of the *Confessions* present only skimpy consideration of the following three books. Pellegrino, for example, covers them in fourteen swift pages (pp. 221–234), though he acknowledges (pp. 225–234) that they must have some organic linkage with the preceding books. The notes in Gibb and Montgomery, pp. 332–449, and Solignac, *BA* 14, pp. 572–634 will be found helpful.

Not for "things of earth" does he ask that God open to his
mind the meaning of Holy Writ; not for gold and silver, fleshly
pleasure or power; "not even for the needs of the body and of
this our life of pilgrimage." No, his "desire arises" from the fact
he seeks God's "kingdom" and "justice," seeks those "treasures of
wisdom and knowledge" which are one with God's own Word,
Law, Truth (4). His motivation is, he means us to understand,
pure: the motivation of a soul intent above all things on returning to contemplative bliss.

Created Words and the Creative Word

Augustine begins his meditation on the *Hexaemeron* with
the words Moses wrote—"wrote them, and passed away, passed
from hence"—that "in the Beginning, God made heaven and
earth." Were Moses here, one could ask him what he meant by
those words. Yet even then, "how would I know whether he
spoke the truth? Even if I knew this, would it be from him that I
knew it?" No, Moses could tell Augustine what he *meant,* what
he *intended to say* by the words he uttered in time, but only the
eternal Truth "within me, within the dwelling place of
thought" (5) would tell whether he spoke truth. Only the eternal Word, beyond all passing syllables uttered in time, is the
Word of Truth; all other words, including those of Scripture,
are "admonitions" uttered to "turn" us inward to where that
Truth is glimpsed. But then, need one understand Hebrew,
need one even study Moses' words to find the truth expressed in
them? The connection between words and truth is still the slack
one proposed in the *De Magistro.* That slack connection will
serve Augustine well as his exegesis of Genesis proceeds.

But all creation is itself an assemblage of words: changing
and varying they "cry out" their creaturely distinction from the
Unchangeable Creator. Their "voice" reminds us that all their
goodness, beauty, being, come from that Goodness, Beauty, Being in comparison with which "they are neither good, nor beautiful, nor real" (6).

God's "making" of them, further, is profoundly unlike the
making of a human artist, who must work with matter God
created, work with faculties He furnished. How, then, did God
make "heaven and earth"? The question shifts abruptly, becomes "where" He made them. Not in the air, not in the wide
world, nor as though holding in a bodily hand "anything out of

which to make it." For "before it was caused to be" there was neither "place where it could be made" nor any matter for the making of it. "[He] spoke, therefore, . . . in [His] Word [He] made them" (7) —in His all-upholding Truth-Hand.

Nor was that creative word uttered in time, made up of "syllables [that] sounded and passed away" in creaturely "temporal movement." Comparing such words "sounding in time" with the "eternal Word in its silence" man's mind finds them far beneath itself. "They do not exist, because they flee and pass away. The Word of my God abides above me forever" (8) . So God calls upon us to understand that Moses is referring to "the Word, God with you, O God, which is spoken eternally, and in which all things are spoken eternally . . . spoken once and forever." "No part of your Word gives place to another or takes the place of another, since it is truly eternal and immortal." Saying "once and forever" all that God says, His Word is coeternal with Him (9) .

We are brought back to the mysterious relationship of eternity to time with which this Book began. God makes nothing except by "speaking," yet "not all things which you make by speaking are made simultaneously and eternally" (9). Why? Augustine "sees" it "in a way" but finds it hard to express. The Word, now equated with "eternal reason" (*ratio aeterna*), knows and ordains eternally when things of time "must begin or cease" in time. This "eternal reason" is, moreover, the *Principium* "in which," Moses tells us, God created all the passing things of time. Christ said the same: He identified Himself as "the beginning, because it also speaks to us" (cf. Jo. 8: 25) .

But in the Gospel he spoke "through the flesh," spoke "outward" words for the "ears of men," spoke in order to be "believed"—all this, however, in order to be "sought inwardly, and found in the eternal Truth where the sole good Master teaches all his disciples." The words of the Incarnate Christ are therefore placed in the same position as Moses' words, indeed, as all temporal, human words, signs, and efforts at "outward" communication. "Admonished by a changeable creature"—including, presumably, the humanity of Christ—"we are led to stable Truth, where we truly learn" if willing to hear. Thus do we "return ourselves back to that from whence we are" (*reddentes nos unde sumus*) , to Him Who is properly termed the Beginning, "for unless He abided when we went astray, there would be no whither for us to return to. But when we return from error, we truly return by knowing (*cognoscendo utique redimus*), and that we may know, he teaches us, because he is the beginning and speaks to us" (10).

A closing *confessio* identifies the "Beginning" in which God made heaven and earth with the Divine Word, Son, Power, Wisdom, and Truth—a light which even now "shines through" Augustine, "cutting through my dark clouds which again cover me over, as I fall down because of that darkness and under the load of my punishments." For thus, he continues, "is my strength weakened in poverty, so that I cannot support my good, until you, O Lord, 'who have been gracious to all my iniquities' likewise 'heal all my diseases.' For you will 'redeem my life from corruption' and . . . 'satisfy my desire with good things' " (11).

From the *De Musica* forward, Augustine's regular practice is to meditate on time's relation to eternity in terms of temporal words as they relate to the one Eternal Word: mankind's conventional fabrications, attempting to create an image of the eternal Truth, they testify to the soul's fall into a world of action, distraction, and dispersion, yet at the same time function as "reminders" to the soul which never loses its thirst for contemplation, its contact with the higher world of recollected bliss. All of these themes he has subtly woven into this introduction to the long *exercitatio* on time and eternity which is to occupy Book XI.

Eternity versus Time

"In the beginning," then, "God created heaven and earth." What, therefore, was God doing "before" He created heaven and earth? That was a stock Manichee question, aimed to point up the absurdities implied in Genesis' account of creation. Augustine reminds us, and the conservative, anti-intellectual Catholics of his day, that he might content himself with making a joke at the objector's expense (14), but the Christian owes the questioner more than that. He must be able to produce some "understanding" of his belief. A question such as this demands an intelligible answer, not some menacing appeal to blind faith.

But the question is difficult, and requires that the mind which has formulated the objection be brought to see the opposing natures of eternity and time. And this in turn demands that one begin, not with the notion of time, but—typically

Plotinian strategy—with the notion of eternity. The less real is always illumined by the real, and not vice-versa.

So Augustine strains to show that the objection implied in the query is valid only if one conceives of God as in time: He is not. Compared with "times that never stand fast," the splendor of God's ever stable eternity is "incomparable," for "in the eternal nothing can pass away, but the whole is present" (13). God is the selfsame, his "years do not come and go . . . [but] stand all at once . . . are one day," an unchanging "today" which succeeds no yesterday, gives way to no tomorrow. Let the objector awaken (evigilet) and see that the all-creating, all-upholding (omnitenentem) God cannot be grasped through temporal "images." "You have made all times, and You are before all times"—ante omnia tempora—but that "before" must be understood a-temporally. "It is not in time (tempore) that You precede time: elsewise You would not precede all times. You precede all past times in the sublimity of an ever present eternity" (15–16).

"At no time, therefore, did You do nothing," Augustine can now conclude. "Why do they ask what You did then," before creating heaven and earth? "There was no 'then,' where there was no time" (17 and 15).

The Nature of Time

But then, what is "time"? We discuss "nothing more familiarly and knowingly" in ordinary conversation, presume to understand what we and others say about it; yet what is it, really? "If no one asks me, I know," Augustine observes, "if I want to explain it to someone who does ask me, I do not know." The remark is a celebrated one, more celebrated than the strikingly similar observation Plotinus makes in opening his treatise On Eternity and Time. But not only is the beginning parallel. As Augustine does, Plotinus treats first of eternity, and only then approaches the nature of time. At that stage he proceeds to evaluate successively the varied notions other philosophers proposed before him: again, Augustine's procedure.

In Augustine's study of time, therefore, the procedure and its successive stages, are remarkably parallel to Plotinus'. More important, however, the same governing intention dominates. Augustine begins with the fact, already exploited in the De Musica, that we do "measure" times, calling some long and others short. Yet we cannot, on the face of it, say that "future"

or "past" times "are" long or short. They do not even exist in
the moment of measuring them (18). Nor can we, on examination, say the "present" is long. Analysis rapidly disintegrates it
into years and days, hours and minutes, till "the present" is
shown to "have no space" (20–21). And yet, we do measure
times and call some long and others short. Can it be that when
the present "comes to be" it proceeds "from some hidden
source" and then, becoming past, "recedes into some hidden
place?" Historians relate the past; prophets predict the future.
"If such things were entirely nonexistent, they could not be
perceived in any way." Therefore, both future and past times
must have "being" (22), but where? Wherever they are, they
must be there "as present" (23).

Time Within the Soul

Perhaps a hint of the solution can be found in this direction: the past is present to my remembering it, through its
image present to me; future things are present to my anticipation of them, through conceptions I form based on presently
existing causes of them (24). Augustine breaks into prayer for
light on all these difficulties. It alerts us we may have come to a
crucial turning in the *exercitatio* (25). The next paragraph
confirms that suspicion. He exploits the hint dropped just before his prayer, proposing that "the present of things" whether
those things be past, present, or future, are all three "in the
soul"; they correspond to the soul's memory, intuition, and
expectation of past, present, and future things, respectively:
memoria, contuitus, exspectatio. This, therefore, is the proper
way to "understand" what "common usage" means in speaking
of "three times," past, present, and future (26). Again, a
common human experience, subjected to analysis, reveals a far
from obvious paradox. Time has been driven back inside the
soul which measures time, just as Plotinus insisted it must.

Time a "Distention"

But this only sharpens the difficulty seen earlier: how can
we call time "long," implying that it has some extension
(*spatium*) to it, when the nonexistent future and no-longer-
existent past can neither of them have such extension, and the
only other choice, the ever-passing present, has been seen to
have no extension at all (*nullum spatium*, 27)? Again, but this

time even more fervently than before, Augustine breaks into prayer (28). He eliminates the possibility that periods of time are constituted by the "movement" (*motus*) of the heavenly bodies, and concludes—the second crucial element of Plotinus' solution—that time is, in any event, "a kind of distention" (*quandam esse distentionem*, 29–30). But distention of what?

Before answering that, Augustine eliminates the definition that identifies time with bodily motion more generally: such motions take place *in* time, but are not time itself (31). Another fervent plea for light (32) and he is ready to take a decisive step forward.

The Soul Itself "Dis-tended"

That step he has carefully prepared his reader to take with him. Touch by successive touch, interspersed with refutations of rival views, he has artfully drawn the Plotinian portrait of time, subtly hinting its "hidden source" is unchanging eternity, later making it something in and of the soul, then vaguely introducing the notion of "distention." Now he feels the reader is ready to take the plunge with him. Discarding the notion that we measure time by time itself—a longer time by comparison with shorter ones—he concludes provisionally that "time is nothing more than a distention: but of what thing I know not, *unless it be of the mind itself*" (33).[2]

What can this mean? Augustine urges his soul to be "steadfast," to "attend firmly," to "look to where truth is beginning to dawn" (34). He takes the example of measuring a vocal utterance. Ambrose's *Deus creator omnium,* from which Monica had drawn her pregnant *Fove precantes Trinitas* so many years ago, is chosen as an example. How do I measure the long and short syllables, which, once they have passed away, "no longer are"? It must be I "do not measure the syllables themselves . . . but something in my memory [of them] that remains fixed there" (35)—it is in the mind itself I measure times! A difficult truth; a "noisy mob of prejudices" cry out against it, and against its implications. But Augustine is firm. It must be a "present state" I measure, hence the "impression" which "remains" in the

2. Having detected the Plotinian character of this entire meditation on time, Gibb and Montgomery note at this point that "The riddle is out!" (p. 357), and rightly refer to Plotinus' *diastasis* notion, from *Ennead* III, 7, 11, 10. Augustine's substantial agreement with Plotinus does not, however, preclude his having worked some modifications; see Solignac, *BA* 15, pp. 581–591 for informed discussion and bibliography.

mind of things that pass. Consider how I utter a verse or poem. The mind first "looks forward" to the part of the verse it is about to utter, then "considers" each passing phase of the utterance, "remembers" what has already been uttered, and does all these things in one abiding act of attention. "It is not, then, future time that is long, but a long future is a long expectation of the future. Nor is past time, which is not, long, but a long past is a long memory of the past" (37). It is the mind itself—looking forward, intuiting the passing present, remembering—it is the mind itself that is "distended," stretched out in the process (38).

The solution, then, is clear. Augustine's excitement is evident in his way of formulating it, and encasing that formulation in a *confessio. Ecce distentio vita mea:* "behold my life is a distention (39)."

That definition is Plotinus' classic διάστασις. It comes from the very treatise *(Enn* III, 7) that has served as Augustine's model, here and in the *De Musica,* for reflecting on the soul's fall from a contemplative eternity into the distraction, dissipation, dispersion of time and the manifold life of action. Not only from that same treatise, the Plotinian definition comes exactly after Plotinus has discarded the various countersolutions Augustine has passed in review, and in a section (III, 7, 11) where he is attributing the soul's being "stretched out" in time to its "curious" or "restless" desire to engage in the activity of creating a temporal image of the eternal pattern of unity. The implication is clear: the soul's existence in time, its immersion in "action," is evidence of its "fallen" state.

The Fall into "Action"

Augustine has already set artfully about the task of making that implication explicit—for those who will understand. First came the cryptic but pregnant phrase, "the life of this action of mine is distended": *distenditur vita hujus actionis meae* (38). Here distention and action are connected, but the application is limited to Augustine himself. The universal bearing of the phrase was then brought out by allusion to all "actions of men" *(actiones hominum)* as comprising "parts" of the "whole life of a man" *(tota vita hominis,* 38). Here the individual application begins to merge with *homo* as man *in general.* This identification is taken one step further when Augustine notes that the entire life of the individual man is itself a "part" of the entire history of the "sons of men in this age": *in toto hoc saeculo* (38). Augustine's situation is that of all men.

And that situation is "fallen." For this reason, his discovery that time is a *distentio* of the soul (39) leads him without a break to speak of God's merciful "right hand" lifting him up, mediating between "us, the many" (who are "dissipated in many ways upon many things") and "God, the One." That mediating action has as its design to "gather together" Augustine's soul, grown "old" by his fall into time, and make him young—a "little one"—again: *ut . . . a veteribus diebus colligar sequens unum.* "Following the One" does not dis-tend, but, in St. Paul's phrase, "ex-tends" him, toward the unchanging things that are "before" all times, but again, not temporally so—"before" in Plotinus' sense, prior and superior in the ontological order, the Eternal. That eternal Father Augustine calls upon as his "comfort" (*solacium*), and then describes his fall from Him. "But I leapt apart into times (*in tempora dissilui*) . . . and my thoughts, the inmost bowels of my soul (*intima viscera animae meae*) are torn asunder by tumultuous variations."

In tempora dissilui: here is another of those Augustinianisms which drive translators into all the by-ways of paraphrase. "I am distracted amid times" is Ryan's conscientious attempt. "I fall into dissolution amid changing times" is the tack W. H. D. Rouse takes. Guilhem Bouissou and Eugène Tréhorel render it as *je me suis éparpillé dans les temps,* thereby respecting the text in much the same way Vernon J. Bourke has managed to do: "I have disintegrated into periods of time."

For *dissilio* means exactly what Augustine meant to say: "to leap apart, burst asunder, be broken up." And the verb is in the perfect tense; there is no warrant for changing it to the present.[3] The preposition *in,* moreover, governs the accusative *tempora.* It denotes motion toward. "Into," not "amid," is the only defensible translation for it.

The background image is the one Augustine embodied in his description of the soul's fall, both in the *De Genesi contra Manichaeos* and in the *De Musica.* He has found Plotinus in *Ennead* V, 1, 1 attributing the soul's fall into the sphere of genesis—"becoming"—to the fault of *tolma.* Coupling that

3. Gibb and Montgomery (p. 363) proffer the puzzling observation that the tense argues against the meaning "flew asunder." They seem to be arguing from the present tense of *dilaniantur* in the following line. But *dilaniantur* expresses the present sundering effect of that "past" fall.

with Ecclesiasticus' image of the "proud" man "spewing forth
his entrails" (*projecit intima sua*) , he has read the whole in the
light of *Ennead* III, 7. There Plotinus compares the soul, falling into time, to a "seed," a "unity self-gathered," unable to
retain within itself the "dense fullness of its possession." "Uncoiling outwards," it "fritters its unity away" and "advances
into a weaker greatness," the impoverishing plurality of time.
In those early works, I submit, the implications are unquestionably Plotinian; here, I suggest, the continuity is substantially
preserved. Augustine is still saying, for those who can clear their
minds of a "mob of prejudices," that man in time is a soul,
fallen through a sin of "pride."

"Return"—to a "Place Aloft"

Hence the appropriateness of his prayer, that God "purge"
and "melt" his fragmented being, making him "flow altogether
into you" (39) . It echoes the allusion in Book X, terminating
the analysis of memory, wherein "continence," God's gift,
"gathers us together," "brings us back to the One, from whom
we flowed downward (*defluximus*) into the many" (X, 40) .
But now the force of that image is unmistakably clear.

The ending of Book XI brings him back to his original
objectors, hoping they will "reach out forth 'to those things
which are before' and understand that you are before all times"
(40) , join Augustine in desiring to "share in the joy of your
light," humble themselves so that God may lift them up: for
"they do not fall down, whose place aloft is you" (41) .

"Whose place aloft is you": if what I am suggesting be true,
Augustine's labors are far from ended. Everything thus far
points to his belief that our souls once dwelt in that divine
"place aloft," before falling into this "region of unlikeness."
This may be quite all right for Plotinus to say, but can Augustine produce any scriptural foundation for such a view? To this
task he sets himself in Book XII.

16 THE SOUL'S
ETERNAL HOME
(BOOK XII)

God, then, made "heaven and earth." Augustine is still eliciting the depths of meaning he claims to gain from that single verse of Genesis. The "heaven and earth" explicitly referred to there would seem to be the visible heaven and tangible earth of our sense-experience: *"this* heaven which I see, *this* earth on which I tread, and from which comes this earth [the body] I bear about with myself" (XII, 2).

But Psalm 113 speaks of a "heaven of heaven" which is the Lord's, whereas "the earth He has given to the children of men." The implication is that there is another, higher heaven "that we do not see." Compared with this invisible realm, "all of this which we see" must be called "earth," and the visible heavens we gaze upon must be termed "the heaven of earth": *caelum terrae* as contrasted with this *caelum caeli* (XII, 2).

Formless Matter

The identity of that "heaven of heaven" will occupy Augustine more directly later. He lays the groundwork for its consideration by turning momentarily to Genesis' phrase: "and the earth was invisible and without form, and darkness was upon the deep." Just as "darkness" means the utter "absence of light," he submits, so Genesis indicates that the first product of God's creative act was a "certain formlessness, devoid of any specific character" (3), the "formlessness of matter . . . from which [God] made this beauteous world" (4).

The job of thinking such "formless matter" devoid of both intelligible and sensible form, is a demanding one. The mind is compelled to "know it by not knowing it, or to be ignorant by knowing it" (5). It must not be conceived, as the Manichees did, and for a while persuaded Augustine to do, as "having countless different forms . . . forms foul and horrid in confused array." The Manichee's so-called "race of darkness," if such existed, would be "formless" only by comparison with "better formed things," but not—as is required by Genesis' text—"from privation of all form": *privatione omnis formae*.

Again, the Manichee's difficulty is that he cannot truly "think." He falls back on imagination. "Genuine reason" (*vera ratio*) persuaded Augustine, on the other hand, to "divest it of every remnant of form," but this he was for a long time unable to do. How indeed conceive of something "deprived of all form" (*quod omni forma privaretur*), something "between form and nothing, neither formed nor nothing, an unformed near-nothing"? Only when his "mind ceased to question [his] imagination," filled as it was with "pictures of formed bodies," and fixed his "thought" on the mutability of bodies, did he make any progress.

The Plotinian Background

Behind his reasoning obviously looms something very like Aristotle's *materia prima,* emerging as it does from an entirely comparable analysis of change. "The mutability of mutable things," Augustine argues, "is itself a capacity for all the forms into which mutable things are changed," a capacity which must be thought of as "something formless," and yet not "absolute nothing," a kind of "nothing-something," an "is-is-not" (6). The constant recurrence of the semi-technical "privation" language would likewise seem to indicate an Aristotelian background to Augustine's analysis. Doubtless there were any number of intermediaries, doxographies among them, where Augustine could have found traces of a similar analysis of matter. What especially recommends Plotinus' treatises on The Nature and Source of Evil (*Enn* I, 8) and on Matter (II,4), apart from

other evidences available that Augustine had them to hand and
read them, is the fact that they both contain those striking turns
of phrase Augustine so regularly delights in. We must "eliminate every kind of form," Plotinus counsels. Then, describing
how this can be done, "to see darkness the eye withdraws from
light . . . its power is rather that of not-seeing than of seeing
and this not-seeing is its nearest approach to seeing Darkness"
(I, 8,9). This is the "bastard kind of thought" required of the
reason which would apprehend what lies at the lowest extreme
of the being-spectrum: "the dim, it knows dimly; this, the dark,
it knows darkly, this it knows in a sort of non-knowing" (II, 4,
10). This latter treatise, which A. H. Armstrong has found particularly influential throughout Augustine's analysis of matter,[1]
also explicitly presents the change-analysis which argues for the
existence of a formless substrate of "receptivity" in all changing
beings (II, 4,6).

Given the likelihood of Plotinian influence, then, it is
especially instructive to observe Augustine's freedom with respect to Plotinus' identification of matter as the principle of
evil. The Saint firmly sets aside the temptation to conceive of
this "formless matter" as made from God's own substance, but
he then goes on to reject the notion that it represents something
existing "beyond" God, from which He made the visible world.
That very independence of the Divine was what permitted
Plotinus to assert that evil must not be thought of—in the
Aristotelian terms Augustine eventually adopted as his own—as
a mere "privation" of good. In *Ennead* I, 8 Plotinus argues
directly against the Aristotelian position, and proves that evil
must, like matter itself, have a quasi-substantial standing in the
universe. Even while very likely borrowing from that treatise,
therefore, Augustine has quite resolutely rejected its central
contention. "You were, and there was naught else out of which
you made heaven and earth" (7). The "formless matter" out of
which God made the formed and ordered sense-world, He made
in its turn "out of nothing into a near-nothing," described in
Genesis as an "abyss above which there was no light . . . close
to non-being since altogether devoid of form." The Augustine
of Cassiciacum [2] toyed with identifying "nothing" as a mysterious "fluid," something strongly redolent of Neo-Platonism's

1. See A. H. Armstrong's "Spiritual or Intelligible Matter in Plotinus and
St. Augustine," *Augustinus Magister* (Paris, 1954), I, 277–283. Also, Solignac,
BA 14, pp. 592–598.
2. *Vita* 8; see *Augustine's Early Theory*, Chap. 7, pp. 186–187.

"non-being." That temptation he has firmly overcome. Formless matter is itself a product of creation, and creation out of
"nothing."

Thus far, then, we have been considering the formless
matter from which God made this visible heaven-and-earth, and
made it "on the third day by giving visible form to formless
matter." That mention of "days" is important, for the statement "in the beginning God made heaven and earth" contains
no such mention of time and days. The "beginning," we have
seen, refers to the Eternal Word. What, then, are we to conclude? Quite obviously, that the "formless matter" in question
God "made *before* the beginning of all days." The understanding of Genesis therefore pushes the mind back to a kind of
a-temporal creation "before" the first of "days." But combine
Genesis with Psalm 113, and the mind is forced to conclude that
something else besides this "formless matter" was made before
the beginning of days, to wit, the "heaven of heaven" (8).

The Heaven of Heaven

What, then, can that "heaven of heaven" be? "Doubtless"
(*nimirum*), Augustine assures us, it is "some kind of intellectual creature": *creatura aliqua intellectualis.* The conclusion
comes with a suddenness for which the modern reader is, to say
the least, ill-prepared. Even granted everything that has gone
before, it has a decidedly abrupt, a faintly arbitrary flavor. What
can be in Augustine's mind, that he finds it so obvious?

Again, Armstrong has pointed out that the background for
Augustine's thinking here is Plotinian: the process of his thinking is illumined chiefly by *Ennead* II, 4, On the Two Orders of
Matter,[3] where Plotinus proves that there must be a spiritual as
well as a corporeal matter, the former to account for the
"potency" present in the higher, spiritual world, the latter
entering into the composition of the visible, corporeal world.
For Plotinus, moreover, both the highest and lowest ranks in
the hierarchy of being are, in his term, "impassible"—not subject to change—and, significantly, for reasons very like those
Augustine gives here. The paradox is a striking one, and he
develops it in *Ennead* III, 6 on The Impassibility of the Incor-
poreals: pure matter has the property of "aping" a number of
the characteristics of *Noûs,* but for precisely opposite reasons. Its

3. Porphyry gives this title in his *Vita Plotini* (4); later, he abbreviates it
to the less informative On Matter.

unchangeability, for instance, is owing to its utter poverty. Without form, it cannot of itself in any way change, because change implies the replacement of one form by another. *Noûs* is unchanging also, but on account of its very perfection: having proceeded from the One, then (a-temporally) "turned about," it is galvanized into un-change by its unwavering orientation toward its Source.

A number of indications in Augustine's text point to this background as having facilitated—for his own mind at least—the exegetical task he has set himself. The trick was not an easy one; his embarrassment will shortly show as he turns to critics of his interpretation and spiritedly defends it at considerable length. Meanwhile he has had to display a certain strained ingenuity to get what he wants from Genesis' text. He has had to ring in the verse of Psalm 113, press heavily upon the alleged lack of time-indication in Genesis 1:1, and in the end will somewhat lamely remind his reader that Scripture later informs us the firmament—what he terms "heaven of earth"—was made on the second day and called heaven. There is, therefore, adequate textual foundation for interpreting the "heaven and earth" of the previous verse as referring to *another*, timeless heaven and earth, the two immutables he is trying to read into the words of Scripture.

The Emanationist Setting

But he has previously, and subtly, attuned our minds to the emanationist background presiding over the being-hierarchy he is working with. He has stressed the contrast between the formless earth and the "superior" celestial bodies which, though bodies, are nonetheless "transparent and brilliant" (*perlucida et luculenta*, 4). Beings, he then goes on to remind us, are more "dissimilar" to God in the very measure they are "distant" from Him in their ontological perfection: "heaven" and "earth" therefore signify "two beings, one near to you, the other near to nothingness, one to which you alone would be superior, the other to which nothing would be inferior" (7).

That same emanationist background shows through references to the being-hierarchy as running from "first to lowest" (11), and to sensible realities in the Plotinian phrase as "latest and lowest things" (14). It will become more evident when we turn to Book XIII; there Augustine describes creation of spiritual beings in terms of a procession from, and turning back to the Word, to be illumined and fixed in changelessness by Him.

This exploration of Plotinianism is only an attempt to conjecture what may be in the back of Augustine's mind as he leaps to a conclusion that might otherwise leave us gasping for breath. Whatever one may think of that suggestion, this much is at all events demonstrated: Augustine had directly at hand a structure of thought that would have prompted him to say, and mean, exactly what he says. It permits us to respect the text as it stands, and leaves without support any residual insistence that Augustine *"could not* possibly have meant *that."*

The Nature of the Heaven of Heaven

To eliminate any question about what he is saying, then, he argues that to understand the first verse of Genesis' creation account, with its absence of any indication of "days," the mind must push back to two pre-temporal products of God's creative activity, one to correspond to the mention of "heaven," the other to correspond to the mention of "earth." The latter will be the "formless" matter from which the "earth," created in the "days" of the subsequent verses, was formed. The former will be the "heaven of heaven" spoken of in Psalm 113. These two God has made "immune to time," though neither is coeternal with Him (15).

What, then, is the nature of this "heaven of heaven"? Here Augustine's text is explicit. For whatever reasons—and we have only tried to propose a likely set of them—he affirms it must be a kind of "intellectual creature" which, "though in no manner coeternal" with the Eternal Trinity, "is yet partaker of your eternity, and because of its most sweet and happy contemplation of you, it firmly checks its own mutability. Without any lapse from its first creation, it has clung fast to you and is thus set beyond all the turns and changes of time" (9).

It is a "sublime creature" which "finds rest in a most veracious contemplation of [God] alone." "It was made" and hence is not "without beginning" (19). It is not the uncreated Wisdom but a created wisdom, "an intellectual nature which, through contemplation of the Light, is light." It is "the rational and intellectual mind of your chaste city, our mother, which is above, and is free and eternal in the heavens" (20) "adapted always to behold your face" and "never turned away from it" (21).

Another description includes a characteristic Plotinian touch. Vision there is "as a whole":

I interpret the heaven of heaven as the intellectual heaven, where it belongs to intellect to know all at once, not in part, not in a dark manner, not through a glass, but as a whole, in plain sight, face to face . . . [knowing] all at once, without any passage of time (16).

God alone is "delight" to that creature who,

with most persevering chastity, drawing its nourishment from you, has nowhere and never asserted its own mutability, and with you yourself ever present with it, to whom it clings with all its powers, having neither future to look forward to nor transferring to the past what it remembers, is neither altered by any change nor distended into any times (12).

"Delight," "nourishment," "clinging"—the lexicon of the "happy life" is with us once again, and once again connected with rejection of all "distention" into times. "O happy creature [Augustine exclaims] if there be such, for cleaving to your happiness, happy in you, its eternal dweller and enlightener" (12).

We would be tempted to suppose that Augustine is speaking solely of the portion of the angelic creation which remained faithful to God. That supposition is immediately weakened once comparison is made with what he has earlier said of human "souls." He found, he assured us in Book VII, the Platonic writings speaking much the same language he has been using here. They showed him that

before all times and above all times your Only-begotten Son remains unchangeably coeternal with you; and that souls "receive of his fulness" so that they may be blessed; and that they are renewed by participation in the wisdom "remaining in herself" so as to be wise (VII, 14).

From Which We "Fell"

Repeatedly throughout the *Confessions*, moreover, he has spoken of his own desire for "return" to the "house" of God from which he strayed and has referred to other souls on this earthly pilgrimage—notably his mother and father—as "fellow-citizens" of the heavenly city. Now he hints more broadly at the meaning of that language when he finds nothing more fittingly called the "heaven of heavens" than "your own house, which contemplates your delight without any fault of going to another, a pure mind, most harmoniously one by the established peace of holy spirits, citizens of your city in heavenly places above these present heavens" (12).

Throughout, however, there are hints that this intellectual creature could conceivably "assert its mutability" (12), and consequently "become dark and cold" (21); could succumb to the "fault of going to another" (12), "turn away" from God's face (21), cease "cleaving" to God in chaste embrace, "detach from him," and "dissolve away"—become "distended"—into the "variation and change of times," "fall away from [God] and to itself" (19).

"O happy creature, if there be such, for cleaving to your happiness." Does the expression (12) imply Augustine doubts any part of the heaven of heavens was always faithul? Too many other texts indicate his belief that part at least of "God's house" "did not go astray," but "unceasingly and unfailingly clings" to God and thus "suffers no change in time" (13), is "forever without defect" because God has "established it forever" with a decree that "will not pass away" (19).

But surely implied in the context is that another part of God's "house" has succumbed to the "fault of going to another" —by a "movement of the will," we may safely surmise, "away from you who are and toward that which is in a lesser way," a movement previously designated "iniquity," but now labeled "crime and sin": *delictum atque peccatum* (11). It has "wandered" from God, but now, if the wandering of its member-souls has undergone the turning Augustine's has, it may more accurately be described as "on pilgrimage" back to the "house" it left.

From this may the soul, whose pilgrimage (*peregrinatio*) has become long, understand that if she now thirsts for you, if her tears are now made her bread . . . if she now seeks of you one thing, and desires it, that she may dwell in your house all the days of her life—and what is her life except yourself? and what are your days except eternity? (13).

There is, in any event, no doubt what Augustine's own situation is: he openly alludes to his having fallen from this "heaven of heaven" into "these things" of earth. He has "wandered" away, been "re-called" by memory's capacity to hear God's voice "behind" (and within) him, and now is "returning" to the place from which he fell.

I flowed downward (*defluxi*) to those [material] things, and I became darkened over, but from there, even from there, I loved you. I went astray (*erravi*), but I did not forget you. "I heard your voice behind me," calling me to return (*ut redirem*) . . . Now, see, I return (*redeo*), burning and yearning for your fountain (10).

Or again, in terms more biblical:

O lightsome and beautiful house . . . May my pilgrimage sigh after you! . . . 'I have gone astray, like a sheep that is lost.' Yet upon the shoulders of my shepherd, your builder, I hope to be borne back to you: *spero me reportari tibi* (21).

Back, that is, to "Jerusalem, my country, Jerusalem my mother."

I will not be turned away until out of this scattered and deformed state (*a dispersione et deformitate*) you gather (*colligas*) all that I am into the peace of her, the mother most dear, where [since Ostia's vision] are the first fruits of my spirit (23).

Did any doubts remain either on his meaning or the unity of the *Confessions*, one need only turn back to the section describing Augustine's vision of the "unchangeable light" in Book VII, 16–17, a section conceived, as we have seen, under the sign of the "happy life," like this one. The terms and images of the former passage repeat in patterns so tightly identical that their repetition is unmistakably intended here. *Ibi legi,* he has said of the *libri platonicorum;* and here we have his frankest endeavor to prove that the understanding eye can read in Scripture the same message of pre-existent bliss, and fall. "Admonished" by the very Platonic books whose doctrine illumines the obscurities of this exegetical effort, he tells us that to know that Light is to know "beloved eternity," God himself, for Whom he "sighs" both day and night (cf. XII, 21). That vision, just as with Scripture's message now of the "heaven of heaven," made him "tremble with love and awe" (cf. XII, 17). At that time, as now, he heard God's "voice from on high," heard "as one hears in his heart" (cf. XII, 11) speaking of Himself as "food" for souls "grown-up" enough to eat. That food would "change"

Augustine, turning him from one who, living in time, "does not
yet exist," into one capable of "cleaving to God" and hence
partaking of God's eternity (cf. XII, 9, 12, 13). How did he
come to live in time? God has "made his soul waste away like a
spider," and the reason is given there, as here. "You have corrected man for iniquity" (VII, 16–17), that is, the same "turning" of the will away from God to lower things (*infima*) as is
here called "crime and sin" (XII, 11).

The heaven of heaven, therefore, is Scripture's term for the
medius locus which up to now has been Augustine's designation
for the soul's ideal situation, the "place" beyond all place from
which, having turned away from God, it "flowed downward,"
and to which now it yearns to "return." At this point, the Saint
is conscious of having filled in the last vital piece of the puzzle.
No longer can the reader mistake the picture he has been drawing. But he is painfully aware, too, that his exegetical exertions
have put something of a strain on his reader's credulity.

Rebellion of the Exegetes

What pains him most is that he cannot claim the adversaries of his view are, like the Manichees, enemies. They are, on
the contrary, "lovers of the sacred books" (XII, 17) he has been
interpreting. They appear, in fact, to have been rather competent exegetes—more competent, by our modern standards,
than Augustine himself, more scrupulous, in any case, of what is
literally meant in Genesis.

There is more than a touch of pique in Augustine's han-
dling of them. What annoys him most is that they do not "assert
to be false" all the things which he asserted in this book. Some,
at least, if not all, would even be willing to "grant that all these
things" which God's Truth has spoken to his inner mind "are
true" (23). Theirs is simply the sober exegetical assertion that
the Holy Spirit "did not will that all this be understood from
these words" (17). "Moses was not considering the two things
you name when by the revelation of the Spirit he said, 'In the
beginning God made heaven and earth.' " "Heaven and earth"
were for him a way of signifying, in an "all-inclusive and brief
manner, the whole visible world" (24).

Now Augustine is prepared to make several concessions to
them: the "heaven" of Genesis 1:1 might coincide with the
"darkness above the deep" to refer to spiritual matter, whereas
"earth" in the same verse coincides with "the earth invisible

and without form" to refer to corporeal matter (25). Or, "if
any other man so wishes," those phrases could signify the "formless commencement of things" (26).

Truth, and Moses' Intention

But these are really side-issues. Augustine's crucial point in
defense of his interpretation turns upon two distinctions, the
first of them between the truth of the matter and the intention
of the one who presumably would, being truthful, report the
truth to us (32). He reminds his "contradictors" they do not
"have a divine spirit" to "see into the heart" of Moses when he
wrote (34). Neither he nor they can therefore "say with confidence" what Moses intended us to understand by his words. "I
do not see him thinking [this or that] within his mind as he
wrote these words, in the way that I see . . . for a certainty in
[God's] Truth" that "in [His] immutable Word [He] made all
things" (33).

Words and Realities

We have been prepared for this answer. But underlying it
is a second distinction which, though never expressly mentioned
here, is crucial to the argument. *Res, non verba,* Augustine
never tires of repeating to his students and readers—not words,
but the realities words are meant to point us toward. Verbal
expression is never adequate to the truth of the matter, never,
in fact, truly *conveys* the truth to us, only reminds us of it. We
must, on the occasion of such reminders—"admonitions"—turn
inward and away from the outward expression, to where the
Truth illumines the soul not totally fallen. This is the function
of all words, read or spoken, from profane or scriptural sources,
even when spoken by Christ himself through the *persona* of the
flesh.

To this distinction between words and meanings Augustine has made appeal several times before, notably at the very
start of his exegetical effort in Book XI, where he regaled us
with a long meditation on "words" and the "Word." Underlying his evaluation of words is the epistemology of the *De
Magistro,* itself an outgrowth of his Plotinian estimate of the
"fallen" condition and its need to work with the opacities of
speech, gesture, and symbol more generally. The same theory
explains why Augustine was at pains to illustrate how he him-

self learned how to speak (I, 8, 13) , to contrast the eloquence of
Faustus against the truths insinuated by Ambrose—a contrast
that pivots on the explicit reminder that there is but one Master, Christ Eternal Word of Truth (VI, 10–13) .

This underlying systematic implies a semi-occasionalistic
connection between words and the truths they attempt to
mediate. It makes it easy to understand why he considers the
strictly exegetical question not only fundamentally insoluble,
but really peripheral. We could not see into Moses' "heart" and
"mind" even were he presently speaking to us, so we cannot
ever have full confidence that we have seized upon the "intention" lying behind his words. But this is relatively unimportant
after all. What is really important is that we reach agreement on
the "truth" of the matter (XII, 33–35) . If "Truth" itself—and
it is hard to resist a temptation to substitute the name "Plotinus" here—if Truth has revealed inwardly to Augustine what is
"true" of God's creative activity, and these same exegetes admit,
as they do, that what Scripture's words have "admonished" him
to see is "the truth," then why on earth continue this uncharita-
ble squabble about the intended meaning of Moses' words?
(35, 43).

Augustine's "Understanding" Challenged

The strictly exegetical question is, therefore, relatively
unimportant, but not absolutely to be dispensed with. Augustine must walk a very careful tightrope here. Were he to make
the connection between the words of Scripture and the Word of
Truth an entirely arbitrary one, then the way of "authority"
would lose all organic continuity with the way of "reason." He
could not claim to present an "understanding" of the "faith"
after having completely blurred the contours of that faith as
proposed in Scripture. And it is central to his view, as well as
essential to his dialogue with Manichees, Neo-Platonists, and
conservative Catholics, that he be able to sustain the proposi-
tion that he is, in fact, presenting an "understanding" of the
"faith."

Hence the extraordinary length and passionate intensity of
his defense. The issue was a burning one for him. At stake is his
entire intellectual project since first he took up the pen to
elaborate a "spiritual" (not to say semi-gnostic) Christianity.
These exegetes have challenged, whether knowingly or not, his
right to pin the label "Christian"—or, more accurately, "Cath-

olic"—on his view of man, the fallen human condition, and the entire economy of redemption.

Hence his anxiety to disarm the exegete's attack on his interpretation, while at the same time leaving room for his claim that he is, in some legitimate sense, presenting an interpretation of Scripture. Even in his way of conceiving it, words do not have a totally arbitrary connection with truth. Not every utterance can serve as "reminder" of any truth whatever. The connection may be loose, but it is there. Here Augustine finds a way out of the impassse. Had he been Moses, he would hope that God would inspire him to use such words as would occasion not just one or another, but several diverse "visions"—all true—on the part of different readers, or even of the same reader at different stages of spiritual development (36). That way, Scripture becomes a fountain for varied thirsts: it replies to the still carnal-minded "little ones" in the nest of the Church with the imaged truth of which alone such souls are capable (37), but to those spiritually more mature, fledged and capable of leaving the nest, the same Scripture points to the intelligible, "spiritual" message that Augustine implicitly claims to have drawn from them (38).

His theory of man, therefore, with its corollaries on words and meanings, is still the base on which his exegetical method rests: it permits him to find in Scripture the very theory of man he is looking for.

17 THE RETURN OF IMAGE TO ARCHETYPE

(BOOK XIII)

GOD, THE GIVER

Augustine's theory of man implies a theory of God as well or, more comprehensively, a theory of man's relationship to God. If man is to undertand his own situation, Augustine never tires of repeating through his earlier works, the first thing required is a right notion of God.

The Manichee notion made man a fragment of the divine substance; it makes creation in its turn a divine strategy to re-capture these sparks of the divine Light, imprisoned in matter. In this view, one can scarcely confess what Augustine does in opening the final book of his *Confessions:* that the soul must be known at least partially by its *contrast* with God. Sinfully, the soul forgot, deserted, but stands in dreadful need of God. God, on the other hand, never forgets, deserts, yet stands in abso-lutely no need of, the soul (1). How can two such beings be conceived of as identical? Indeed, to understand that the soul, or anything distinct from God, exists at all, requires our grasp-ing something of the "fullness of [God's] goodness," poured out incessantly to beings of every rank, though none of them can lay claim to what He gives them initially, or to what He works on their behalf to "convert" them back to Him (2–3).

Augustine is at pains throughout the early portions of Book XIII to lay to rest for once and all the fundamental Manichee contention and its corollaries. For if souls are truly "of [God's] substance and thus equal" to Him (2), they do have a "claim" on Him. He does need them for the reintegration of His own Being. No, Augustine emphatically repeats, no! God alone "exists absolutely," whereas both the life and happiness of created spiritual beings are owed "entirely to [His] grace" (4). Neither His creating nor informing of them shows something was "wanting" or "needy" in Him, "as if [His] joy were to be fulfilled in them," or as though He had been "imperfect and were to be made perfect by their perfection" (5). *Praesumptio, confessio*: the idea of God in either case results in a profoundly different religious attitude.

One may legitimately ask, however, whether Augustine is not making a subtle point against the Neo-Platonist as well. Surely, inasmuch as Neo-Platonists would consider the soul in the same self-idolatrous manner as a few unfortunate phrases suggest, he would be. Yet no one stressed more than the Plotinus of *Ennead* VI, 9 that the One stands utterly "without need" of the beings emanating from It. Hence this question might better be left open for the moment: it is, at all events, secondary for our purposes.

Creation and "Conversion to Form"

But the text suggests yet another reason for leaving that question open. Augustine is plainly putting something very like the Plotinian emanation-image to work in his description of creation.[1] Creation here, as in Book XII, occurs in two distinct (though not temporally successive) stages. Because we are principally interested in the creation of the soul, we shall stay with it for now. In the first stage God created a formless "inchoate spiritual creation . . . to float and flow about, darksome like the deep" (3). But along with its being "inchoate and formless," this first product of creation is described as exhibiting a kind of downward-flowing tendency, as cascading down from the Creator, and in danger of "running off into immoderation and unlikeness far distant from [God]" (2), "darksome accord-

---

1. See Solignac's *Note* on "création," *BA* 14, pp. 572–581, and on "Conversion et formation," *ibid.*, pp. 613–617. Cf. Charles Couturier, "Structure métaphysique de l'être créé d'après saint Augustin," in *Recherches de Philosophie* (Paris, 1955), I, 57–81.

ing to the inconstant downflow of its spiritual formlessness"
(6).

The second moment in the creative process is described, as
Plotinus himself describes the procession of the hypostases from
the One, in the image of "conversion." This stage Augustine
finds expressed in the biblical "Let there be light" (Gen. 1:3).
The downflow of spiritual formlessness was checked, or in
Augustine's terms, "recalled" (2), "restrained" (5), "converted
to" the Light of the Divine Word. In this second stage it is converted "to form" (5), recalled to God's "unity and given form"
(2), "enlightened by [the Word] and made into light, although
not equal to the form equal to [God], yet conformed to it" (3),
"by His illumination made a beauteous life and become his
heaven of heaven" (6).

"Aversion" to Formlessness

This "first conversion" is, however, constitutive of the very
process of "creation." Augustine then suggests the possibility
that this spiritual creation, formed by the first, creative conversion, could subsequently turn away from the Divine Light, "by
aversion from [God] lose the light gained by conversion, and
fall back into the life similar to the darksome deep." This in
fact, has been our fate: "For we also, who are a spiritual creature
as to the soul, being turned away (*aversi*) from you, our light,
were sometimes darkness in this life. Still do we labor (*labora-
mus*) amid the remains of our obscurity" (3).

Again, he airs his conviction that some portion of the
heaven of heaven never fell: it "knew no other state" than
blessedness, because "as soon as it was made"—that is, was informed by being "converted"—"without any intervening time,
it was raised up . . . and made light" (11). But again, too, he
speaks of the soul's fall in terms perfectly coordinate with the
fall of the angels. *Defluxit angelus, defluxit anima hominis:*
"the angel flowed downward, man's soul flowed downward."
Had there been no "obedient intelligences in [God's] heavenly
city" which "cleaved to [Him] and found rest in [His] Spirit,"
the entirety of the heaven of heaven would have become a
"darksome deep" (9).

The Gift of God and "Return"

What, then, is the way of "return" to that light? What does
Scripture say? It tells us that God's "spirit was borne over the

waters" (Gen. 1:2) —over them, not borne up by them, as though depending on them. The "waters" signify the "life" of that fallen portion of the spiritual creation, as it "floats about in its own darkness." The text already suggests the Spirit's function will still, as in the early Augustine,[2] be linked with the need of those darkened creatures "to be converted . . . and more and more live by the fountain of life, in his light to see light, be perfected, enlightened, and made happy" (5). For it is said of Him that he is "borne above," an expression recalling the "supereminence" of that knowledge and love of Christ the Spirit brings us when charity is "poured forth into our hearts" (Rom. 5:5), a charity that "lifts us up" from the deep abyss to which the "weight of lust dragged us down." Charity's effect is described as "raising us aloft" from the "places into which we are plunged" by the "filthiness of our spirit flowing downwards with a love that brings but care" (8). This connection between "weight" and "love" is the reason "a sort of place . . . has been affirmed" only of the Spirit, not of either Father or Son. So at least Augustine assures us, and he proceeds to rehearse the ancient-world physical image wherein "by reason of its weight [every] body strives toward its . . . proper place"; only when that proper place in the order of things has been attained does the body naturally come to "rest." In the spiritual order, "my love is my weight. I am borne about by it, wheresoever I am borne," so that, by analogy with the relative weights and consequent "proper places" of the four material elements, "enkindled" by the Spirit's "fire," we "glow with inward fire" and "go upwards" to the rest and "peace of Jerusalem" (10).

Image of the Trinity

Thus is man's being and situation limned in Scripture, if we would but understand it aright. Distinct from God, destined in the Beginning to be soul enlightened, light in his Divine Light, even now the greatness of the "rational creature" is shown forth by the fact that no being less than God can give it rest. All abundance that is not God is but want (9). This is the deepest depth of that *grande profundum, homo.* His being, knowing, and willing still manifest the unity-in-distinction that testify he is made to the "image" of the Trinity itself (12), Father Son and Spirit, present for those who will understand, in

2. *Sol* I, 3 (*Deus per quem accepimus . . . a quo admonemur* etc.) assigns to the Holy Spirit all these functions touching the return of the soul. See *Augustine's Early Theory,* Chap. 7, pp. 197–199.

the first verses of Genesis (6) , and in whose triadic name we
are baptized as first step of our return (13) . "In his image": no
longer can Manichees scoff that this would endow God with ears
and nose and hair. The Platonist, too, can see that he need but
correct the subordination in his Trinity, eliminate all hints of
the soul's consubstantiality with God, and all pretended differences with Scripture have, on this central issue, vanished.

"RETURN" AND THE SECOND CREATION

Now Augustine sets about presenting a fuller view of that
economy of the fallen soul's "return." For this also is spoken of
in Genesis, prophetically: not only the first, but the second, the
new creation in Christ, is the burden of the *Hexaemeron.*
Augustine will devote the major portion of Book XIII to eliciting from the text a figured description of the means God has set
afoot to bring the fallen soul "back" to Him.

Why does he vault over the subsequent verses of the
Hexaemeron—he has interpreted only the first three verses—in
order now to take up at the beginning with a "prophetic" interpretation? Perhaps because he thought the literal sense of the
rest was perfectly obvious. Or was it because he might find
certain of Scripture's sayings somewhat difficult to square with
the view of man he is proposing, God's blessing placed on the
marriage act, for one? Whatever the reason for his having left
them to one side, it is certain that he has avoided some of the
scriptural affirmations which most solidly attest to man's having
been conceived, from the very beginning, as incarnate person
rather than as "fallen soul."

In any event, Augustine assures us that God in this "second" creation started by making "heaven and earth," the spiritual and carnal" parts of His Church. "Let there be Light," He
said, and through the Spirit "borne over the waters" of our
sinful abyss, the Incarnation was accomplished, the "mountain
equal to [God]" was "made small in our behalf," and the light
of the Word shone through flesh for our conversion (13) .

Carnal and Spiritual Christians

But that conversion to Christ brings us only to the initial
stage of our return. Even Paul confesses to being thereby saved
only "in hope." He groans, reaches out to "the things that are
before," calls to "the lower deep"—souls still carnal in their

understanding of Christianity—to "be reformed in the newness of [their] mind," be no longer "children in mind," but grow, as we shall see, to the spiritual understanding of salvation Augustine is about to show is Scripture's message.

For Paul is not only zealous, he is fearful for that "other deep" of carnal-minded Christians, fearful "lest as the serpent deceived Eve by his guile" so they too might allow their "minds" to be corrupted from "chastity." "Chastity" here, like the "continence" which functioned as its synonym earlier, purifies our love until it settles for nothing less than contemplative return to the "light of beauty" our souls aspire "to see," not with the eyes of flesh or even of faith, but with the spiritual eye which will see him "as He is" (14).

In this way, therefore, God has already set about "separating the light" of the saved "from the darkness" of the damned (cf. Gen. 1:4). It is not for us, however, at this stage at least, but for Him alone to distinguish between the two "on this pilgrimage," calling "light day, and darkness night" (15; cf. Gen. 1:5).

"Let there be a firmament" (Gen. 1:6), that is, a "firmament of authority" in the form of Scriptures, those "heavens [that] shall be folded together like a book" at the end of times, but now are "stretched over us like a skin." But ever since God "clothed men with skins" in Eden, skin is the sign of mortality. This puts Augustine in mind of those dispensers of the divine word who have sealed their witness with their deaths, and thereby "extended" the authority of Scriptures over all the earth (16).

The Function of Authority

But the regime of authority, be it scriptural or otherwise, is a provisional one, "giving wisdom to the little ones" and prompting God's praise from "babes and sucklings" (17). The words of Scripture are, like "clouds" against the face of heaven, God's Word "under the dark figure of the clouds and in the mirror of the heavens" (18). Luminous they are with heaven's light, yet half-concealing it as well, as words and signs of every sort inevitably do. One must be humble enough to take this initial approach to eventual vision (17) and still keep one's aim high, one's aspirations directed to those "other waters above this firmament," that God placed "between the waters" as a "division" between them (Gen. 1:6). The waters above that firmament signify the "supercelestial peoples" who have "no need to look up to this firmament" of Scripture, nor "by reading to know your Word." Unfallen, reminders to us of what will be when we too have been liberated from this world of body, time, and symbolic communication, "they always behold [God's] face," reading "without any syllables of time," the "book [that is] never closed," God's own immutable Word which "shall not pass away" but "endures forever." Like the words of God's Son who "looked through the lattice of the flesh" and spoke to arouse our love, the whole regime of Scripture, body, time, and symbol, will at the last be "folded up," and only the Eternal Word remain, seen face to face. "We shall be like Him, because we shall see Him as He is" (18), "in [His] Light we shall see Light" (19).

Action of Men among Men

Then God said: "Let the waters below the heavens be gathered together into one place so that the dry land may appear" (Gen. 1:9). In reference to the second creation, the sea-waters represent the "embittered" against God, the denizens of the "city of man" whose end is "temporal and earthly happiness." The "gathering" action is God's, restraining their lusts, fixing limits on them, and thereby constituting them a "sea," a "society" (cf. Gen. 1:10).

But this very act of "gathering" creates a boundary distinguishing the "sea" from the "dry land," the "earth" which "thirsts" after God. Under these conditions "the earth may bring forth its fruit" (cf. Gen. 1:11), the faithful may, in obedience to God's command, "germinate works of mercy." It should be observed, though, that each performs those works of mercy "according to its kind": love of neighbor and relief of "bodily necessities" are proportioned to the "likeness" men in their "earthly" state bear to one another (20–21).

But "let there be lights made in the firmament" (Gen. 1:14). Those works of mercy and mutual human assistance are "the lower fruit of action." Our business is to "pass" from them "to the delights of contemplation" and in that process "appear like lights in the world," capable of distinguishing between "intelligible and sensible things," or (at least in general terms) between two classes of souls, those "dedicated to intelligible things" and those "given over to the things of sense." Now, "not only [God] in [His] hidden judgment," but his "spiritual children also" are "with [His] grace" equipped to "distinguish between light and darkness"—in Genesis' terms, "separate the day from night" (22). But Augustine will shortly return to this power to distinguish carnal from spiritual souls, and in terms far more precise than here.

Wisdom and Knowledge

And so God made, in the second creation also, "two great luminaries, the greater luminary to rule the day, and the smaller one to rule the night—and the stars also" (cf. Gen. 1:16). The Saint assures us that the diversity of the Spirit's gifts to which St. Paul alludes is here foretold in Genesis. The "word of wisdom" Augustine equates with "the greater luminary," and describes it in terms of the "delight" some have "in the light of manifest Truth."

Paul's "word of knowledge," on the other hand, becomes a "lesser light," while the "stars" symbolize the gifts of faith, healing, miracles, prophecy, discernment of spirits, and finally, the gift of speaking with tongues. All these, however "profitable" they may be, are given to "rule the night." Their profit is directed toward those whom Paul referred to as "carnal" men, those "babes in Christ," "drinkers of milk," not strong enough for "solid food." They are incapable of steadying their eye "so as to look at the sun," the Sun, we may safely presume, of that "manifest Truth" for whose vision only the "wise" are fitted. The night of these "little ones" is not entirely bereft of light, Augustine notes, but their gifts remain "lesser" when compared with the "brightness of wisdom" (23).

From Action to Contemplation

But how does one pass from the lower stage of "action" to the "wisdom" of the contemplative manner of life? The parable of the rich young man reminds us one must first pass *through* the lower stage. But then, to cut the final moorings to the earthly manner of existence, one must do as Augustine himself found necessary: "root up all . . . covetousness," all the "thorns" of temporal cares that choke the word, set one's heart on "treasure in heaven" and become "comrade of those among whom He speaks wisdom" (24). "Shine in the firmament," Augustine urges us, "making division between day and night" as only "perfect," that is, spiritually mature, contemplative

Christians can. These are, admittedly, "not yet like the angels," but only "not yet." They are the "lights in the heaven" symbolized by the "tongues of fire" at Pentecost, the Lord's lights sent as witnesses to all nations (25).

The Regime of "Sacrament"

Then God said: "Let the waters bring forth the creeping creatures having life (*reptilia animarum vivarum*) and the fowls (*volatilia*) flying over the earth beneath the firmament of heaven." And so it was. God created the great sea-monsters (*coetos magnos*) and all the various kinds of creeping creatures having life (*omnem animam animalium repentium*) which the waters brought forth, each according to its kind, and every winged flying creature (Gen. 1:20–21).

The "creeping creatures having life" Augustine likens to the sacraments (*mysteria*) which, through the instrumentality of God's saints, have "crept amid the waves of the world's temptations, to imbue the nations with [His] name in baptism." Sea-monsters, like "whales," symbolize the great "wonders" wrought by God's messengers, but among their wonders must also be listed the "voices," that is, the varied "speeches" and "languages" in which they spoke, as they flew like "winged creatures" with a "sound gone forth into all the earth" (26).

How is it that the "sea," thus far the symbol of sinful, fallen humanity, could bring these forth? The waters did bring forth these things, but "in [God's] Word"; the "needs of people alienated" from Eternal Truth have "brought them forth," but "in [God's] Gospel." The "bitter disease" of these waters caused them to come forth—but to come forth "in [God's] Word" (27).

"For by your blessing, O Lord, you multiplied them" (cf. Gen. 1:22), making them come forth even from the embittered waters of sinful humanity. But "If Adam had not fallen away from" God, there would have been no "people alienated" from Eternal Truth to need such corporeal sacraments and miracles. "From his reins there would not have flowed that salt sea water, the human race," active, stormy, and "restlessly flowing." The unfallen spirit—contemplative, peaceful, and partaking of God's eternity—would have had no need for "mystical deeds and words" of this sort (28). Again, the whole economy of symbol, sacrament, miracle, and scripture, is linked to the fact that the children of Adam are fallen souls, needing to be "consoled for the weakness" of having to seek truth through "mortal senses"

(27). Augustine assigned this meaning to Adam's curse in the *De Genesi contra Manichaeos*.[3] He must "labor" for the "bread" of supernal Truth through the thickets of sense and symbol. That meaning has held firm; but more than that, the suggestion is growing more and more overt that we, laboring under the same curse, are somehow mysteriously identical with our father, Adam.

From Sacrament to Reality

That allusion to the fallen condition brings once more a reminder of how upward progress must be made. The "soul" at first is "subject to corporeal rites" on account of the fall. It needs to be "instructed and initiated by such signs," but the way of progress demands that it pass beyond this stage, "begin to live spiritually upon another plane, and after words of admission, look forward to their consummation" (28). That consummation, as we have seen and will see again, implies liberation from this entire economy of sense and symbol, arrival at vision of the "single thing" that is "pictured and expressed in many ways by bodily motions" (27), the "manifest Truth."

The "Pure of Heart"

The passage to a higher, "spiritual" form of the Christian life, is insinuated in the following verse of Genesis. In it the "earth" was commanded to bring forth the "living soul" (*animam vivam*); so Augustine's translation apparently read (Gen. 1:24). The "living soul" figures the baptized believers, who have gone beyond the unbeliever's need of "signs and wonders" and "tongues." They no longer even need the "flying fowl," the gospel messengers whose task is to "narrate God's works." Now God Himself "works in them." The messenger's function consists in "sending [God's own] Word" into the "earth." The earth must itself then "labor" to "produce," which in this case means to become, a "living soul" (29).

At first, Augustine may seem to be suggesting that the Christian at this stage has gone beyond the need of sacraments and signs of any sort whatever. The "living soul," one might infer, depends no longer on "creeping creatures" and "fowls."

---

3. *Gen Man* II, 30; see *Augustine's Early Theory*, Chap. 6, pp. 161–166. Gibb and Montgomery (p. 428) rightly note that "Adam" is used more "generically" than "personally" here; compare my earlier suggestion, Chap. XII, n. 5, above.

There may, indeed, be some salutary hesitation on his own part as to what he means, for the Christian experience must have taught him something of the perennial value of the sacramental economy, even for the most advanced believer. His theory would have him say—and he does say—that the Evangelists begin their gospels with the exhortation to "repent and be converted" because they are speaking to the unbeliever. It may be, however, that he implies a certain residue of unbelief even in the "earth" becoming a "living soul"; this would account for their still benefiting from the "exhortation and blessing" the gospel messengers impart. In any event, this much is clear: those "flying creatures," though originally "offspring of the sea," still are "'multiplied upon the earth," and even the "earth" engages in the sacramental eucharistic rite of "feeding upon the Fish" drawn from the sea.

But even if Augustine means to admit that certain residue of unbelief, and a consequent dependence on the sacramental economy, these are not the features that properly characterize the "earth" on its way to becoming "living soul." Rather than urging them to conversion and repentance, the gospel messengers far more frequently encourage and bless them. For they have taken their beginning now, not from the embittered waters of infidelity, but from the "earth." Their special virtue now is a "continence" which keeps them from "the love of this world" and of its "death-bringing pleasures" and makes their soul "live to God," seeking only the "life-bringing pleasures of the pure of heart" (29).

The gospel "ministers" should therefore adapt their approach. At the stage to which these souls have progressed, "preaching and speaking through miracles and sacraments and mystic words" is no longer appropriate. The minister should strive, rather, to be a "pattern to the faithful," by "living before them and by arousing them to imitation," stimulating them to "seek God." His conduct should incite the believers "not to be conformed to this world" but to "keep [themselves] from it." And, predictably, this transfer of loves will be accomplished by "keeping clean" of the triadic sin: of pride, sensuality, and the "curiosity" which parades under the "false name of knowledge." For these were the "motions" which caused the soul to fall "by forsaking the fountain of life," God's own Eternal "Word," to be "taken up by the passing world" of time to the extent of being "conformed to it" (30).

This "departure" of the fallen soul has been "restrained by

[God's] Word" telling it to be no longer "conformed to this world," but to become "a soul continent in [God's] word." That "continence" requires that "reason" keep under its "obedience" the lower progeny of the "earth" spoken of in Genesis, the wild beasts signifying the "monstrous savagery of pride," the domestic "cattle" signifying "lustful delight," and the "serpents" figuring "poisonous curiosity." The "continence" proper to the earth becoming a living soul will issue, accordingly, in meekness, self-restraint, and the wisdom to search "only so far into temporal nature as suffices for eternity to be 'clearly seen, being understood by the things that are made'" (31).

Imitation of God Himself

A certain measure of imitation, therefore, each "according to its kind"—imitation of men who are themselves "imitators of . . . Christ"—is appropriate to this stage (31). But it becomes quickly apparent that such imitation must soon yield to another type of "conformity." For in Genesis (1:26) we are reminded that God made man, not "according to his kind," but to His own "image and likeness." This means that "by living well" the soul will in time have "begun to exist." It will, we may assume, achieve that power of contemplative unity with God that eventually will result in its fully "existing," partaking of God's own eternity by "cleaving to Him." As soon as such progress begins to show, the soul is urged to "be reformed in the newness of [its] mind." No longer must it be content with imitating the "neighbor who goes on before . . . living according to the example of some better man." It must conform itself to nothing less than the supernal Truth its developed power of contemplation has permitted it to glimpse, enjoy, and embrace.

Augustine finds the same message in St. Paul. As God's "dispenser," he begot "children in the gospel," but he would not "keep them as babes, whom he would have to nourish with milk and cherish as a nurse"—echoes of the *fovere*-image. No, he urged them to be "reformed in the newness of [their] mind" so that they might "prove" (Augustine adds a significantly unbiblical "for themselves") "what is God's will," good, acceptable, the "perfect thing." To be "renewed in mind" means the Christian now "perceives your Truth that he has understood." Having passed from the stage of simple, childlike faith to this measure of understanding, "he does not need a man to point∠

the way so that he may imitate his own kind." By God's own
"direction" now, "he himself establishes what is [His] will."
Now become "capable of receiving it," he is taught to "see" the
Trinity-in-unity which is insinuated in the very way Genesis'
expressions shift from plural form (Let *us* make man to *our*
image) to singular (God made man . . . to the image of
God). "Being made spiritual," therefore, man is "renewed unto
knowledge of God, according to the image of him who created
him." He has reached the stage where he " 'judges all things,'
that is, all things that are to be judged, but 'he himself is judged
by no man' " (32).

The Spiritual Man's Judgment

This power to "judge all things" is what Genesis prefigures
in according to man "dominion" over fishes, fowls, beasts, and
creeping things, "the whole earth" (Gen. 1:26). The soul exer-
cises its dominion "by the mind's understanding, through which
it 'perceives the things that are of the spirit of God.' " For
Augustine, the term "judgment" is regularly used, and is here
being used, in the sense of "approving" or "disapproving" by
comparison with some norm (cf. 34). And the power to "judge
spiritually" is not confined to those in God's Church, the hierarchy of jurisdiction who "preside spiritually"; it extends as
well to those who "spiritually are subject to those in authority."
For this is the prophetic meaning of the passage in Genesis that
God made man "male and female": just as "there is neither
Jew nor Greek, neither slave nor freeman," so (as Augustine
previously exemplified in Monica) "as to bodily sex," there is
"neither male or female" in the second, "spiritual" creation.

What does this power to "judge spiritually" imply? Augustine answers that question by enumerating the objects to which
it does and does not extend. The underlying principle governing that enumeration seems to be that the soul can judge nothing "above" its station, but everything "below" it. It cannot, for
example, judge the "forms of spiritual knowledge" because of
their "sublime authority." Those forms of understanding are
clearly, as Solignac has suggested,[4] the *rationes aeternales,*
intelligible principles in the light of which Augustine earlier
informed us (VII, 23) he passed judgment on the various
grades of created beauties. The crucial axiom in that particular
instance was that the unchangeable is superior to the changeable. Such intelligible truths act as the norms of judgment and

4. *BA* 14, p. 631.

never themselves become the object of judgment. The mind must accept, consent to them, and then judge all "inferior" realities in their light.

But Augustine remains confident that those "forms of spiritual knowledge" coincide in intelligible content with what "God's book"—properly understood—conveys to the matured soul. Hence we must "submit our minds" also to what the "book" contains. Even those things in it that are "closed to our sight" we must hold to be "rightly and truly spoken," thus becoming "doers," not "judges" of the Law which here, as in Book XI, is God's Eternal Word, Son, and Logos of all that is.

That Eternal Logos above the soul determines, as we have already seen, all that occurs in time, including the predestination of those God intends to be saved and damned. This superiority of the Logos would seem to be the reason it lies outside the scope of the soul's judgment to discern, within the Church, those who will prove to have been "spiritual men" from those destined to remain forever "carnal." And for the same reason, among "those who are without" the Church, the soul cannot tell which will come into God's "sweet grace," and which remain in the "everlasting bitterness of impiety" (33).

What, then, does the spiritual man "judge"? His dominion, Augustine has previously noted, extends to the "whole" of what Genesis (as he interprets it) symbolizes by the term "earth"— to fishes, flying creatures, beasts, and creeping things, in short, to all those features of the salvation-economy that belong to the sensible, corporeal order. Having risen above that sensible order, he has all of it now under his sway. Thus, "subject" always to the "authority of [God's] book," he is empowered to approve or disapprove of all the "signs and utterances of words" the Church employs, of the way the sacraments are administered (baptism and the Eucharist particularly), of the sensibly observable "deeds and habits of the faithful" as well as of their "meditations on things perceived by the bodily senses." Having passed to the higher stage of contemplation, he may judge all that pertains to the "living soul" still engaged in the lower life of action: the life of "earth bringing forth fruit" in works of mercy, fasting, almsgiving, and the like.

The Spiritual and the Hierarchic Church

All of this, it must be pointed out, the spiritual man does thanks to the stage which, "according to [God's] grace," he has reached in his spiritual development, not in virtue of any

official place that has been accorded him in the hierarchy of the
Church. When it comes to the power, not only of "judging,"
but also of "correcting" (*potestatem corrigendi*, 34) , Augustine
explicitly sets aside any distinction between "those who preside
spiritually" and those who are "subject to those in authority,"
between "those in authority" and "those who obey" (33) . Both
of them exercise the same power of judgment, and precisely in
virtue of their developed "spirituality." The spiritual man can
obviously judge upon actions of the ordained minister, even of
the Bishop, but he himself is "judged by no-one": *a nemine
judicatur* (32) . In terms of the classic problematic of Church-
hierarchical and Church-charismatic, the Plotinian flavor of
Augustine's anthropology commits him squarely to the latter
alternative, to a frankly "spiritual" Church. Or, put more
exactly, the corporate and hierarchic nature of the Christian
body, however vital and important it would seem for those
("carnals") at lower stages, becomes progressively less relevant
to those at higher echelons of spiritual development, until it is
virtually sublimated.[5]

Multiple Signs, One Reality

Now Augustine comes to the blessing God bestowed on the
man and woman, bidding them "increase, and multiply, and fill
the earth." Once again it is well to remember that a literal
interpretation of this text would have compelled him to face the
annoying topic of sexual reproduction. That challenge he has
adroitly side-stepped, and he is now free to give that blessing a
figurative meaning. He does so, in one of the most tortured
pieces of reasoning to be found in the entire *Confessions*, and in

5. To attenuate the "spiritual" nature of Augustine's ecclesiology here,
Solignac (*BA* 14, pp. 633–634) stresses that Augustine locates the "spiritual"
Christian "in" the Church: (*in ecclesia* 33) , as though that term meant what it
means today, particularly for a twentieth-century Roman Catholic: the Christian
body, corporate and hierarchic from top to bottom. But this is exactly what Augustine's entire scheme calls into serious question. Solignac then brings to bear
a text from *Sermo* 4, questions Adalbert Kunzelmann's dating of that sermon
(between the years A.D. 410 and 419) , suggests it *may* have been preached as
early as between A.D. 405 and 410—still some five years after the completion of
the *Confessions*—and interprets this section of Book XIII in the light of what
Augustine says *there*. The procedure is questionable from start to finish. What
it may point up, however, is that when faced with the principle of the "spiritual
church" as concretely embodied in the Donatist heresy, Augustine may have begun having serious second thoughts on the ecclesiology enshrined in Book XIII
of the *Confessions*. And well he might. But the evidence for such second thoughts
here is so slender as to be nonexistent.

the course of his argument even manages to suggest that no literal interpretation of the text is really admissible.

For the interpreter must take into account not only the beneficiaries of this blessing, but those as well on whom it was *not* bestowed. It cannot be "that it was stated" in exactly the way it was "to no purpose" (36). Now were we to insist that the statement was meant to be understood literally, "properly," according to the "actual natures of things," then "the words 'Increase and multiply' would hold for all things that are be-gotten from seed" (37), in which case the same blessing *should* have been accorded to "trees, plants, and beasts of the earth" (35). The Bible does not accord it to them, when, were the blessing to be taken literally, it *should* have. There must be a purpose in Moses' not having done so and that purpose must have been to warn us not to take it literally (36). We are driven therefore to conclude that this is one of the "figurative statements" found in Scriptures (36).

What interpretation, then, must we give to this "figurative statement"? Augustine lets a certain embarrassment show. He once again protests against the opposition he feels his interpre-tation will arouse, yet he refuses to "be silent." Perhaps he does not understand it after all. Let his betters do better with it "according as [God] has given to each of them to understand." Yet it cannot be "in vain" that God has "spoken to [him]" the way He has, on the "occasion of reading" the text of this bless-ing (36).

Now, Augustine cautions, not every figurative interpreta-tion will do. Consider, for instance, the interpretation which would say God's "blessing" to increase and multiply goes out to all instances, both spiritual and corporeal, where "multitudes, fertility, and increase" can be found (37). This interpretation forgets that these three properties are to be found in spiritual and corporeal creatures, just and unjust souls, in the society of the embittered, and so on. Were this the interpretation Moses *meant* us to give this blessing, he would surely have depicted God bestowing it on all the created entities which figure these: on "heaven and earth," "light and darkness," the "waters," and all the rest.

Why then was the same blessing, to "increase and multi-ply," conferred on the animals "brought forth by the waters" and on "man"—on these two, and these two only? It must sug-gest a kind of "increase and multiplication" peculiar to what these befigure, both to fallen souls and to man inasmuch as he is made to God's image, man considered as endowed with reason. Now we are coming closer to the answer. The "generations of the waters," we have already seen (XIII, 29), symbolize fallen souls whose embodiment demands that they communicate through words and symbols. But symbols and words can signify one intelligible reality by a multitude of different bodily expressions, rites, languages, turns of speech (36). The "fecundity of reason" (37) works in the opposite direction. It permits any single statement to be "understood in many ways . . . by various kinds of true interpretations" (36). The blessing therefore refers to the "power and the faculty [which] have been granted to us to express in manifold ways what we understand in but one, and to understand in manifold ways what we read as obscurely uttered in one way" (37).

Gift and Fruit

That hurdle crossed, Augustine girds himself for another. Again, he will "speak out, and have no fear." He obviously feels many will reject his way of interpreting the statement in Genesis that God gave us for food "every herb bearing seed which is upon the whole earth, and every tree that has in itself fruit of its own seed" (Gen. 1:29).

Not only to us was this "food" given, but also to the birds, beasts, and serpents of the "earth." Why not, Augustine asks, to the "fishes and whales" of the sea? The "fruits of the earth," he then reminds us, have already been interpreted as the works of mercy aimed at filling the needs of "this life" in the body. So St. Paul was "fed" by Onesiphorus and by the Philippians, and rejoiced at being fed by them (38). What precisely made him rejoice, however? Paul himself gives us a clue, when he assures the Philippians he sought, "not the gift, but . . . the fruit" (Phil. 5:17). It was not, therefore, the fact that they had filled his bodily needs, for God had taught him how to live in want as well as in abundance. It was not the "gifts" they gave him that made him rejoice. It was the fact that he saw that their giving gave evidence they were "bearing fruit," "doing well," "flourishing again, like a field" which for a time had withered but now was "again producing life" (39–40).

There is, accordingly, a decisive difference between giving "gifts" and bearing "fruit," the difference residing in the "good and right will" (41), the "right and holy will" (42) —the motive for the giving. Only those who know why "bodily refreshment" and all such bodily "aid for the present life" must be given can do their giving with the motivation that makes it "bear fruit" (42).

This, then, is why Scripture omits the "fishes and whales" as recipients of these "fruits of the earth." For fishes and whales now symbolize the dispensers of the initiatory sacraments, the workers of wonders. Their mission is to the "unlearned and unbelievers" who simply cannot have the knowledge required for the motivation which turns gift to fruit (42).

The effort is strenuous; once again Augustine has put all his ingenuity to work. But the result thus far is hardly shocking. The importance of a right intention should not have been such startling news to his readers. Why, then, all the show of embarrassment, the protestations that he will "speak what is true" in God's sight, whatever others may say?

"Right Will" and Soul's "Return"

The reason may lie in what exactly Augustine understands by a "right and holy will." He explains it in quite scriptural terms at first. It means giving to a prophet "in the name of a prophet," to a just man *because* he is a just man, to a disciple precisely *qua* disciple. But what does that, in turn, imply? Augustine's systematic as we have thus far seen it leads us to suspect it may mean that the giving of money, food, lodging, in short anything which is "useful" for the "necessities of this life" in the body, must not be considered as an end in itself. The giving must be accompanied by insight into why such "aid for the present life" is valid and virtuous. What makes it valid is its orientation toward the spiritual progress of both giver and recipient, an orientation that corresponds to the orientation Augustine has already established, whereby the "lower fruits of action" must eventually flower in the "delights of contemplation," the works of mercy flower in the "continence" which "collects" the soul from its scattered, dis-tended state, and returns it from "this life" to the "happy life" it enjoyed before its fall. This passage from action through continence to contemplative union with God corresponds to the spiritual infant's growth from "earth" to a "living soul" thoroughly "renewed in mind," capable of being "nourished" by the spiritual "food of grown men"—of "rejoicing" in the vision of eternal "Truth."

All this we might *expect* Augustine to have in mind, not only from what he has been saying throughout the *Confessions,* but from the way he has been describing the soul's progress in Book XIII. Is there, in the text itself, positive indication that he *does* have all this in mind?

What follows may seem like an Augustinian exegesis of Augustine, but then, there might be no more appropriate field for such an exercise. The summary presented above resumes an involved argument that runs through five numbered paragraphs (38–42) of text. In presenting it, a host of elements were deliberately omitted. They did not of themselves contribute to making what is evidently the main point of the argument, the need of a "right and holy will." But the very fact that so many elements seem superfluous may itself be significant. Are we, Augustine would ask, to conclude that they are put down "to no purpose"?

The purpose for which Augustine put them down, I submit, was to illumine not only *that* a "right and holy will" was needed to validate the active works of mercy, but to insinuate, to those who would "understand," *what* the inner structure of that right intention is: the giver must bear in mind the liminal value of the life of action, intend all bodily benefits to aid the soul's eventual passage from the active to the contemplative life. In any case, were this his presiding intention, he could not have chosen his language more appropriately.

For throughout his argument here he constantly links the works of mercy with the "needs" of "this life," presumably, the life of soul in the "mortal" body. The language of passage to the contemplative life is met at every turn. Paul is evidently one of those who "minister rational doctrine by means of their understanding of the divine mysteries" (38). He is expressly referred to as a "living soul," and "of great continence," a "man," in the sense of Book XIII, "renewed 'unto the knowledge of God, according to [God's] image' " (40). "The mind feeds on that in which it finds joy" (42), Augustine remarks. He tells us Paul is "fed" a food in which he "rejoices," "is nourished upon that in which he rejoices." In the next phrase the Apostle is said to speak "in all truth." Bearing in mind that "truth" is the "food" of such grown-up souls as Paul was, and happiness for Augustine is "joy in the Truth," it is difficult to keep one's suspicions from being aroused. Moreover, Paul tells the Philippians that their "thought" for him has "flourished again" (39). This revival in them of Christian activity betokened that they too were "like a fertile field again producing life"—earth, in the sense of Book

XIII, in "labor" toward producing, or becoming, a "living soul" in the fullest sense, "renewed in mind." Thus, both for Paul and for them, their "gift" bore "fruit" in progress toward that contemplative union with God which, for Augustine, is the perfection of charity.

Surely the only justification for so over-subtle, even precious, a piece of Augustinian interpretation is the supposition that Augustine can himself become both precious and over-subtle, in the present instance on the grounds of attributing those same qualities to the Moses whose words he is interpreting. One has to admit, if all we had of his works was Book XIII of the *Confessions,* his own claim upon those qualities would be secure.

IMAGE ABSORBED IN ARCHETYPE

Loving God "in" All Creatures

"And you, O God, saw all the things that you had made, and behold, 'they were very good.' " So Augustine comes to the final comment in Genesis on God's creative activity: having pronounced each part good in itself, now God "sees" that the harmonious assemblage of all created beings is "very good" (43).

The phrase was calculated to make a Manichee chortle. Here was God exclaiming with wonder over something He had "learned," as though He had not known it previously. Seven times He pronounces each successive stage of creation "good." And now, this eighth expression of appreciation: surely this implied that God Himself was involved in time? The Manichees are, in fact, very much on Augustine's mind as he finishes his interpretation of Genesis. A few paragraphs later, he will refute their "insane" opinion that the beings "in the lower portions of the world" are products of a "hostile intelligence, different in nature" from God (45). Not evil, these beings are not good in the sense that man should consent to "enjoy creation rather than [God]." And still, God Himself should be "loved in that which he has made": *ut ille ametur in eo, quod fecit* (46).

The phrase has an unsettling ring. God has been made present, not "to," but "in" all things. Augustine seemed about to correct any misapprehensions such expressions may cause. The Eternal God must not be made subject to time. In the case of these successive appreciations of creation, for example, it is Scripture which "speaks in time," whereas time does not "affect God's Word."

Yet how understand the fact that Scripture's words say what God's Eternal Word expresses also? The problem of relating the Eternal and the temporal cannot be solved merely by setting them off one against the other. The final portion of the *Confessions* shows Augustine boldly trying to suggest how they relate positively to one another. That effort will bring him to pursue one side of the omnipresence insight to some of its most radical, and frightening, corollaries. He has always been very careful that the Eternal not become temporalized. Now, however, the temporal is in serious danger of being swallowed up in the Eternal.

He first interprets the statement in Scripture that God "sees" creation is "good" as meaning that "we," through His Spirit, "see" creation that way (45). But this expression is immediately balanced by another: "when men see these things through [God's] Spirit, [God] *sees in them*" (*tu vides in eis*). God then has become the "seer" in all our "seeing." A moment later, He becomes the "seen" as well: "whatsoever things are pleasing because of You, You Yourself are pleasing." Not content with that, Augustine makes his statement even stronger: "It is rightly said to those who know in the Spirit of God, 'It is not you who know,'" and "to those who see in the Spirit of God, 'It is not you who see' . . . but God who 'sees that it is good'" (46). Here our human agency seems to have vanished altogether. God has become the only actor on the scene. The distinction of Creator and creature has, it would seem, been effectively canceled.

Again, Emanation and Omnipresence

We have seen how the Saint regularly corrects such unilateral statements by shifting out of the omnipresence mode of thought into the emanation mode which makes it easier to envisage levels and distinctions in the real, makes it possible to conceive of soul not only as distinct from God but "fallen" into the world of bodies. But because he never seems to have squarely confronted the problems involved in synthesizing these two modes of thought (if, indeed, they can be synthesized at all), it may have been inevitable that now the one, now the other, succeeded in gaining their secret vengeance on him.

When thinking out the fall, the emanation style of thought regularly has the last word. Even here, in the finale of the *Confessions,* it is not entirely absent. Creation's ascending grades of being, and radical distinction from God, is implicit in the injunction that no creature must replace God as object of the soul's "enjoyment" *(frui)* ; they are all for "use" like rungs of a ladder which serve toward arrival at the highest. So too, the principle of "ordered love" *(ordo amoris)* is what presides over the entire process of the second creation. Its purpose is to restore the original order: lower subject to higher, material to spiritual, the active appetite represented by "woman" become subject again to the rule of the masculine "reason" (47). This order a timeless Providence is progressively reinstating amid the disordered things of time. Scripture, the Incarnation, the Church, sacraments, and miracles all conspire to form "living souls" of the "earth" we have, through the fall, become, to "renew us in mind," make the soul's "rational actions" once more "subject to the primatial intellect, as woman is to man" (49)—in short, to lead us back from the feverish actions of time to the eternal sabbath rest of joyful contemplation.

But then, the rightful conclusion should be that we shall become "light in His Light," never Light Itself. So strong is the grip of omnipresence thought upon him now, however, Augustine presents a sketch of how the hierarchic strata of the visible world mystically prefigure the second creation in Christ, only to conclude roundly that "we see all these things" as "very good" because God Himself "sees them" in our seeing of them (49).

A similar unilateral use of omnipresence insights governs the final meditation on the mention in Genesis of the Sabbath rest. This is, of course, a prophecy of the "rest" and "peace" to follow when all the "things that are very good," their temporal measures finally accomplished, eventually "pass away" (50). We also, "after our works" which God has "given" to us, "will rest in [Him] on the sabbath of eternal life" (51). This, put in denser fashion, means that God Himself, Who is "forever at rest," indeed, is identical with His own "rest," will "rest in us, even as now [He] works in us" and "through us" (52).

But then, what is left of that "us"? Is it our very selves, or only our temporality which is destined to "pass away" in the final return of all to God?

It would be tempting to resolve this problem in the way similar problems of Augustinian interpretation are so often resolved: by brushing it away as a momentary extravagance of

language. He is in the grip of an exegetical difficulty and has
found an inviting way out. His words ought not be taken so
literally as I am taking them. Besides, his mind is very probably
dominated by descriptions of the eschatological consummation
such as St. Paul's allusions to the figure of this world "passing
away," and God becoming "all in all." Why push the matter
further?

The matter must be pushed because the language used
here recalls too forcibly language used in earlier books of the
Confessions, language which emerges from deeper layers of
Augustine's theology than may at first sight seem to be the case.
Who, for example, fed the infant Augustine? Not his nurses.
The milk came "through" them, if you will, but *tu mihi per eas
dabas:* God was the true "giver" (I, 7). When Monica, his
dying friend, and Ambrose all "unknowing" admonished him,
the warning reminder came from God Himself. *Tu egisti, tu
fecisti, tu!* Well may Augustine complain that the Manichees
confuse God and creature. He seems also to have been alert
enough to see when the omnipresence insight, driven to what
might seem its logical conclusion, tended in Plotinus' thought
to obliterate all meaningful distinction between God and creature.[6] But there are times when the drive of that same insight
seems to have impelled him to something very like what he has
rightly censured in his adversaries, times when the creature's
substantiality is volatilized, the shimmering veil of created
realities is suddenly parted, and the "un-knower" become
"knower" sees exactly what Plotinus claimed he would: that in
all that is or comes to pass, God is the one true reality, seer and
seen, designer and actor.

This may be the ultimate metaphysical reason the
"weights" which are our loves can coincide perfectly with the
"goads" whereby God's eternal plan works out in us, the reason
we choose internally what He would have us choose, the reason
our wills seem radically at one with the Logos which eternally
rules all passing times, so that what God predestines is inexorably accomplished. One wonders if there is any genuine place in
such a scheme of thought for that autonomy of human will
whereby its actions are, in a true sense, its own. That Augustine
wished to find place for freedom is one thing; whether his
metaphysic *allows* of it is another question. Our merits, he
never tires of saying, are God's gifts. But then, are they truly
"merits" after all? If God be both seer and seen in all things,

6. See *Augustine's Early Theory,* Chap. 3, pp. 87–111.

lover and loved, how is a wrongly directed love even thinkable? If it is God who works "in" and "through" us, what do *we* do? When Augustine goes to great lengths to prove that the will's "turning away" is at bottom a "nothing" (*Lib* II, 53; cf. *Conf* XII, 11), has he truly solved this problem, or quite frankly acquiesced in the logic of a position which accords the creature no genuinely positive contribution of its own?

If the interpretation presented here is at all accurate, then the second of these alternatives is the only choice: creaturely activity, including man's free action, has in the end been swallowed up in God's unique activity. But then, a serious difficulty must be dealt with. Augustine would hardly have wanted this to happen, would very likely have been most uncomfortable on realizing that his metaphysics had brought him to such an impasse. It could only have occurred, then, contrary to his daylight intentions. The process that led him to such formulations must have been a dark and sinuous one, following a logic he was unable to dominate with full lucidity. What could that process have been?

Route to an Impasse

It would, first of all, oversimplify matters to explain that process as a direct outgrowth of those features in Plotinus' omnipresence thinking which momentarily encouraged the evaporation of all limited beings into the All. When dealing with those precise features of Plotinus' thought, in fact, Augustine exhibits a wariness which does him credit. The evidence suggests that here he finds Plotinus guilty of what he terms "idolatry." [7] A brief recall of how he puts *Ennead* VI, 4–5 to use will show that.

One of the slight anomalies in that treatise was Plotinus' resort, at crucial junctures, to the Stoic *Pan:* the "All." He keeps firmly in mind throughout most of his treatise—speaking in terms of classic Platonic notions such as the Ideas and the Soul seems to have kept him alert—that bald identification of "Being" in the Platonic sense with the "All" in the Stoic sense would abolish the transcendence of "Being" and thereby make the Omnipresent as extended as the "All"—present not integrally, but part-for-part. The thesis of integral omnipresence he is arguing for requires the transcendence of the Omnipresent. If it is to defy the ordinary corporeal mode of presence part-by-

7. *Ibid.*, pp. 99–109.

part, it must be a Being of another order entirely. Again and again Augustine shows unmistakable evidence of having grasped that need of keeping God transcendent, distinct from the world "to" which, rather than "in" which, He is present.

Only when Plotinus slides into the Stoic vocabulary and speaks of the "All" as everywhere present does he lose something of his sureness of touch. Then we are assured that did he know his true situation a man would see "at once God, himself, and the All." Once "we find no stop at which to declare a limit to our being we cease to rule ourselves out from the totality of reality" (*Enn* VI, 5, 7). "In that you have entered the All, no longer content with the part" you may be convinced you have attained to the Omnipresent. "You cease to think of yourself as under limit but, laying all such determination aside, you become an All." One must "put away" the "non-Being" whose admixture accounts for that limitation which defines him off from the All (VI, 5, 12).

All too close to the surface here is the logic of thinking about God and "creation" on the lines of the part-whole relation. Elimination of the barrier between individual and God then requires elimination of limit, stop, determination, part-icularity, and results in the individual's re-absorption in the All.

But these two loci where Plotinus' expressions seem to verge on "outspoken pantheism" are hardly typical of his omnipresence doctrine. We have seen evidence to suggest that Augustine was alert to their implicits, and categorically rejected the radical identification of soul and God they would imply. It is remarkable how, on the whole, the Saint has avoided the pitfalls of this part-whole kind of thinking, at least in the *Confessions*. He avoided it, that is, when *directly* engaged in thinking out the corollaries of omnipresence theory. Plotinus' more characteristic insistence on transcendence, his earlier animus against the Stoics, coupled with Augustine's own rejection of the Manichee view of soul as "part" of God—all these were factors calculated to caution him against a part-whole line of thought. Only once, to my knowledge, does the *Confessions* come close to portraying the soul as having left the "whole" and fallen into possession of the "part" (III, 16), and even there, Augustine stops well short of saying it. Far more normally, the "whole" Augustine refers to is the visible, sensible "universe" which, from the various contexts, is clearly distinct from God. The part-whole dialectic, then, when used, does not expressly refer to God as the "whole" in question.

How, then, understand that when thinking out the omni-presence relation itself, Augustine so regularly respects the distinction of creature and Creator, whereas a whole array of expressions argues that, in other contexts, his usual balance may have deserted him?

A careful review of those contexts may suggest an answer. Admonitions, nurses' care, "goads" and weights, and the way they operate in our turning-away-from or turning-back-toward God—the common characteristic of them all is that they express how Eternal Providence (God's Logos or Law) acts through and "in" the actions of all temporal realities. And in all cases, Providence is envisaged as—not only omnipresent, but—quite literally "omnipresence."

The last of those features, the "omnipresence" character of Providence, points once again to the importance that doctrine had for Augustine's thinking. He has thought out all of Plotinus' other treatises in terms of, through the lens of, *Ennead* VI, 4–5. More crucial, perhaps, he has allowed that insight to saturate his powerful artistic imagination which, I have more than once suggested, is far more active than his theory of soul could have countenanced.

But the idea of Providence, especially when held, as Augustine and Plotinus hold it to be, universal—extending to every mouse that runs or leaf that falls in the night—requires that both of them explain how the actions of all temporal beings can coincide in some mysterious fashion with the Logos that rules their every action. That problem the imagination too readily translates into its own terms. How can the Eternal be envisaged as acting "in and through" all things of time?

The "things of time": the fact that our sense-experience deals with changing temporal realities introduces a further complication. Coming to be, flowing onward, and passing away, all temporal realities are, in the Plotinian scheme, mere "images," half-real when compared with the only "True" reality. This doctrine, when combined (especially in imagination) with the notion of an immanent Divine Logos, an Eternal become present "in" them, only serves to accent their insubstantiality, their "transparency" to the Divine working "in" and "through" them.

The result: temporal realities come to be conceptualized, or, more accurately, imagined, as a kind of "mask" for the Divine ingredient in them. This permits Augustine to picture the sinner trying to flee "away," but succeeding only in fleeing always "toward" God, but a God Who is angry now instead of being kindly. In all his punishments he unwittingly "finds" God's omnipresent "Law" (IV, 14). Blind, sinners do not "know" that on all the "rugged ways" they travel they encounter God, "stumble upon [Him]," "stumbling," that is, "upon [His] righteousness, and falling upon [His] severity" (V, 2).

The imagination now has placed God as the True Reality to be uncovered "in" things. Only one more step is needed to reinforce the process. The Divine Logos has ordained that passing, temporal realities all have their being "From here, unto there": *hinc, et huc usque* (IV, 15). Each of them is part of the visible, temporal Whole. The phrase recalls Plotinus' "limit to our being," as resulting from our alienation from the All. Augustine has himself described the soul's punishment as confining it to a similar "particularity" (IV, 15–17; cf. I, 3), its "return" as enabling it to see the "whole" again (IV, 15–17 and XII, 16). That "whole," however, hovers uncertainly between the visible and intelligible worlds. It seems, in fact, to be the reality that the visible world will have when all its temporal measures shall have passed away. And one more imaginative circuit has been set up whereby the Whole, in Augustine's metaphysical imagery, threatens to become identified with God as present "in" things of time; one more impulse has been added to the undercurrent dynamism whereby the "particularity" of temporal beings is in danger of being viewed as the decisive feature discriminating them from God. If, accordingly, their "temporality" were to "pass away," the temptation is to think of them as being re-absorbed into the One, True, Eternal Reality.

God, All in All

The final sections of the *Confessions* show that Augustine was far from immune to that temptation. The foregoing examination of his sensitivity to the various strands in Plotinian thinking is intended to show, not *that* he succumbed to it, but *how* that evident capitulation can be accounted for. If that explanation is the right one, the factors that made for Augustine's eventual capitulation were pursuing their subterranean labor long before he came up against the problem of explaining our "Sabbath rest" in God as God's eternal rest "in us." It may not be entirely clear what St. Paul meant by saying that in the end God would be "all in all." It is all too clear what Augustine came to mean by it—clear, and profoundly disturbing. I have tried to reconstruct the process through which he very likely came to say what he says, and thought himself entitled, indeed, compelled to say it. That reconstruction represents a final reason for asking whether he has not, as much if not more than Plotinus, welded together in his theory of man a set of internal tensions which at the last run up against an "undeniable contradiction." [8] He has given us, I suggest, far less a synthesis than a dexterous juxtaposition of basically divergent orientations of mind.

He seems to have been vaguely conscious that his reader would be baffled by this closing set of radical affirmations. His final questions betray a reticent admission. He has led us, in the quest for knowledge of the human situation, as far as he can. "What man will give it to a man to understand this? . . . What angel to a man?" He must now content himself with merely "pointing the way" to a vision beyond all that can be seen "through a glass, darkly," beyond all that words and symbols can stammer. His *Confessions* ends with the refrain on which it, and his entire intellectual project, opened:

From you let it be asked, in you let it be sought, at your door let us knock for it. Thus, thus it is received, thus it is found, thus it is opened to us.

8. Emile Bréhier uses this phrase of Plotinus' theory of soul, *La philosophie de Plotin* (Paris, 1928) , p. 68. See "Plotinian Fall," pp. 6–8.

18 CONCLUSION

Augustine, Everyman, Adam. This secret identity governs the subtle development of the *Confessions*, harmonizes its themes, blends them into a symphonic unity, discloses their profoundest sense. A theory of man, indeed; man as Prodigal, lost sheep, soul in odyssey, *peregrinatio*, ambiguous term which can mean either "wandering" or "pilgrimage" depending on the direction of its movement, away from or back to God.

For Adam is "man," archetypal man, or, more precisely, archetypal soul, *ratio*. Created in a *medius locus*, a *media regio salutis*, that contemplative *ratio* was meant to govern the inferior sensible world of time and action—symbolized by "woman," Eve—without any of the difficulty and resistance which we now experience. Human nature as we know it is a state of misery, not to be attributed to God's original design, but to the execution of a penalty which followed inevitably from the intrinsic nature of our primal sin. The proportions of that sin we must acknowledge before we can adequately "confess" our fault, the greatness of God's tireless mercy toward us, the marvels of His work both in and through us, the omnipresence of His providence which, like a faithful mother, refuses to desert the child that has deserted her.

But how are we to understand that a soul, blissful in the ✔
splendor and repose of eternal contemplation, should "turn
away" to the misery of this life of action? This ultimate
anomaly the Platonist must face, and Augustine with him.

One feature of that answer has been added to the theory of
man enclosed in Augustine's earlier works. He drives it home
laboriously in Book II of the *Confessions*. Without the shame-
less prodding of companions he would never have stolen those
pears when there were better aplenty at home; alone he would
never have perpetrated that senseless act of malice, *iniquitas*.
Nor, he means to suggest, would Alypius have "fallen" to the
lure of *curiositas* which for a time again undid him, had he not
met certain "friends" returning from a banquet, who dragged
him *familiari violentia* to the circus with them (VI, 13).

The mystery of iniquity, then, leads straight to the mystery
of companionship, of the "society of souls" both in the other
world and this. From "heavenly city," we have become an
"earthly city," an embittered sea flowing from the loins of that
Adam *in quo*, St. Paul reminds us (and Augustine translates),
"in whom we have all sinned" (Rom. 5:12).

Here, it would seem, lies the source of man's mysterious
unity with his fellow-men. That unity Augustine was once
tempted to characterize by the term "human society." Despite
the soul's natural equality with the angel, he warned his readers
in the *De Quantitate Animae* (73), the *societas humana* which
issued from its fall must be held in high esteem. He appeals to
the same esteem for the *societas humana* when trying to persuade his friend Honoratus to take the slower route of belief on
the authority of the Catholic Church, despite the fact that his
mind may well be suited for (*idoneus*) pursuing the upward
way to vision without the need of such authority (*Util* 24).

But this was a note not destined to last. The pressure of his
disincarnate view of man soon gets the better of him. Some
short months afterward, in the *De Vera Religione,* he has only
the most searing contempt for all temporal, human relationships. What, then, is left to ground the universal need of sub-
mitting to the Church's care, a need implicit in the fact that
baptism is now decreed as the only portal for the soul's salvation?

That ground is supplied by all men's unity as fallen souls,
indeed, as one soul. At their deepest, they all bear the single
name of Adam. No longer the *societas humana,* now it is the
societas animarum, the kinship of fallen souls "in" Adam,

which would seem to make intelligible the otherwise arbitrary
divine decree which constitutes the Church the universal and
unique way by which souls can make their journey homeward.

But then, if we "sinned" in Adam, we must somehow have
been contained in him; been happy in him with a happiness we
still obscurely recall; been cursed with his curse so that now we
"sweat and labor" for the self-knowledge so necessary to our
return; been, in short, one soul with him in a unity every
friendship dimly figures: *dimidium animae*.

No superficial "carnal" reading of such dark sayings will,
Augustine thinks, disclose the true depths of our human condition. Nor will it fully answer to the Manichee objections. The
easy and obvious assumptions we usually bring to the understanding of our experience need correcting. Only a "spiritual"
exegesis, performed in the light of the Plotinian theory of one
universal soul a portion of which fell from eternity into time,
can illumine that *grande profundum* which is man. But so
attuned is man to the "customary" view which accepts corpo-
reity, language, labor, carnal procreation, and the rest as "natural" and resulting from God's original creative design, that a
patient *exercitatio animi*—long and subtle and difficult—is
needed to invert that view and bring self-awareness to the
"interior man" who was made to "the image of God." The
human condition must be limned in images that suggest, more
and more overtly, the true dimension of our misery. Platonism,
or Christianity? The two, for Augustine, are substantially at
one. The images of both must be made to alternate, then inter-
weave and fuse until their fundamental identity is established—
until Augustine *becomes* the Prodigal, the Prodigal *is* Ulysses in
pilgrimage back to his longed-for *patria,* and Ulysses Adam, a
portion of the "whole soul" fallen into time and body. "All
men" must coalesce in "one man" before we are prepared to see
that the *Hexaemeron* is prophetic history, the history of each
individual soul and of "soul" entire, the key, for those who will
"understand," to the *Confessions* and to Augustine's theory of
man.

That theory, again, strikes the contemporary ear as strange.
A post-Freudian, post-Darwinian century can scarcely be expected to resonate with sympathy to such a view of man. And
yet, have we forgotten how strange it sounded at first to hear
that man was totally creature of this earth, product of its bil-
lions of years of evolution, and not some being half this-
worldly, the other half sprung from and headed back to a spiritual world, "up there" or "out there" as the case may be?

Man's self-image has in the past century changed with remarkable rapidity. But the comfort with which we settle into a twentieth-century image of ourselves should not prevent our crediting the possibility that another age could seriously have entertained a self-image at antipodes from our own.

But, the objection returns in another form, human experience is such that no one, not even a fourth-century man, could ever have viewed his life as meaning what Augustine thought his own to mean. The reader of the *Confessions* finds the notion of his having portrayed his life-experience in terms of so artificial a theory of man difficult to countenance. And yet, there were precedents, Plotinus being one of them, and one of many. The contours of human experience reveal themselves to one who looks at it square, and along its entire spectrum. But who is genuinely capable of this? In all too many instances we wind up seeing what we were looking *for,* and the cues which operate in keying out inspection of experience are legion: adult beliefs, language, reading, all the bewildering variety of implicits that come with living in a certain age, a certain culture.

Of the cues that operated in Augustine's case, a number served to cushion the shock involved in seeing himself the way he did: Manichaeism, the strands of Platonism he would have found in Cicero, Plotinus. Even Ambrose reads at times like a soul, estranged and alienated in the life of body, yearning for a "flight from this world." Year upon year of meditating on his own experience through the lens of Plotinian theory have brought Augustine genuinely to "see" his life that way. There are no grounds for setting the "personal tone" of the *Confessions* over against the "typical" bearing he thought his life embodied, as though the first argued against his having conceived of his life-story as (more or less artificial and didactic) illustration of the second. We must not envisage Augustine sitting down and first outlining a semi-abstract theory of man, then selecting and forming the episodes of his past to fit, and prove, that theory. Granted, his theory of art would argue for some such stiff and stilted process, but if anything follows from what I have tried to show respecting the *fovere*-image that dominates the *Confessions* it is that Augustine was much too great an artist to observe the canons of art his theory set up for him.

I am saying, but now in another register entirely, that there is, after all, a gap between experience and theory in the *Confessions*. The crucial point of breakdown we have seen in a number of instances. His theory cannot do justice to the work of human imagination and sensibility. His polemic against the products of *fantasia* combines with Plotinus' (earlier) insistence on lunging for a vision beyond all reach of sense. The result is a theoretical divorce, quite literally the *Chôrismos* which Aristotle complained of in Platonism, between what we humanly experience "here" and what "truly exists" (in Plotinus' adverb) "There." But some relation must exist between those realms. Augustine wavers between two relations: the first, a stark contrast (that Light was *aliud, aliud valde,* "other, wholly other") ; the second, a relation of image-to-Archetype. In the latter case, at crucial points the temptation catches up with him to "collapse" the reality of the image so that it loses all substantiality, and hence, all intrinsic value. Monica, Ambrose, even Augustine himself, risk becoming pure transparencies through which there streams the Light of the only True Reality, the power of the only genuine agent in the drama, God. The world of creatures, the landscape of human experience, are drained of all intrinsic interest, human life becomes a desert or stormy sea, heaven a haven for the weary soul.

A churning poetic imagination, a stunning gift of artistic conception and organization, a wide-ranging and thoroughly human sensibility, all operating within a theoretical frame which would radically relativize those very endowments—here we have the paradox of the *Confessions,* a paradox which also discloses its peculiar power. For like any poetic masterpiece, it can "communicate" before it is "understood"; its feel for life invades our sensibilities even—perhaps especially—in passages where we cannot confidently conceptualize what Augustine is driving at. It forms our vision, keys our evaluations, leads our affectivity along unsuspected pathways, pathways which, once they have been mapped, we might legitimately prefer to avoid.

Few books have done more than the *Confessions* to shape the sensibility and fashion the subjective world of Western Christianity—to elaborate its mighty images, articulate its religious moods, express its instinctive feeling for life, for man, and for man's historical adventure. We are far from having read the final chapter on its influence. Indeed, the very boldness of the thesis advanced here may be thought to argue strongly against any pretensions it might have to being that last chapter. It may not, though, be too rash to hope that even its errors may fertilize the minds of whatever future students may be drawn to clarifying our understanding of Augustine's towering masterpiece.

INDEX

INDEX

Academics: crypto-Platonism of, 14; Augustine's attraction to, 61; skepticism of, 61, 64, 65

Action, life of, 53, 106, 176; and contemplative life, 68-70, 92-93, 164-166, 175; and fall of soul, 142-144. *See also* Contemplation

Adam, 47, 57-58, 61, 113, 116, 119, 126, 128, 167, 167n, 187, 188; as archetypal soul, 97n, 186; and soul's alienation, 166

Admonition, 31, 38-39, 44, 55, 60, 74, 75-79, 101, 136, 153, 183; and sensible reality, 17; and memory, 39, 124; and omnipresence, 47

All, the, 181-182. *See also* Being

All-Soul, *see* Soul, Divinity of

Alypius, 67, 69, 78, 93, 97, 100, 116, 187

Ambrose (Saint), 4, 5, 38, 38n, 62, 63, 91, 96, 106, 107, 109, 156, 180, 189, 190; Biblical exegesis of, 14, 20, 64; and Plotinianism, 14; *Deus creator omnium* of, 141

Anamnesis, see Memory

Angels, *see* Soul, mid-rank station of

Anthony (Saint), 96, 100

Archetype (and image), *see* God; Images

Aristotle, 59, 190; *Categories* of, 57; *materia prima* of, 146

Armstrong, A. H., 85n, 130n, 147, 147n; on Plotinus' influence on Augustine, 148

Augustine

  Christianity of, 12, 53, 64, 65, 71, 91, 100; and Donatists, 13; and Pelagians, 13; episcopacy of, 22, 134; on human experience, 31, 32, 36, 190; as catechumen, 54; as "unknower," 60, 62, 67; Academicism of, 61, 64, 65; on marriage, 68; lust of, 69; faith of, 70, 72; superstition of, 72; Catholicism of, 72, 91; and women, 90; celibacy of, 91; on temporal relationships, 105-119, 187; self-control of, 108, 109; on sexes, 113; friendships of, 116; self-examination of, 133; influence of Aristotle on, 147; ecclesiology of, 172; subtlety of, 177; sensibility of, 190; and Monica, *see* Monica; use of Bible by, *see* Bible

  Intellectual development of, 12, 53; corporeal thought of, 57, 61, 64, 65, 70, 77, 146; conversion of, 35-36,

51-54, 63-64, 91, 94, 103; and the quest for understanding, 63-65, 71-74; *Weltanschauung* of, 75-79, 120, 188-190

  Literary artistry of, 9-11, 189-190; use of language by, 120; artistic imagination of, 183, 184; esthetic theory of, 189. *See also* Images

  Manichaeism of, 13, 53, 60, 61, 64, 72, 91, 107, 133, 189. *See also* Manichees

  Neo-Platonism of, 1, 4, 81, 101, 151, 159; Plotinian influence on, 3, 4, 12, 14, 27, 47, 74, 146-148, 150, 172, 181, 184, 189; possible influence of Porphyry on, 4. *See also* Plotinus; Porphyry

  Works of:

  Confessions, 4, 13, 113, 122, 190; historicity of, 4-5; meaning and unity of, 5-12; addressees of, 12-22 passim

    BOOK ONE, 37-45; *I, 1,* 127; *I, 1-3,* 184; *I, 17,* 91, 107; *I, 28,* 87

    BOOK TWO, 46-50; *II, 4,* 107

    BOOK THREE, 51-54, 101, 102; *III, 3-4,* 56; *III, 7-8,* 92, 94, 142; *III, 11,* 142; *III, 16,* 46, 182; *III, 19-21,* 107

    BOOK FOUR, 55-58; *IV, 14,* 184; *IV, 15,* 184; *IV, 20,* 102; *IV, 31,* 59, 104

    BOOK FIVE, 59-62, 72, 102; *V, 2,* 184; *V, 15,* 107; *V, 21,* 68; *V, 24,* 64; *V, 25,* 54, 63, 64

    BOOK SIX, 63-70, 92, 102; *VI, 2,* 107; *VI, 6,* 73; *VI, 7,* 42; *VI, 13,* 187; *VI, 18,* 92; *VI, 19,* 93; *VI, 20,* 93; *VI, 21,* 93; *VI, 23,* 92; *VI, 23-25,* 107; *VI, 24,* 93; *VI, 25,* 107, 113

    BOOK SEVEN, 71-80, 8, 91, 101, 102, 120; *VII, 10,* 100-101; *VII, 11,* 123; *VII, 13-26,* 4, 75-80; *VII, 14,* 151; *VII, 16,* 1, 84, 85, 102, 103; *VII, 16-17,* 87, 153, 154; *VII, 17,* 84, 85; *VII, 19,* 84; *VII, 21,* 84, 85; *VII, 22,* 84; *VII, 23,* 85, 102, 118, 123, 170; *VII, 24,* 29; *VII, 26,* 102, 104

    BOOK EIGHT, 90-104, 8, 53, 120; *VIII, 1,* 76

    BOOK NINE, 105-119, 102, 120; *IX, 1,* 101

Truth: enjoyment of, 8, 14, 28, 43,
103; possession of, 14; as Way, 14,
18, 30, 34; embrace of, 15; soul as
dwelling place of, 15; as Light, 15,
16, 165; as soul's food, 29, 48, 62,
117, 176; finding of, 67; as eternal,
77; as "above," 85; as non-spatial,
85; Christ as, 94; and custom, 98
Truth-hand, 77, 85, 103, 137. *See also*
Hand, image of; Omnipresence
Turn (*vertere*), 52, 59. *See also Aver-
sio;* Conversion; *Fovere*

Ulysses, 188. *See also* Odyssey
Understanding, 16, 19, 34, 38, 70, 117,
118, 170; of faith, 12, 14, 19, 62,
94, 138, 156, 169; Augustine's quest
for, 19, 63-65; as step toward vision,
15-17, 28-29, 34, 73-74, 117. *See also*
Disciplines; Faith; Knowledge; Reason; Way

Van der Meer, F., 22, 22n
Varro, 32
Verecundus, 105
Verheijen, Melchior, 7n
Vision, 2n, 3n, 4, 77, 79, 80, 115, 117,
151, 185; at Ostia, 8, 53, 104, 115-
118, 115n, 119, 153; as accessible in
this life, 34, 66; of Truth-hand, 103;
"return" to, 118

Want, 29, 30, 45, 48, 161, 174; region
of, 49
Watts, William, xi, 143
Way, the, 12; Incarnate Truth as, 14,
18, 30, 34; of many and few, 18-19,
66, 79; universal, 18, 19, 67; of faith
and understanding, 30; of learning,
44; "upward," 98. *See also* Authority;
Faith; Reason; Understanding
"Weight (s)," 25, 26-27, 84, 101, 103;
and iniquity, 2; of pride, 57; and
soul's fall, 57, 78; and charity, 57,
161; and "seeing," 100; of custom,
102; and "goads," 180; and Providence, 183
Whole-part, 57, 76, 142, 182, 184; and
fall of soul, 182, 188
Wicked, *see* Evil; Iniquity
Will, 47, 174, 178, 190; freedom of, 71-
74, 78, 101, 180, 181; divided, in
man, 96-98; and conversion, 97;
"right," 174-177; and Logos, 180
Williger, Eduard, 10
Wisdom, 7, 30, 102, 117, 150, 165
Within-without, *see* Interiority
Women, 113-115, 179
Word, the, 136-138, 148, 163, 178
Words, *see* Language
Wundt, Max, 7n